Cooking for
a Crowd

BOOKS BY ANNETTE LASLETT ROSS and
JEAN ADAMS DISNEY

Cooking for a Crowd

The Art of Making Good Cookies — Plain and Fancy

Cooking for a Crowd

Annette Laslett Ross
and
Jean Adams Disney

Doubleday & Company, Inc.
Garden City, New York

PREFACE

Why does a good cook need a special quantity recipe collection? This question has teased more than one individual who justly deserves the title, "Good Cook." Knotty though the problem is, there remains a very explicit answer.

Household-size recipes cannot be relied on to perform in doubled and larger batches exactly as they do in a single mixing without a prior testing. There may be too many ingredients to blend adequately in the suggested mixing time and the careful cook will be concerned that it may be necessary to double the mixing time if ingredients are doubled. Only careful, repeated testing will tell. There can be out-of-balance proportions in a larger volume and, worst of all, inadequate yields for desirable size individual servings.

Recipes in the following section that may be doubled or otherwise prepared in larger quantities are so indicated.

Festive foods for many may require that the host (hostess) plan a menu in which consideration of cost is an overriding factor. When this is true, all the more care must be exercised in the selection of recipes to ensure success.

The differences between a doubled recipe and a quantity recipe for a particular dish may be slight, but vital. Give success in quantity cookery greater probability by following recipe proportions exactly—even to use of suggested pan sizes and methods of cookery. Like a talisman for happiness, the practical pointers to success that are in the following sections on arrangement will lead to the kind of entertaining that encourages more gatherings involving festive foods for many.

Time and temperature charts for baking, broiling, deep frying, roasting and cooking of vegetables are grouped together in the Appendix. Use these to plan preparation timetables and to utilize equipment efficiently. They will help ensure that all foods are ready at serving time and frequently enable cooking an entree and an accompaniment course at the same time.

ACKNOWLEDGMENTS

The assistance of the test kitchens and home economics departments of the following firms is acknowledged with grateful appreciation:

American Dairy Association; American Dry Milk Institute, Inc.; American Institute of Baking; American Molasses Company; California Cantaloupe Advisory Board; California Wine Advisory Board; Evaporated Milk Association; Florida Citrus Commission; General Foods; Kellogg Company; Knox Gelatine, Inc.; McIllhenny Tabasco Company; National Canners Association; National Live Stock and Meat Board; The Nestlé Company, Inc.; Oscar Mayer & Company; Ralston Purina Company; Standard Brands, Inc.; Swift & Company; United States Brewers Foundation.

Drawings for meat carving are courtesy of the National Live Stock and Meat Board.

CONTENTS

PREFACE   vii

  I. WHAT THIS BOOK WILL DO FOR YOU   1

 II. EQUIPMENT FOR QUANTITY COOKERY   17

III. MENUS FOR ALL OCCASIONS   23

     Menus for 12 Servings   29

     Menus for 12 or 48 Servings   31

     Menus for 24 Servings   36

     Menus for 48 Servings   48

IV. QUANTITY SERVING CHARTS AND
    PURCHASE GUIDE   61

 V. RECIPES   69

     Appetizers and First Courses   71

     Beverages   81

     Breads   89

     Desserts   117

     Egg and Cheese Entrees   188

     Fish Entrees   194

     Meat Entrees   205

     Meat Carving Techniques   205

Poultry Entrees   244

Poultry Carving Guide   244

Relishes and Accompaniments   256

Salads and Salad Dressings   260

Sandwiches   300

Soups   310

Vegetables and Pastas   314

APPENDIX   339

Cooking Charts   341

Wine Charts   354

INDEX   357

Recipes marked with an asterisk (*) may be found by consulting the Index.

ILLUSTRATIONS

Piquant Flavor Calls Guests   *following 82*

Delicate Desserts Delight Eye   *following 130*

Party-Pretty Buffet Easy to Prepare   *following 226*

Fruits Star at Brunch or Lunchtime   *following 274*

Photographs listed are reproduced through the courtesy
of the American Dairy Association

CHAPTER I

What This Book Will Do for You

The purpose of this book is to meet the needs of those who THINK BIG, as one must do when cooking food for a large group. Besides recipes, there are included detailed steps for planning, purchasing and preparing for such events:

1. AT HOME PARTIES
2. ORGANIZATIONAL EVENTS
3. COMMERCIAL FOOD ENTERPRISES or INSTITUTIONAL FOOD MANAGERS
4. BIG FAMILIES or FREEZER-FILLING DO-AHEAD COOKING

This book is designed to enable all those who COOK BIG, to do so successfully. It has been said that anyone who can read, can cook. We would add . . . anyone who reads *carefully* can cook well . . . and for a crowd.

While quantity cooking recipe proportions are somewhat different and sometimes require special utensils, there are many recipes included in this book that require neither unusual talent nor tools, and all could be served in any company without apology.

CHECK OUT GUIDELINES

Specific guidelines to planning and preparations are found in the ensuing chapters, which include *quantity charts, menus* and *recipes*.

1. Quantity charts are included to tell servings obtained from prepared, packaged, canned and frozen foods and to answer such questions as "How many cups of coffee can you make from 1 pound?" Use the charts as a marketing guide and to estimate costs for money-raising events.

2. Menus are suggested for a variety of occasions, ranging from breakfasts and brunches to formal dinners and receptions.

They are suggestions of possible pleasing combinations of foods to serve together, each one of an infinite variety.

3. Formulate your own menus to suit your tastes and needs, adding or deleting items from the suggested menus. For instance, if one of the *buffet menus* appeals to you, but you are planning a *tea,* delete the entree and salad. If a *luncheon menu* suggestion appeals to you, but you are planning a *dinner party,* add a soup, an hors d'oeuvres course and dessert that will give more substance.

4. Menus are grouped according to the number of servings for each of the items. Keep this in mind in switching foods from one menu to another so that you do not select a recipe for 48 when you are planning an event for 12. When recipes permit doubling, tripling or halving with safety, a footnote on the recipe will so indicate.

5. Menus are grouped according to type of dish and number of servings, 12, 24 or 48, as shown in the table of contents. They may be used for planning both home and organizational events. Simply adjust the menu plan to fit each particular set of circumstances.

6. Recipes are grouped according to their category of use. A complete listing by the name of the recipe is to be found in the Index at the back of the book. Recipes are given for all items that are starred in the menu section.

7. Amounts to plan and prepare for those foods that require no special directions may be determined by consulting quantity serving charts preceding the menus.

8. A number of menus suggest ways of enhancing such foods by some simple addition, such as a garnish or topping. Where a special method is required, this will be shown in the Index as a recipe.

REMEMBER . . . no matter how expertly a recipe is formulated, nothing takes the place of careful measurement with standard kitchen equipment. This is particularly true when working with large amounts.

In preparing quantity recipes, what would normally be "just a little off" is magnified.

Care in mixing is essential, also, in order that larger amounts are properly blended.

PLANNING POINTERS FOR SUCCESS

Regardless of whether the function you are planning is to be held in a home or is a group event, the following are the steps which must be given careful thought to make all run smoothly, from the time the idea is first formed to the satisfying conclusion that everyone who participated enjoyed it, guests and hostesses alike.

Watch Out for the Outlook: It is not so much what you do but the way that you do it that counts. If party-giving and organizational events are done with a grin-and-bear-it attitude, it manifests itself grimly to all. The one insurmountable obstacle to the success of any occasion is a harried hostess or a committee with gritted teeth and the mien of frenzy.

AT HOME PARTIES

Hospitality is the key to successful entertaining. The wish to extend a sincerely warm welcome expresses itself in the extra attention which distinguishes any occasion and makes it pleasantly memorable to all those present.

The expressions of care for your guests do not mean necessarily elaborate foods or lavish decorations. The casual gaiety of a soup luncheon before a sports event or an informal patio buffet can still convey this special quality of thoughtful, genuine hospitality.

CHECKLIST: Use the following pointers as your checklist, listing your own plans with pencil and paper so you don't have the mental strain of trying to remember every detail.

TIMETABLE: Separate the various jobs to be done into steps to be prepared over several weeks, doing each phase as you have time for it. This makes every part not too big in itself and often the tasks may be combined with part of the regular routine, such as shopping for the party done at the same time with the regular weekly shopping. However, to attempt such shopping without a careful list invariably leads to overlooking something and an emergency trip.

THEME: The "when" of a party and the reason for its being are closely interrelated. Give some thought to "off-season" entertaining, such as a "Christmas in July" party or a "Sun-Breakthrough" indoor picnic for those friends not "going south for the winter." Not only is the novelty of approach appreciated, so is the fun of a party at a time when everyone isn't worn out from too much entertaining.

Anniversaries, promotions, a new house, new neighbor, a cheerup after April 15 or an "Auld Lang Syne" time for friends one hasn't seen for too long all could provide the starting point for a memorable occasion.

INVITATIONS: Unless the occasion is one where a formal invitation is obligatory, the decision to phone or write invitations depends on convenience and whether or not there is a way you might wish to set the stage for a special type of party with a related invitation. Written invitations have the advantage of providing all details in a form which may be referred to readily, as to time, date, etc.

However, if using written invitations for informal events, make it easy for guests to RSVP by phone, when possible, to answer questions about what to wear, transportation, and other arrangements. Suggest times when you expect to be home and a date by which you'd like to hear, so that you aren't in a quandary about who is coming or whether you can leave the house or not. Two to three weeks prior is a good rule for informal events, three weeks' minimum is obligatory on formal events, such as receptions.

MENU PLANNING: The type of event determines in part the kind of menu you will want. Browse through the menu section with this in mind. Keep in mind, also, the serving procedure: whether it will be buffet or a sit-down meal. Picture the serving containers and table settings, mentally planning (or make sketches) the table arrangements and all appointments. This will provide a list of necessary items such as candles and flowers, which you may want to get. It also will prevent a last-minute scramble to decide what foods will be served in what. Naturally, seasonal choices will have some effect on menu choices, too, as well as your own taste and known preferences of guests.

FOOD PURCHASING: Here, once more, careful planning pays off, both in time saved in preventing extra trips for things forgotten, and in the peace of mind of having what you need at hand, when you need it. Once the menu is determined, make a complete list of all items, including decorations, silver polish, and other household supplies. Make a separate list or note of perishable items, then put both the far-ahead and last-minute shopping trips into your timetable. This also spreads the cost over a longer period, and for a big party, this can be a considerable budget item. Sometimes, it also enables one to take advantage of special sales as they come along by knowing well ahead just what is needed. However, it is hardly necessary to point out that when one is entertaining this is a poor time to make any purchase of doubtful quality.

DECORATIONS: Whether these are flowers or other table and room decorations that relate to your chosen theme, planning and arranging is required. It is helpful if these are done the day before the big event and the less perishable decorations are, the farther ahead they may be done, another factor to bear in mind in planning. Art objects, banners, posters, fresh fruits, and vegetables, items from novelty or import stores all offer a fresh approach for center-pieces. It is well to remember that their purpose is to add attractive color, not to be overwhelming.

TABLE SETTING: Arranging dishes and silver is another detail that should be done well in advance. If a variety of dishes will be used, a look of clutter can be avoided by grouping them. Check quantities and wash and polish in advance. For big buffet parties, stacking plates all of one kind in clusters on the buffet works well, or a number of smaller sit-down tables may be set, each with a different pattern where several sets of china may be used. Of course, matching silver, dishes and crystal may be obtained from party rental services. Sometimes use of paper and plastic ware suffices, particularly if the new, color-cued disposable tableware is chosen with care.

FOOD PREPARATION: Planning the times to do each item on the menu is part of the listing which should go into the timetable.

Many of the recipes may be done ahead, as indicated on the recipes themselves. Many, also, may be frozen and thus prepared even further in advance. By planning what will be done when, the problem of trying to do too many things at once is eliminated. Put into play any special appliances which will be helpful, such as warming trays and insulated servers.

SERVING: The hostess will need to plan the ways and means to keep the necessary foods flowing from the kitchen with a minimum of running. The special serving containers, mentioned above, are one. Serving carts or side tables are another. She may wish to ask a few close friends to share in these tasks, unless she has engaged kitchen and serving assistants.

CLEANUP: A great deal can be done to smooth the serving and the cleanup by having all preparation utensils washed and put away before guests arrive. Plan where you will have returned dishes, silver, glassware and food go as it is brought into the kitchen. As soon as possible, at the end of the meal one can proceed to stack dishes and put food away, leaving a minimum of confusion for the actual dishwashing. This takes only a few minutes if the advance thinking has been done and the hostess can return to her guests, smiling and serene.

ORGANIZATIONAL EVENTS

The sage advice of having fun at your own party applies to large group functions as well. Overcomplicating or straining too hard are the most likely causes for making an event seem like work and not a festive occasion, enjoyed by those attending and those responsible for it. Don't try to use all the good ideas suggested at one affair. There will be other opportunities, so pick the ones that fit this time, and save the others for the future. Regard your event as an opportunity to use skills and share talents with those who will appreciate them.

Phase I The general chairman must take note of the various areas of work and assign a committee or individual, depending on how much is to be done, for each. The overall planning committee then must decide:

WHEN

WHERE

WHAT TYPE OF PARTY

Set a timetable and establish deadlines so that work can be done without any last-minute crises.

Particularly for a money-raising event or other occasions when a conflicting calendar could be a problem, it is important to check the tentative date to be sure that there is no major conflicting attraction. Most Chambers of Commerce maintain an activity calendar that shows such city-wide events. If the night you have in mind is the date of a major football game, concert or another club's big ball, better move the date than to buck the conflict of interests.

The "where" is usually fairly obvious, although sometimes groups thrive on a change of setting from the usual spot to an available room that may be loaned or rented for special occasions.

The type of event usually sets the theme for decorations and the general plan of the menu so it must be determined early in the planning.

For organizational events, a special theme can be a valuable asset in adding sparkle to all aspects, including the publicity. Sometimes the best themes are those closest at hand—a "barn-raising" for those with a building project to aid; an "East-Side West-Side" party to send a delegation cross-country; an "Oh, to be young again" teen-age type party to raise funds for young people's needs, to suggest a few as a starting point for your own imaginative theme to fit your purposes.

Phase II For each of the following responsibilities, an individual or committee must be picked. If the latter, it is often wise to combine experienced persons with new ones, relying on the latter to add bright, new touches and learn the ropes for future events and on the former to share their experience from past participation. As you check these off, think through the processes involved for the occasion coming up, making notes of any special factors to be considered.

Invitations or Tickets: The type of event determines whether formal or fun kinds of invitations are in order, or whether just simple tickets will suffice. Party supply shops and printers can offer good advice. Rolls of tickets may be purchased pre-printed from business stationers, either in single or double rolls. The latter provide duplicate numbers for door-prize drawings or other occasions when 2 tickets with identical numbers would be helpful. Often it is an impetus to sales if tickets can be purchased at the door and needed reservations made by phone, when a precise count is necessary. Usually experience from past years or other groups will provide a reasonable estimate of attendance.

Publicity: This is important to the success of organizational events where a large turnout is desired. The form it will take depends on your community but putting together all the details as to what will take place, when and where, and who will participate, provides the facts which will interest newspapers, radio stations and perhaps even television stations, especially those with women's programs, and when you can offer something with unusual visual interest. Look for the unique in planning and publicizing your event to set it apart from the passing parade. It is helpful to time first publicity announcements for release when tickets go on sale to pave the way by creating enthusiasm.

Menu Planning: Much of this will be determined partially by your general planning session for the type of event. From the menus in the book, select those that attract you. By choosing foods that will be plentiful for the time of year, budget costs will be lower.

How to Price Right: If the event is a benefit, determine costs carefully in advance and add a fair margin of profit. If you need only to cover your costs, a 5 to 10 per cent leeway is precaution against a deficit. Food costs of 50 to 60 per cent of admission price are a good average for a profit-making event. If the food is good, the price will be right regardless of the figure at which it is set. If you cut corners too closely, both the budget you hope to boost and the attendance at any future events will suffer.

Food Purchasing: If the event is for 24 or more, it will pay you to buy from a food wholesaler who supplies restaurants and hotels. Such purveyors are glad to quote costs in advance on staple items and give you a reasonable estimate on fresh items so that you can establish your budget, even though the price may fluctuate somewhat from the time when you first make your plans until your purchases are made. Often there is a courtesy discount to nonprofit groups, too, which is worth checking on when you are making your preliminary cost plans. Avoid purchases of questionable quality for the same reasons you would for an at-home party. Naturally, detailed lists are a "must."

Decorations: Whatever the occasion and its theme, simple and striking decorations that avoid lots of little clutter are the most effective. They also require a minimum of time to put in place. Planning decorations that do not droop readily is also important. Consider non-floral decor when it is appropriate: flags, art objects, posters and any of a wide variety of paper novelties are among the possibilities. It is helpful if the decorations are in place no later than the morning before the big event to eliminate added confusion and traffic in kitchen and dining areas.

Table Setting: Check quantities and wash and polish dishes, glassware and silver in advance. Plan table arrangement and placement so that traffic flows smoothly. If food will be served buffet-style, a double line or dual serving tables speed service and ensures that food is more appetizing. Placing silver, coffee cups, glasses and condiments on tables also facilitates buffet service. Dishes and silver should be placed well in advance of food preparation, to eliminate extra kitchen traffic. When a number of different patterns of china will be used, a cluttered look can be avoided by grouping them, in clusters on the buffet or at a number of sit-down tables, each with its own pattern. Party supplies of virtually all kinds are available from rental services in most cities of any size. Disposable plastic and paper ware are also suitable for many occasions and become more attractive each season.

Food Preparation: An important aspect of this all-essential phase of operations is to check out all equipment needed to be sure that it is in working order, of the right size, etc. It is essential to know ahead of actual cooking time that the utensils required are at hand. Refrigerator and oven space must be considered. Be sure, too, that any unfamiliar equipment is pre-tried and its timing checked. Large coffeepots, for instance, may take as long as an hour to make coffee. Portable appliances such as ovens may be needed, but watch out for adding so many that the wiring load becomes dangerous. A blown fuse can really cause confusion!

Responsibility for keeping the foods supplied throughout the meal usually is designated to those preparing it, but this should be included in the planning so that serving of hot rolls, coffee-pouring, platter-filling and so forth are handled smoothly.

Serving: At any large event, this becomes a responsibility for several persons; depending on how much self-help there is by guests, one person is needed for each 10 to 20 guests. Even at a buffet-type meal, servers to fill coffee cups, replenish the buffet, remove main course dishes and help serve dessert will be required.

These specific detailed serving pointers may be helpful:

1. For a group of 20 or more, plan dual or quadruple buffet lines to keep traffic moving. The quadruple lines require two tables with guests able to serve themselves from either side of the table. This requires having dual or quadruple serving dishes for every item on the menu, at least; more if they need to be kept at a special temperature.

2. Have serving dishes of moderate size to enable their being replaced with a fresh, attractive new dish, instead of using very large ones which look woebegone as they get down toward the last serving or two.

3. Place buffet tables near kitchen to facilitate replenishing and save steps.

4. Napkins and silver may be placed on tables where guests will be seated to avoid crowding the buffet.

5. Cream and sugar, rolls and butter, relishes and other condiments are usually most conveniently placed at the tables where the guests will be seated.

6. Beverages may be served to guests after they have been seated or placed on a separate table or tables from which guests can serve themselves. If the group is large and helpers are available, it makes for less confusion to serve them.

7. When just one kind of salad is to be served, these may be placed at the table before guests are seated. By passing the dressing or a choice of dressings, salads stay crisper and guests may choose the amount and/or kind they prefer.

8. Dessert may be served buffet-style, also, letting guests help themselves after they have finished their main course. These should go on a table set only with dessert, either a separate one or the main buffet, which has been cleared.

9. If guests will be seated simultaneously and the group is large, serving desserts from a tray or cart will cause less congestion.

10. Have a place cleared to stack dishes, silver and glasses in the kitchen and a separate area for returned food to be taken home or otherwise disposed of.

11. Avoid an overzealous clean-up crew. Nothing shatters a pleasant occasion as rapidly as dishes being whisked away with undue speed or clatter.

12. Allow enough time so that there is not a feeling of pressure. If your party is a double feature with bridge, perhaps, or a fashion show following the meal, it is ideal to serve in one room or one section of a large hall, then move to an adjoining area.

13. Providing fresh hot coffee and clean ashtrays provides a relaxing atmosphere for guests, even though the clean-up committee may be beginning to clear tables.

14. Using carts and trays is helpful to save steps but try to use them unobtrusively to retain a "gracious" atmosphere.

Clean-up Crew: The foregoing pointers help make short work of the actual cleanup by having dishes stacked and food cleared away as they are returned to the kitchen. Glasses and silver should be washed first to retain their shine, then dishes. Be sure that adequate supplies of tea towels are available if no dishwasher is at hand. Even then, some towels will be required for large pans and other pieces that won't fit into the dishwasher or are part of a "leftover" load. If the kitchen you are using is unfamiliar, be sure that instructions for using this vital piece of equipment are obtained in advance.

CHECKLIST FOR VOLUNTEER HELPERS

1. Be sure all persons who have volunteered to assist in serving are supervised directly and constantly by an individual thoroughly familiar with the task at hand and experienced in directing this work.

2. Plan some safe place to leave helpers' coats, hats and handbags. (No one can do his best worrying about personal belongings.)

3. Be sure servers have on clean clothes and are supplied with clean aprons. Be certain hands are scrubbed with soap and water immediately before helpers take their places in the dining room. See that clothes are neat and suitable for the occasion.

4. Direct helpers' attention before guests arrive to sources of supplies they will need: Silverware, cups and saucers, table linen, condiments, clean cloths or sponges for taking care of spills, refuse containers, trays for dish removal and dessert service and perhaps, floor mops for really serious spills. If tea, coffee, milk and other beverages are stored in several places, be sure dining room helpers know the whereabouts of all of these.

5. Kitchen helpers: Direct attention to source of supply of all items needed for the specific job helper is assigned. A simple sketch of kitchen and dining room and sources might be useful to inform workers quickly.

COMMERCIAL FOOD ENTERPRISES

The majority of persons engaged in commercial and institutional operations are experienced professionals and have ready access to skilled help from such sources as commercial food companies' test kitchens and well-informed representatives of major suppliers, both of food products and equipment. Although we will not attempt to go into operations for such enterprises, a number of the recipes included in this collection are ones of interest to such culinary operations. Both guidelines and menus may prove to be of help, also, in suggesting new ideas which may make dining more pleasant.

BIG FAMILIES OR FREEZER-FILLING
DO-AHEAD COOKING

Both large families and those preparing ahead for a party or organizational event find advance preparation and freezing a boon.

With a few exceptions, the recipes found in this book may be frozen successfully. The foods NOT TO FREEZE include all salads, except those which include freezing in the directions, such as those listed in the Index; avocado dip or sandwich filling; stuffed celery; any dessert with a gelatin base, including chiffon pies; melon balls or watermelon; any salad dressing; tomatoes or zucchini, raw or cooked.

For all other items, follow these general guidelines, in addition to the recipe instructions. When dish is completed, cool, wrap and freeze quickly, in moisture-vapor-proof paper or packaging containers.

1.   Recommended storage time is 2 to 3 months for most cooked foods.

2.   Let prepared foods thaw slowly in refrigerator or cold place, allowing about 2 hours per pound to defrost.

3.   Once foods have been thawed, they should not be refrozen.

4.   Heat main dishes and casseroles, loosely covered with foil, in 350° F. oven about 1 hour per each 12-serving amount in single container.

5.   Fried or crisp baked individual servings of food are best reheated on shallow baking pans in 375° F. oven about 15 minutes.

6.   Thawed baked pies should be reheated in 350° F. oven until warmed through, about 30 minutes.

7.   Sauces and soups should be reheated in broad, heavy skillets or saucepans, over low heat, stirred occasionally.

8.   Iced breads and cakes should be unwrapped before thawing to prevent frosting from sticking as it thaws.

9.   Un-iced breads, cakes and rolls should be thawed in wrappings, at room temperature. Individual servings thaw in about 15 minutes. Frozen cakes take about an hour to thaw sufficiently to

slice. Rolls to be reheated, wrapped in foil or heavy paper bags, may be placed directly in 300° F. oven for about 20 minutes.

10. Frozen vegetables or pasta dishes should be thawed slowly and then heated, either on top of the range or in a 350° F. oven, until hot through, 15 to 45 minutes, depending on quantity.

CHAPTER II

Equipment for Quantity Cookery

Sanitation, durability and ease of handling are three equally important qualities of utensils and equipment for a kitchen, whether they are to be used for foods for a family or for larger groups of persons. Good appearance in the piece may be of significance as well when it is called on to serve as well as cook food.

The inherent quality of a material can be emphasized to bring all of these to a particular item. Consider the nest of stainless steel bowls for home mixers that actually was designed in copy of their commercial kitchen counterparts. These are recognized as handsome as well as functional in use. Stainless steel is used widely, not only for kitchen utensils but for large equipment, surfacing of work areas and sinks in modern commercial kitchens. Initial cost is high, but maintenance is not. Other materials which may prove satisfactory given proper design and weight are aluminum and glass. Glass and ceramic containers may shatter if sharply banged and have limited capacity to withstand sudden heat changes.

Specific requirements of individual items may vary, but one should select equipment and furnishings to provide surfaces resistant to corrosive action of foods, beverages and cleaning materials. If the considered material could damage any food by imparting off-odor or taste or cause a color change, then it is not suitable for food preparation.

Kinds of equipment one expects to find in a kitchen designed for quantity food service (as in a church, clubhouse or school) include the following:

Surface heating units, one or more ovens (separate or combined with the top units), automatic coffeemaker of at least 50-cup serving capacity, refrigerator, freezer, automatic hot water heater, work counters, worktables, rolling carts (preferably equipped with several shelves), a heavy duty food mixer and one or more sinks.

Desirable but optional may be one or more of the following:

Meat slicer, pressure cooker, deep fat fryer, automatic broiler, griddle and steam-jacketed kettles.

Adequate containers for disposal of discards must be provided for so that scrupulous cleanliness in preparation, storage, serving and cleanup is observed. A room fan is desirable for air change. Adequate towel drying space, broom closet space and conveniently stored china, glass and flatware in addition to drawers for utensils and shelves for pots and pans are essentials. Food storage spaces must be designed for both convenience and sanitation. In general, these need not be overly large because it is wiser to plan on using up most items at widely separated affairs rather than have them grow old in storage. A consistent and frequently held dinner meeting in such an area could result of course, in reduced costs if one bought in quantities to meet demand.

Be aware that foods that are brought in fresh from a garden or orchard will require more space for making table-ready than if only packaged or processed foods are chosen. Poultry purchased rough-dressed or meat that is to be cut into cooking-size portions frequently requires both cold storage space of unusual dimensions and additional kitchen work area. Unless one wishes to embark on a continuous career of food service in quantity, it is recommended that the precise skills of meat cutting be left to the experts. It is wise to order meat in cuts that are usable without much additional attention or that can be handled without specialized saws and knives.

Although the recipes in the following sections are concerned with preparation of a large number of servings, containers specified are mainly those used in home-size kitchens. Cakes are to be baked in 8- or 9-inch rounds, $8 \times 8 \times 2$-inch squares, 11×15-inch rectangles, $9 \times 5 \times 3$-inch loaf or 10-inch tube pans. Pie pans are standard 9-inch rounds.

If one wishes to double recipes in mixing (and for many kinds of foods this is perfectly satisfactory and so noted on the recipe), then be sure that the equipment for doing so is adequate to the task. Bowls must be large enough and the food mixer powerful enough to do as complete a mixing as if a lesser amount of ingredients is involved.

Food mixing equipment comes in standard rated capacity, ranging from 5, 10 and 12 quarts clear up to 140-quart capacity. One 60-quart machine, for example, is designed to mix 50 pounds of pie dough with splendid efficiency.

Some of these mixers have extra, optional equipment to perform other tasks such as chopping, slicing and dicing of meat and vegetables and an attachment that will slowly drip in oil for preparation of mayonnaise. Very large mixers may be bolted to counter or floor, giving great stability to the machine.

Before plunging into the mixing of any food to be baked, the cook must check the oven space to be sure that the required number of pans for all the dough prepared can be put in to bake under proper conditions. Good baking in a conventional oven requires adequate movement of air over and around baking pans. To achieve this, place pans in the oven so that 1 inch of space is open between pans and the sides of the oven including front and back.

Ideally, four 9-inch layer cake pans will be arranged on two shelves so that each pan is freely exposed to heat on top, bottom and both sides—not one among the group is placed over another. The two pans on the top oven shelf will be opposite the two cake pans on the lower shelf, exposing all four to even movement of heated air.

Top-of-stove cookery in the following recipes requires outsize equipment for very few items, one of these being preparation of pastes which are boiled in water. Macaroni and the like require sufficient cooking water so that they may turn readily in response to the rapidly moving cooking liquid. A kettle that will hold from 6 to 8½ quarts of water is required. A good grade canning kettle may suffice and be useful other than at times of entertaining. In any case, choose a saucepot with a cover ensuring versatility in its use.

For baking of puddings or oven-glazing of cooked vegetables, a baking pan sized approximately $12 \times 18 \times 2\frac{1}{2}$ inches is an excellent choice. Four-quart casseroles may be used, and these fitted with tight lids are useful for holding baked foods at serving temperature for a time. Casseroles of larger than 4-quart capacity are available, but remember they tend to be extremely heavy and awkward to handle when hot and full of food.

Consider the amount of refrigerated shelf space before undertaking a dessert such as Strawberry Chiffon Pie and the like. The 48 servings come from eight filled pie shells mounded high with a gelatin-thickened whipped fruit mixture. Chilling is essential. If there is not enough refrigerated shelf space for storing these several pies, then an alternate dessert should be selected for the menu.

Roasting pans for meat and poultry can be chosen in a variety of sizes up to those measuring $16 \times 20 \times 4\frac{1}{2}$ inches. This is adequate for most roasting of meat and poultry. Measure the oven shelf and select any roasting pan so that it, too, will leave the required free area for movement of heated air. The broiler-roaster pan supplied by many range manufacturers may be adequate to the needs of a sometimes quantity cook so that no additional pan is required for the few times that very large meat cuts are baked.

CHAPTER III

Menus for All Occasions

HOW TO USE THIS CHAPTER

Menus are grouped according to numbers of servings expected from recipes given. Asterisk (*) indicates recipe is in following section. See Index.

Menus in the 12- or 48-servings section are planned around recipes developed for preparation in both a medium and large quantity.

Amounts to purchase may be determined by consulting "Quantity Serving Charts and Purchase Guide," Chapter IV.

Many menus are suitable for several occasions as noted under featured entree headings.

Planning a menu for guests is a road to pleasure and a challenge that never fails to intrigue the accomplished cook and excite the mind of the creative. Food can lead one to travel-like change of something new, something exotic, something particularly delectable. It is possible to turn an ordinary affair into a special fete, an occasion for which a theme will make a pleasant party a unique affair.

In planning, make the most of seasonal foods and vary a good recipe by substituting a plentiful food for a scarce or expensive one. Most persons who dine out frequently will choose a restaurant for a particular food or a particular menu. It is quality that tells. On the other hand, a good cook may have grown famous for the superb variety on the table each time entertaining is done. If there's Italian-style spaghetti one time, there might be a menu of Oriental foods the next time, or a great roast of fine rare beef to carve thin and serve very hot.

Successful menu planning owes as much to the appetizing appearance of the several foods served as to the contrast or blend of flavors. Work hard to preserve inherent colors of fruits and vegetables, their inimitable texture, shape and fresh flavor. Guard these as if they were precious—they are. Overcooking is the most serious threat to these when cooked; too soon dressing with acid-based sauces, when raw. It is true that everything can't be left to the last minute for a bit of attention. Consider which foods require special care and then, if the decision is to include that food in spite of its extra-care requirement, detail someone to see that it gets the required supervision at the proper time. However, if there's a decision to be made between risking flavor and wrecking the time-table, change the menu to something less demanding.

Menus may acquire a totally new look simply from the way the several foods are cooked and served. Picture a browned, quarter chicken on a large plate, a mound of mashed potatoes beside it and a caress of creamy chicken gravy over all. Now contrast it with this: Petite casserole lined with dry toast points, butter-baked chicken pieces laid over them and all garnished with broiled mushroom caps. Serve a crisp green salad with the first plate and let the casserole be accompanied by a tart fruit mold served on its own chilled plate. Cost-wise, there's scarcely a difference. Preparation is about the same. Equipment for making either is standard. The serving dishes contrast largely. Gleaming china plates are required for the first menu, individual casseroles or ramekins for the second on a companion service plate. The chicken used for these two menus looks different and will taste different and, in fact, it is different because its accompaniments are different. The two menus each cast an individual mood—one of warm Southern hospitality, the other reminiscent of its European origins. Accentuate the positive qualities of each by emphasizing the innate qualities of goodness in other foods served. Split biscuits buttered and dressed with honey please one with the first menu; consider crusty salt or poppy seed finger rolls with the chicken en casserole. When it comes to desserts, make the most of the mood created by the above choice. Carry the quality to a superb close with deep dish apple pie wrapped in a bit of its own spicy juice for the chicken with gravy. Make it Pears Helene for the second.

Menu variety can arise from including foods prepared by a variety of cooking methods. Consider dishes that are baked, broiled, fried, sautéed, braised, steamed, creamed, buttered, escalloped or topped with a variety of sauces or garnishes. Check the menu to determine if a cooking method has been repeated too often—a change may be indicated.

Guests will always feel more at ease if there are ample portions of less expensive foods than when there is an obviously limited quantity of an expensive one. A hard lesson of this kind was learned by a young hostess when she gave her first formal tea party. She had put only a few of the pretty petits fours (the real star of that particular menu) on the serving table, thinking she would replenish the plates often. A young person asked her hostess breathlessly, "Did you mean for us children to have cake, too?" And of course she had. How much more gracious to have had plenty in view so that the quantity says, "Please have some!"

Again, if there must be a choice between a satisfactory serving of crab or shrimp in a cocktail and a skimpy one, choose a less expensive fruit cocktail for an equally good beginning without the risk of disappointingly small servings. A great gourmet once wrote that if one had to scrape a thick sauce off an entree to find it, the effort was seldom worth while. This could be said of fish cocktails, too. A half-cup of sauce cannot make up for the lack of shellfish that should be nestled underneath it all.

One only disappoints a guest with a too-small serving of pie even if it means that an expensive whipped topping can be added. Better choose a serving adequate in size even if it means dispensing with the elaborate topping.

Menus must fit the realm of possibilities of the kitchen's physical arrangement and equipment. What's the good of a menu lifted from an accomplished chef if the kitchen work space and supplies are inadequate for its preparation? With the services of a salad chef, a sauce chef, a baker and a general assistant, miracles can be wrought, but that's another world. In the realm of actuality open to most part-time quantity cooks, real danger may lie in a too-ambitious menu. Perhaps nothing will break down harmony behind the scenes faster than giving an inexperienced work crew too much to do unless it's asking an expert crew to accomplish miracles with just the materials ordinary mortals find in everyday settings. Consider a one-oven kitchen called on to produce at one and the same moment perfectly broiled steak for four as well as golden-topped, light biscuits. Should the steak cool while the biscuits bake or the biscuits grow limp while the steak broils? How much wiser to slip ready-baked buns into a warmer to accompany that steak and have the best of both worlds.

Much the same kind of crisis (only with more serious consequences) can occur when preparing festive foods for many if the menu has not been planned realistically in relation to facilities as well as know-how. The more elaborate the menu plan, the more demanding the requirements for its production. Plan well *within* the outside limit of possibilities—simplicity in production wins over too-elaborate kitchen maneuvers every time. Put the dramatic touches on the front line in fresh flavor, perfect service and ample-size servings.

Knowing food and liking it, a good cook plans a menu from a sense of bounty and a feeling of goodwill. It is helpful to be alert to innovation—there's a new quick-frozen food at the supermarket? Try it: it may open an undreamed-of vista to one's personal entertaining. Skills of many persons gifted in the use of foods and busy pushing out the old familiar limitations are developing new versions of old favorites as well as seeking innovations. The tedium of slow preparation of sauces, where has it gone? Food frontiers may have new horizons undreamed of yet—even by those dreamers who have succeeded in making a freezer a necessity in the modern kitchen and a new mix an eagerly anticipated event.

Menus that follow tell how to plan for today, but they are ready to be adapted for tomorrow, too, by substituting prepared and packaged foods. The following menus make full use of both hot and cold dishes to ensure variety. Themes can be emphasized with food, but never let these interfere with the quality of food. If theme garnishes are employed, let them be edible. Added flavor, heightened color and texture change can be brought to a menu this way. More importantly, these are the means to a subtle reminder that someone really cares. Individual touches convey most heartily the welcome and warmth of gracious entertaining.

MENUS FOR 12 SERVINGS

Featuring **Cheese**

LENTEN SUPPER
(Add Meat for Informal Supper or Buffet.)

Fruit Platter
*Lenten Dinner Casserole**
*Green Salad, Rosy Roquefort Dressing**
Salty Bread Sticks
*Coconut Cake or Easy Spice Cake**
Ice Cream
Coffee   Tea

Meats may be added: *Meat Loaf, Roast Beef or Ham, Ground Beef Patties, Meat Balls, Brown and Serve Sausages or Wieners.*

Featuring **Fish**

BRUNCH, LUNCH OR LATE SUPPER

*Hot Spiced Tomato Juice**
*Crab Suzettes**
Oven-browned Potatoes
Buttered Asparagus
Melba Toast   Butter   Orange Marmalade
*Pears à la Cumberland**
Coffee   Tea

Featuring **Meat**

HEARTY LUNCH OR LATE SUPPER

*Cole Slaw in Lettuce Cups**
Hot Corned Beef or Pastrami on Rye Bread*
Hot Mustard   Horseradish   Mayonnaise
Dill Pickle Wedges
Raspberry Sherbet
Vanilla Wafers
Coffee   Tea   Beer

Featuring **Turkey**

BUFFET SUPPER, DINNER OR MIDNIGHT SUPPER
(For LUNCHEON Omit Hot Vegetables.)

*Turkey en Casserole with Broccoli**
Oven-browned Potatoes
Parsleyed Carrots
Celery, Pickles, Olives
French Bread   Butter
*Hearts of Lettuce with Green Goddess Dressing**
*Schaum Torte**
Coffee   Tea

MENUS FOR 12 OR 48 SERVINGS

Featuring **Chicken, Duck or Goose**

DINNER

Sparkling Cranberry Cocktail
Chicken en Casserole*
Mock Wild Rice*
Spinach à la Suisse*
Orange-Avocado Salad on Endive
Chocolate Whipped Cream-filled Angel Cake Loaf*
Coffee   Tea

AL FRESCO OR INDOOR BARBECUE SUPPER

Sherried Grapefruit Halves
Charcoal or Oven-barbecued Chicken*
Herb Seasoned, Skewered Vegetables*
Dinner Rolls*
Pineapple-Cottage Cheese Lime Molded Salad*
Baked Apples in Port*
Coffee   Tea

DINNER

Fruit Cup
Wild or Domestic Roast Duck or Goose*
Wild Rice
Green Peas
Crescent Dinner Rolls*
Molded Fruit Salad*, (Apricot-Orange) Nutted Cheese Balls
Schaum Torte*
Coffee   Tea

Featuring **Fish**

HEARTY LUNCHEON, DINNER OR BUFFET SUPPER

Marinated Artichoke Hearts
Fillet of Sole in White Wine*
Shoestring Potatoes
Glazed Carrots*
Tomato Aspic on Greens*
Cloverleaf Rolls*
Pineapple Meringue Torte* or Icebox Cake
Coffee   Tea

Featuring **Meat**

BUFFET OR COCKTAIL SUPPER, LITTLE OR LATE DINNER

Shrimp Dressing* on Mixed Salad Greens
Burgundy Beef Balls*
Bulgar Wheat Casserole*
Green Vegetable
French Bread
Sherry Chiffon Pie* or Tarts
Coffee   Tea

DINNER

Seasoned Tomato Juice Cocktail
Chef's Salad—Choice of Dressings
Burgundy Sirloin Tips*
Mashed Potatoes
Green Vegetable
Dinner Rolls*
Lime or Mint Sherbet
Punch Bowl Cookies*
Coffee   Tea

AL FRESCO OR INDOOR BARBECUE SUPPER

Baked Stuffed Tomatoes*
Butter-browned, Whole Small Potatoes
Skewered Lamb or Beef Cubes with Mushrooms*
Tossed Green Salad*, Anchovy-Parsley Dressing*
Garlic or Plain French Bread
Strawberry Glazed Cheesecake*
Coffee   Tea

HEARTY LUNCH FOR MEN, DINNER OR BUFFET SUPPER

Lamb, Beef or Veal Pie Topped with Cornmeal Biscuits*
Cole Slaw*
Pickled Crabapples or Spiced Peaches or Apricots
Pound Cake*
Frozen Lemon Cream*
Coffee   Tea

BUFFET SUPPER OR DINNER

Black Olives, Celery Hearts, Gherkins
Shrimp Cole Slaw in Tomato Aspic Ring
Veal Scallopini*
Poppy Seed Noodles* or Steamed Rice*
Bread Sticks
Spumoni Ice Cream
Almond Macaroons

Featuring **Party Specialties**

TEA OR STAND-UP LUNCHEON

Fruit Bread* Sandwiches
Bite-size Chicken-filled Buns* or Petits Choux*
Pinwheel Sandwiches*
Ribbon Sandwiches
Rolled Sandwiches*
Miniature Cupcakes*, Petits Fours* or Frosted Bar Cookies
Salted Nuts   Candies
Tea   Coffee   Fruit Punch

LUNCHEON, LATE SUPPER OR WEDDING BREAKFAST

Red and Green Madrilene* or Clam Bisque
Thin Wafers
Turkey or Chicken à la King* with Toast Points,
Patty Shells or Biscuits

or

Chicken-Almond Salad* in Petits Choux* or Toast Baskets*
Marinated Cooked Fruit Halves on Romaine
Frosted Yellow Layer Cake* or Bar Cookies
Coffee   Tea
Note: Adapt for Wedding Breakfast as follows: Substitute
Tiered Cake* for Layer Cake or Cookies
Add: *Ice Cream, Ice Cream Molds or Ice Cream Balls**
Nuts   Candies
Champagne, Champagne Punch* or Fruit Punch*

MENUS FOR 24 SERVINGS

Featuring **Cheese**

LUNCHEON, INFORMAL SUPPER OR BUFFET

Cheese Soufflé*
Green Beans Amandine* or Buttered Asparagus Spears
Bran Muffins* or Scones*
Butter   Orange Marmalade or Fruit Jelly
Pear-Grape Salad*
Chocolate Upside-down Pudding*, Whipped Cream Garnish
Coffee   Tea

BRUNCH, LUNCHEON OR MIDNIGHT SUPPER

Cheese Blintzes with Sour Cream*
Assorted Jams
Honey Celery Seed Dressing* over Fruit Compote
(Grapes, Apples, Mandarin Oranges, Nuts)
Coffee   Tea

LUNCHEON OR BRUNCH (Omit Hot Vegetable),
INFORMAL SUPPER OR BUFFET

High-hat Macaroni and Cheese*
Green Beans Julienne
Waldorf Salad*
French Rolls
Orange Rum Bavarian*
Coffee   Tea

BRUNCH OR LUNCHEON

Melon Cup
Mushroom Noodle Kugel Supreme*
Lyonnaise Green Beans*
French Rolls or Bread Sticks
Date Squares*
Coffee   Tea

Featuring **Chicken**

LUNCHEON, BRUNCH (Omit Soup) OR LATE SUPPER

Herbed Tomato Soup—Saltines
Chicken-Almond Salad*
Grape Clusters
Small Rolls or Biscuits*
Butter   Currant Jelly
Orange Chiffon Cake or Lazy-Daisy Cake*
Coffee   Tea

PATIO OR PARK PICNIC

Relishes
Potato or Macaroni Salad*
Cold Fried Chicken or Sliced, Cold Meats
Buttered Bread
Fresh Fruits in Season
Frosted Loaf Cake
Coffee   Lemonade

LUNCHEON, DINNER OR MIDNIGHT SUPPER

Aloha Barbecued Chicken*
Corn on the Cob or Parsleyed Rice*
Cooked Vegetable Salad Platter*
Crusty Rolls
Butter   Tart Jelly
Orange Cake or Fruited Caliloupe Mold*
Coffee   Tea

DINNER, BUFFET OR COCKTAIL SUPPER

Chicken Livers Sauté* or Beef Balls Epicurean*
Stuffed Mushrooms*
Green Beans à la Victor*
Cherry Tomatoes Italienne*
Dinner Rolls*
Peppermint Parfait*
Coffee   Tea

BRUNCH, LUNCHEON OR MIDNIGHT SUPPER

*Chicken-Ham Supreme**
Buttered Rice or Noodles
Green Vegetable
*Cheese Sticks**
*Baked Fruits**
*Pound Cake**
Coffee   Tea

DINNER OR BUFFET SUPPER

*Baked Chicken Bombay**
*Bacon and Prune Broiled Garnish**
Relish and Olive Platter
*Grapefruit-Avocado Salad**
Euphrates Wafers—Assorted Crackers   Butter Balls
Lemon Sherbet—Crème de Menthe Parfait
Coffee   Tea

LUNCHEON OR DINNER

Chicken Polynesian or Pork Chops Hawaiian**
*Rice**
Buttered Peas
*Cherry Tomato-Cucumber Salad**
Dinner Rolls   Butter*
*Chocolate Mousse**
Coffee   Tea

Featuring **Fish**

LUNCHEON, DINNER OR BUFFET

Baked Fish Stroganoff* or Flounder Rolls Rarebit*
Pimento Rice*
Green Beans à la Victor*
Marinated Cucumbers with Onions*
Pickled Beets*
Crescent Rolls*
Strawberry Glazed Cheesecake*
Coffee   Tea

BRUNCH, LUNCHEON OR SUPPER

Shrimp Creamed with Oysters* or Shrimp Tallyho*
Toast Baskets*
Broiled Tomatoes Parmesan*
Grapefruit Cucumber Mold*
Coffee   Tea

LUNCHEON, BUFFET OR MIDNIGHT SUPPER

Crab Louis* or Molded Seafood Salad*
Deviled Eggs and Cherry Tomatoes
Caraway Cottage Cheese Sticks*
Cherry Upside-down Pudding* or Lemon Crunch Pudding*
Coffee   Tea

LUNCHEON, DINNER OR BUFFET SUPPER

Cold Spiced Salmon* or Baked Salmon Steaks*
Potato Salad Stuffed Tomatoes*
or Buttered New Potatoes with Green Onions and Peas*
Cole Slaw* or Tossed Green Salad*
French Rolls
Cherries Jubilee*
Coffee   Tea

INFORMAL DINNER OR SUPPER FOR TEEN-AGERS

Baked Tuna Casserole*
Hot Vegetables with Parsley Butter Platter
Green Salad, Thousand Island Dressing*
Dinner Rolls* or Biscuits*
Peach Crisp*, Whipped Cream Garnish
Beverage

Featuring **Meat**

LUNCHEON, INFORMAL BUFFET OR MIDNIGHT SUPPER

Oven-barbecued Burgers*
Savory Rice* or Baked Beans*
Broiled Tomatoes
Sour Cream Cole Slaw*
Hot Buttered French Bread
Blueberry Crisp*
Coffee   Beer

BUFFET DINNER OR SUPPER

Rye Bread and Wafers
Cheese Platter
Herring with Onion Rings
Waldorf Salad*
Cole Slaw*
Swedish Meat Balls*
Baked Whole Salmon*
Swedish Brown Beans*
Wine Jelly with Fruit* or Lingonberry Sundaes
Spritz Cookies
Coffee

LUNCHEON, DINNER, BUFFET OR MIDNIGHT SUPPER

Swedish Meat Balls*
Buttered Noodles
Tiny Beets
3-Bean Salad*
Applesauce
Cottage Cheese Mold*
Assorted Breads
Heavenly Ambrosia* or Bananas à l'Orange*

INFORMAL SUPPER OR EVENING REFRESHMENT FOR TEEN-AGERS

Chili Beefburgers*
Cole Slaw*, Potato Salad* or Molded Fruit Salad*
Chocolate Frosted Layer Cake* or Ice Cream and Cookies
Coffee   Milk   Punch or Lemonade

INFORMAL DINNER OR SUPPER FOR TEEN-AGERS

Raw Vegetable Relishes and Pickles
*Tamale Pie**
Mixed Fruit Salad on Greens
Sesame Bread Sticks
Baked Apples in Port or Ice Cream with*
*Mexican Cinnamon Crescent Cookies**
Coffee   Milk

INFORMAL DINNER OR BUFFET

*Pot Roast of Beef**
*Potato Pancakes**
Buttered Asparagus
Cinnamon Apples with Sour Cream*
*Tropical Orange Puff**
Coffee   Tea

DINNER

Melon Wedges on Greens
*Pot Roast of Beef with Brown Gravy**
Mashed Potatoes or Broad Noodles
Buttered Sliced Beets
*Hot Rolls or Muffins**
*Deep Dish Fruit Pie**
Coffee   Tea

DINNER OR INFORMAL BUFFET SUPPER

Raw Vegetables and Olives Relish Platter
Italian Meat Sauce* on Spaghetti
Green Salad Bowl
French Bread with Pimento Cheese Topping*
Biscuit Tortoni*
Red Wine   Coffee

LUNCHEON, INFORMAL SUPPER OR MIDNIGHT BUFFET

Deviled Eggs
Celery, Pickles, Cherry Tomatoes, Marinated Artichoke Hearts
Italian Pizza*
Fresh Fruit and Cheese Tray
Beer or Burgundy   Coffee

DINNER OR BUFFET SUPPER

Pork Chop Spaghetti* or Lasagne*
Green Salad
Bread Sticks or French Bread
Sherried Pears with Custard Sauce* or Lemon Cake*
Coffee   Tea

LUNCHEON, DINNER OR BUFFET SUPPER

Veal Paprika* or Beef Stroganoff*
Buttered Noodles
Glazed Carrots and Small Whole Onions*
Molded Minted Pears*
Crisp-crusted Dinner Rolls
Mocha Chocolate Chiffon Pie*
Coffee   Tea

DINNER OR FATHER-SON BANQUET

Shrimp or Crab Cocktail or Fruit Cup
Hungarian Goulash* with Noodles or Rice
Buttered Peas
Dinner Rolls*
Deep Dish Fruit Pie*—Apple with Cheese
Coffee   Milk

LUNCHEON, INFORMAL SUPPER OR BARBECUE

Teriyaki Beef*
Corn on Cob or Foil-baked Potatoes
Cucumber and Tomato Salad*
French Rolls
Watermelon-Cantaloupe Balls with Sherbet*
Coffee   Tea   Lemonade   Fruit Punch*

BRUNCH, LUNCHEON, DINNER OR MIDNIGHT SUPPER

Baked Ham or Orange Ham Loaf*
Harvest Casserole*
Tomato Aspic Rings with Cucumber Slices*
Crisp French Rolls
Strawberry Melon Mold*
Coffee   Tea

LUNCHEON, INFORMAL SUPPER OR AL FRESCO BUFFET

Hot Tomato Juice*
Salami Shrimp Supper Salad*
Cheese-Mustard French Bread* or Corn Muffins* or Biscuits*
Tropical Gingerbread* with Orange Sauce*
Coffee   Tea   Beer

LUNCHEON, DINNER OR BUFFET SUPPER

Shish Kebabs* or Deep-fried Shrimp*
Fluffy Rice
Peas with Onions*
Raw Vegetable Salad*
Dinner Rolls*
Coffee Soufflé* or Lemon Snow*
Coffee   Tea

BREAKFAST OR BRUNCH

Canned or Fresh Stewed Fruit
Pancakes from Commercial Mix*
Ground Sausage Patties
Cinnamon-Sugar, Jam, Syrup, Butter
Coffee   Milk

BREAKFAST OR BRUNCH

Fresh Whole Strawberries or Grape Clusters
Breakfast Crepes* or French Toast*
Orange Sauce*
Maple Syrup*
Broiled Ham Slices
Coffee

BREAKFAST, BRUNCH OR LUNCHEON

Melon Cup*
Corn Fritters*
Maple Syrup*
Broiled Ham Slices, Bacon or Sausage Links
Coffee   Tea

Featuring **Party Specialties**

RECEPTION, LATE DAY AT HOME OR COCKTAIL PARTY

Wassail Bowl* (cold)
Cantaloupe on Smoked Salmon Canapés
Deviled Eggs
Celery, Pickles, Olives
Appetizer Meat Balls*
Broiled Cheese Puffs*
Spanish Sticks*
Coffee   Tea

BRUNCH, LUNCHEON OR MIDNIGHT SUPPER

Hot Mulled Punch*
Eggs Florentine*
Toasted English Muffins
Glazed Orange Peaches*
Coffee   Tea

MENUS FOR 48 SERVINGS

Featuring **Breakfast Foods**

BREAKFAST, BRUNCH OR EARLY OR LATE SUPPER

Citrus Fruit Compote
Pancakes*
Butter, Maple Syrup*
Sausages
Coffee   Milk

BREAKFAST, BRUNCH OR EARLY OR LATE SUPPER

Apple Juice
Buttermilk Pancakes*
Butter, Syrup
Ham Slices
Coffee   Milk

BREAKFAST, BRUNCH OR EARLY OR LATE SUPPER

Fruit Platter (e.g., Strawberries and Melon in Season)
French Toast*
Butter, Fruit Jam or Jelly
Bacon
Coffee   Milk

BREAKFAST, BRUNCH OR EARLY OR LATE SUPPER

Orange, Cranberry or Pineapple Juice
Scrambled Eggs*
Canadian Bacon
Stollen* or Spicy Coffee Cake*
Coffee   Milk

Featuring **Fish**

LUNCHEON, BUFFET SUPPER OR DINNER

Hot Bacon-Cheese Canapés*
Shrimp Creole with Rice*
French Rolls
Layered Lime-Pear Salad*
Chocolate or Butterscotch Sundaes
Thin Nut Cookies
Coffee   Tea

LUNCHEON, BUFFET SUPPER OR MIDNIGHT SUPPER

Macaroni Salad* on Lettuce Cups
Chilled Salmon Loaf* or Molded Ham Loaf*
Cranberry Horseradish Relish*
Hot Crescent Rolls*
Frosted Layer Cake*
Coffee   Tea

LUNCHEON, DINNER, OR EARLY OR LATE SUPPER

Baked Prawns*
Rice Pilaff*
Mixed Green Salad with Cherry Tomatoes or Tomato Aspic*
Squares
Sourdough or Plain French Rolls
Mocha Chiffon* in Nut Pastry Crust* or Strawberry Chiffon Pie*
in Plain Pastry Crust*
Coffee   Tea

Featuring **Chicken and Turkey**

DINNER OR BUFFET SUPPER

Shrimp or Crab Cocktail with Red Sauce*
Chicken Sauté*
Buttered Noodles
Green Peas, Beans or Broccoli
Poppy Seed Rolls
Port Wine Cranberry Mold*
Black Bottom Pie* or Chocolate Spanish Cream*
Coffee   Tea

Note: Eliminate fish cocktail for buffet supper and add *Green Salad Dressed with Olive Oil and Wine Vinegar Dressing.*

DINNER

Fresh Fruit Cup
Coq au Vin Rouge*
Butter-browned Small Whole Potatoes and Onions
Julienne Green Beans
Caesar Salad*
Dinner Rolls*
Coffee Soufflé* with Whipped Cream
Coffee   Tea

LUNCHEON OR LATE SUPPER

Avocado-stuffed Celery Sticks*
Chicken Alexandria*
Cranberry Apricot Molded Salad*
Pineapple Sherbet—Cookies
Coffee   Tea

LUNCHEON OR DINNER

Oven-fried Chicken*
Baked Stuffed Potatoes*
Buttered Broccoli or Asparagus
Cranberry-Apple Salad*
Dinner Rolls, Butter, Mint Jelly
Rum Chocolate Chiffon Pie*
Coffee   Tea

LUNCHEON, INFORMAL SUPPER OR BARBECUE

Charcoal or Oven-barbecued
Chicken*
Potato Salad on Tomato Halves*
Celery, Pickled Beets, Cucumber Slices
Green Beans or Grilled Zucchini*
Strawberry Shortcake*
Coffee   Lemonade

LUNCHEON OR MIDNIGHT SUPPER

French Onion Soup* with Parmesan French Bread*
Chicken Grape Almond Salad Supreme*
Wheat Muffins*, Butter, Assorted Jams
Black Bottom Pie*
Coffee   Tea

LUNCHEON OR DINNER

Tomato Bouillon*
Chicken or Turkey Salad Mold*
Black and Green Olives, Gherkin Pickles
Cheese-stuffed Finger Rolls*
Lemon Chiffon Pie* in Graham Cracker Crust* or
Eggnog Chiffon Pie* in Baked Pastry Crust*
Coffee   Tea

LUNCHEON, DINNER, BUFFET SUPPER OR MIDNIGHT SUPPER

Boned Turkey Roll
Stuffed Mushrooms*
Broiled Tomatoes Parmesan*
Whipped Potatoes or Shoestring Potatoes
Cucumber Lime Vegetable Salad*
Peach-Blueberry Parfait*
Coffee   Tea

LUNCHEON OR LATE SUPPER

Turkey Sandwich Supreme*
Grapefruit and Orange Segments on Bed of Lettuce
Grape Clusters
Charlotte Russe*
Coffee   Tea

Featuring **Meat**

HEARTY FARE FOR MEN'S LUNCHEON OR GENERAL DINNER

Chilled Vegetable Juice
Meat Loaf*
Delmonico Potatoes*
Green Beans Caesar*
Molded Beet Salad*
Bran Muffins*, Butter, Honey and Fruit Preserves
Apple Crisp*, Whipped Cream
Coffee   Tea

DINNER OR BUFFET SUPPER

Roast Beef or Baked Ham
Mustard Sauce Supreme*
Baked Stuffed Potatoes*
Herbed Carrots
Waldorf Salad* or Fruited Caliloupe Mold*
Pumpkin Pie—Old-fashioned* or Chiffon*
Coffee   Tea

DINNER OR BUFFET SUPPER

Boned Leg of Lamb or Roast Sirloin of Beef
Rice Pilaff*
Beans with Mushrooms* or Ratatouille* (mixed vegetable casserole)
Sherried Apple Mold with Pineapple and Mandarin Oranges*
Crusted Rolls, Butter, Mint Jelly
Chocolate Mousse*
Coffee   Tea

DINNER OR BUFFET SUPPER

Stuffed Shoulder of Lamb
Glazed Carrots and Small Whole Onions*
Browned New Potatoes and Mushroom Caps
French Bread Slices
Green Endive Salad with Rosy Roquefort Dressing* or Blue Cheese
Dressing*
Lemon Snow*, Mixed Fruits Topping
Coffee   Tea

LUNCHEON, INFORMAL SUPPER OR LATE SNACK FOR TEENS

Hot Dogs, Hamburgers or Ham-Stuffed Buns*
Cooked Vegetable Salad Platter*
Deviled Eggs, Cherry Tomatoes, Pickles
Potato Chips
Apple Crunch à la Mode*
Coffee   Lemonade   Beer

INFORMAL DINNER OR SUPPER FOR TEEN-AGERS

Chili con Carne*
Toasted French Bread Slices or Saltines
or Chili Beefburgers*
Sour Cream Cole Slaw*
Ice Cream with Fruit Toppings, Cookies*
Coffee   Milk

LUNCHEON OR DINNER

Sweet-Sour Pork* or Beef Balls Oriental*
Rice, Boiled* or Steamed*
Green Beans with Water Chestnuts*
Harlequin Salad*
Bread Sticks
Heavenly Ambrosia*
Coffee   Tea

BUFFET, SIT-DOWN DINNER OR CASUAL SUPPER

Consommé Cup
Pork Chop Suey Amandine* on Crisp, Fried Noodles or Rice
Spiced Fruits (Plums, Apricots, Pineapple, Peaches, Pears)
Lazy-Daisy Cake*
Coffee   Milk

SUMMER PATIO PARTY OR DINNER

Barbecued Spareribs*
Corn on the Cob or Baked Potatoes
Cole Slaw with Cherry Tomatoes*
Hot Buttered French Bread
Orange Layer Cake*
Coffee   Beer   Lemonade

CASUAL DINNER (Frankfurters Popular with Teen-Agers)

Relish Plate
Sour Cream Cole Slaw*
Hot Baked Ham, Grilled Frankfurters or Small Meat Balls*
Vintner's Beans*
Corn Bread* Squares or Muffins*
Apple Crisp* with Sherry Spice Sauce*
Coffee   Beer   Lemonade

INFORMAL BUFFET OR COCKTAIL SUPPER

Deviled Egg Salad Squares*
Cherry Tomatoes or Tomato Wedges
Sliced Cold Ham or Boiled Tongue*
Hot Corned Beef* or Frankfurters in Beer*
Baked Beans*
Sesame Corn Bread* and Boston Brown Bread*
Frozen Fruit Salad*
Coffee   Tea

DINNER OR LATE SUPPER

Baked Ham Slices with Broiled Peaches*
Buttered Potato Balls*
Asparagus or Green Beans Amandine*
Orange Tea Biscuits*, Butter
Petits Fours* or Chocolate Chiffon Pie* or Tarts
Coffee   Tea

LUNCHEON OR SUPPER

Broccoli and Ham or Turkey en Casserole*
Toast Points
Harlequin Salad*
Pound Cake* and Pears Rosé*
Coffee   Tea

LUNCHEON, DINNER OR BUFFET SUPPER

Hot Spiced Tomato Juice*
Ham-Veal Pot Pie*
Grapefruit Molded Salad*
Apple Crunch à la Mode*
Coffee   Tea

DINNER OR HEARTY LUNCHEON FOR MEN

Sherried Lamb Fricassee* or Burgundy Beef Stew*
French Bread or Hot Biscuits*, Butter and Mint Jelly
Celery, Pickles, Radishes
Peaches Melba*
Coffee   Tea

LUNCHEON, MIDNIGHT SUPPER OR COCKTAIL SUPPER

Cold, Sliced Meat Platter
Jellied Cottage Cheese and Vegetable Salad*
Butter Flake Rolls*
Melon Balls in Watermelon Shell*
Coffee   Tea

Featuring **Hearty Soup**

LUNCHEON OR EARLY OR LATE SUPPER

Oyster Stew*
Corn Bread* or Garlic Bread
Cinnamon Apple Salad with Cream Cheese Balls*
Lemon Snow*, Chocolate Chip Cookies*
Coffee   Tea

LUNCHEON OR EARLY OR LATE SUPPER

Clam Chowder*
Toasted Crackers and Boston Brown Bread*
Cheese Tray
Cranberry-Apple Mold*
Lemon Cake*
Coffee   Tea

LUNCHEON OR EARLY OR LATE INFORMAL SUPPER

Split Pea Soup with Ham*
Bread Sticks, Saltines
Celery Stuffed with Blue Cheese*
Deviled Eggs, Pickled Beets
Chocolate Mint Mousse*
Coffee   Tea

Featuring **Party Specialties**

BRUNCH, LUNCHEON OR LATE SUPPER

*Pineapple-Strawberry Kebabs**
*Curried Eggs in Rice Nests**
or
*Creamed Chipped Beef with Mushrooms**
Melba Toast
Coffee   Tea

WEDDING BREAKFAST, LUNCHEON OR LATE SUPPER
(Add Wedding Cake in place of Peppermint Chocolate Icebox Log*,
if desired, for Wedding Breakfast)

*Red and Green Madrilene**
*Fruited Frozen Cranberry Orange Mold**
or
*Layered Lime-Pear Salad**
Orange, Date* and Banana* Breads Tray*
Blue, Cheddar and Cream Cheese Platter
*Peppermint Chocolate Icebox Log**
Coffee   Tea   Punch

RECEPTION OR COCKTAIL PARTY

*Rum Punch**
*Gourmet Cheese Ball**
*Avocado Dip**
*Crab Roll-Ups**
*Ham-filled Cream Puffs**
*Assorted Sandwiches**
*Decorated Cake or Petits Fours**
Coffee   Tea

RECEPTION OR COCKTAIL SUPPER

Wine Punch*
Blue Cheese Balls*
Deviled Deckers*
Cheese Sticks*
Molded Ham and Liver Paté*
Crackers
Fresh Fruit Tray
Decorated Cake, Miniature Cupcakes* or Petits Fours* or
Cookies*, Frosted
Coffee   Tea

CHAPTER IV

Quantity Serving Charts and

Purchase Guide

The Quantity Serving Charts provide information to take the guess-work out of grocery-shopping when buying foods in quantity. Note quantities suggested are for 24 medium-size servings. Halve suggested amounts for 12 servings, double suggested amounts for 48 servings.

Whenever possible, purchase foods from a source accustomed to selling in large units in order to gain the advantage of quantity pricing. These sources may be listed in shopping directories under headings, such as "Grocers—Wholesale," or "Meat—Wholesale Purveyors to Schools and Institutions," for example. Do not hesitate to discuss large-scale purchases with the managers of food markets. Many persons are eager to accommodate this type of customer and give cooperative service as well as bringing specialized knowledge to the supply question.

Quantities suggested will make 24 moderate-size servings unless otherwise noted.

BEVERAGES

Item	Amount Needed
Chocolate	5 quarts
Coffee, ground	½ pound to 5 quarts water
Coffee, instant	2 ounces to 5 quarts boiling water
Fruit Juices, canned	2 46-ounce cans
Fruit Juices, frozen concentrate	5 6-ounce cans
Milk	1½ gallons
Punch	1½ gallons
Tea, instant	¾ ounce to 5 quarts boiling water or cold tap water for iced tea
Tea, leaves	½ cup to 1 gallon boiling water

FISH

Baking piece or large, whole	8 to 10 pounds
Fillets	8 pounds
Cooked, boned fish (fresh or canned) in salad mixtures	3 pounds
Oysters for frying	Allow 3 per person medium size, 2 large or 4 small
Oysters for stew	1½ quarts
Shrimp for cocktails	2 to 3 pounds
Shrimp for frying	6 to 8 pounds

FOWL

Chicken for boned, cooked meat for salad or casseroles	7 to 9 pounds, drawn weight
Chicken, fricassee	12 to 16 pounds, drawn weight
Chicken, fried	15 pounds, drawn weight
Chicken, roast	12 to 16 pounds, drawn weight
Duck, roast	20 to 24 pounds, drawn weight
Goose, roast	22 to 24 pounds, drawn weight
Turkey for boned, cooked meat	13 to 18 pounds, drawn weight
Turkey, roast	20 to 25 pounds, drawn weight

NOTE: 5 pounds dressed fowl yields 1¼ pounds cooked, bone-free meat or approximately 4 cups (1 quart).

MEAT

Beef, chipped	3½ pounds
Beef, ground for balls or patties	9 to 10 pounds
Beef, roast (bone in)	10 to 13 pounds
Beef, roast (boneless)	9 to 10 pounds
Beef, steak	12 pounds (6 to 8 ounces per serving)

MEAT (*continued*)

Chopped, cooked meat for mixture for 24 sandwiches	1 pound
Ham (bone in)	12 pounds
Ham (boneless)	8 pounds
Lamb, leg roast	12 to 14 pounds
Lamb, shoulder roast	14 to 18 pounds
Sliced, cooked meat for 24 sandwiches (prepared or processed meats)	1½ to 2 pounds
Veal, leg roast	12 to 14 pounds
Veal, crown roast	14 to 18 pounds
Wieners (frankfurters)	7 to 8 pounds (2 per serving)

FRUIT

Apples, sauce	8 pounds
Apricots	5 to 6 pounds
Bananas	7 pounds
Cranberries, sauce	2 pounds
Grapefruit	3 to 4 dozen to 1 crate
Grapes	6 pounds
Oranges	7 to 10 dozen to 1 crate
Peaches	5 to 6 pounds
Rhubarb, sauce	5 pounds
Strawberries, shortcake	5 to 6 pounds

FRUIT, CANNED

Fruit cocktail mixture	4 1-pound-14-ounce cans (No. 2½)

FRUIT, FROZEN

Commercial frozen fruit
  packages

6 10-ounce packages yield
  4 to 5 servings per 10-ounce
  package, approximately
  ⅓ cup each

VEGETABLES

Asparagus	6 to 8 pounds
Beans, green	5 to 6 pounds
Beets	6 to 7 pounds
Cabbage for slaw	7 to 8 pounds
Carrots	7 to 8 pounds
Carrots for relishes	1 to 2 pounds
Cauliflower	12 to 14 pounds
Celery for cut relishes	1 to 2 pounds
Celery stalks 1 per person	3 pounds
Corn on cob	24 ears
Lettuce, leaves	4 heads
Lettuce, shredded	8 heads
Peas in pods	12 to 14 pounds
Potatoes, sweet	8 to 10 pounds
Potatoes, white	8 to 10 pounds
Radishes	5 bunches
Spinach	8 pounds
Squash, summer	8 pounds
Squash, winter	12 to 15 pounds
Tomatoes, slices	5 pounds

VEGETABLES, CANNED

One No. 10 can vegetables yields approximately twenty-four ½-cup servings.

VEGETABLES, FROZEN

Two 2½-pound commercial frozen food packages yield twenty-four ½-cup servings, approximately.

Eight boxes 10-ounce size frozen vegetables yield twenty-four ½-cup servings, approximately.

MISCELLANEOUS FOODS

Beans, dried	2½ pounds
Biscuit Mix (2½ pound package)	48 2-inch biscuits
Bread, 1 pound loaf	16 slices
Bread, 1½ pound loaf	20 to 24 slices
Bread, 2 pound loaf	30 slices
Butter, 1 pound	48 pats
Butter, ¾ pound	spreads 1 slice bread for 50 sandwiches
Butter, ¼ pound (1 cube)	seasons vegetables for 24 servings
Cake, angel (large)	2 cakes, 16 servings each
Cake, 9-inch 3-layer	2 cakes, 16 servings each
Cake, 8-inch 2-layer	2 cakes, 12 servings each
Cereals, to cook variety	1 to 1½ pounds
Cereals, ready to eat	3 packages 6-ounce size or larger
Cheese, brick for sandwiches	1½ pounds
Cheese, brick, cut in cubes 1-inch size for garnish	¾ pound
Cookies	6 to 7 dozen (3 per person)
Cream, coffee (1½-tablespoon serving)	¾ quart
Cream, whipping (1-tablespoon serving)	½ pint
Dip for crackers	1 cup makes forty-eight 1-teaspoon servings

MISCELLANEOUS FOODS (*continued*)

Ice Cream, brick	4 quarts (6 to 8 slices each)
Ice Cream, bulk	1 gallon
Macaroni, packaged	6 pounds
Marshmallows, 1 pound	50 to 75
Mayonnaise, garnish	1 pint
Mints, small after-dinner size	½ pound
Noodles, packaged	6 pounds
Nuts, mixed (for small nut cups)	1 pound
Olives	1 quart
Pickles	1 quart
Pie, 9-inch	4 pies, 6 to 7 servings each
Pie, 8-inch	5 pies, 5 to 6 servings each
Potato or Corn Chips	2 pounds
Rice	2 to 2½ pounds
Rolls, dinner	36 (1½ per person)
Salad mixtures	1 gallon (½ cup serving)
Sandwiches and canapés, small	100
Sandwich mixtures	1½ quarts (2 rounded table-spoons per serving)
Soup	1½ gallons
Spaghetti	6 pounds
Sugar for coffee	½ pound granulated, ¾ pound cubes
Syrup for pancakes	1 quart
Tea sandwiches, small	100

CONTENTS OF COMMERCIAL CAN SIZES

Can size	Cups	Approx. Net Weight
No. 303	2	16 to 17 ounces
No. 2	2½	1 pound 4 ounces
No. 2½	3½	1 pound 13 ounces
No. 10	12	6½ pounds to 7 pounds 5 ounces

CHAPTER V

Recipes

APPETIZER MEAT BALLS
(24 servings)

1 pound ground beef
½ pound ground veal
¼ cup minced onion
1½ teaspoons salt
1½ cups fine dry bread crumbs
2 eggs, beaten
2 tablespoons butter or margarine
1 pint dry red wine or tomato juice
1 tablespoon minced parsley

Combine meat, onion, salt, bread crumbs and eggs. Shape into balls about 1 inch in diameter. Brown a few at a time in melted butter. Chill until serving time. Heat wine or tomato juice with parsley in chafing dish, using 1 cup initially. Add as many meat balls as chafing dish will hold without crowding and heat well, keeping warm as guests serve themselves. Add additional wine or tomato juice and meat balls, as needed. Makes 48 small meat balls.

Recipe may be doubled, as required.

AVOCADO DIP
(48 servings)

6 ripe avocados
½ cup lemon juice
¼ cup finely minced parsley
¼ cup minced chives
2 teaspoons salt

½ cup minced onion, if
desired
2 cups mayonnaise or salad
dressing

Mash avocados and blend with lemon juice. Stir in remaining ingredients. Chill until serving time. Dip will hold its color well 4 to 6 hours. Serve with crisp crackers or raw vegetable sticks. Makes 1 quart.

Recipe may be doubled. Amount required for group depends on number of other foods to be served.

AVOCADO-STUFFED CELERY STICKS
(48 servings)

5 to 6 pounds celery
2 large or 3 medium fully
ripe avocados
Juice of 2 limes
2 teaspoons grated onion

1½ teaspoons chili powder
For garnish, if desired:
pimentos, pearl onions,
parsley, green pepper,
anchovies or paprika

Wash and trim celery stalks. Cut into 48 fairly uniform pieces. Mash avocados and stir in lime juice, grated onion and chili powder. Taste and increase seasonings to individual preference. Spread mixture on prepared celery stalks. Cut into 2-inch chunks. Garnish with suggested foods or dust with paprika.

Recipe may be doubled. Keep stuffed celery chilled for top quality.

Lime juice keeps avocado from darkening for a while. For best results, prepare mixture about 1 hour before serving.

BACON-BROILED PRUNE GARNISH
(24 servings)

24 large dried prunes
24 whole toasted almonds or filberts (optional)
12 strips bacon

Cook prunes until barely tender. Cool, drain and pit. Replace pits with nuts, if desired. Cut bacon strips in halves. Wrap prunes with bacon strips, fastening securely with toothpicks. Broil until bacon is done. Serve hot.

These may be pre-broiled not quite done, drained on paper toweling and reheated under broiler or in 425° F. oven at serving time. Heat on broiler pan rack so that bacon is crisp. Warming may be done at lower temperature, allowing longer time to reheat, about 15 minutes at 325° F., if oven is being used for other food at lower temperature.

Double or triple recipe for additional servings. Do not crowd rack. Broil in several batches, keeping first warm while others are cooking.

BLUE CHEESE BALLS
(48 servings)

¾ cup crumbled blue cheese   *1 cup finely chopped filberts*
¾ cup butter or margarine   *or pecans*
1 cup sifted all-purpose flour

Cream together room-temperature cheese and butter. Gradually add flour and nuts. Work with hands to blend, if necessary. Chill 1 hour.

Shape into 48 small balls about ¾ inch in diameter. Place on ungreased baking sheet. Bake at 350° F. 12 to 15 minutes, until firm and golden-colored. Cool on racks.

Recipe may be doubled.

BROILED CHEESE PUFFS
(24 servings)

4 cups grated Cheddar
cheese
2 teaspoons prepared
mustard
1 cup mayonnaise or salad
dressing

4 egg whites
½ teaspoon salt
48 toasted bread rounds or
crackers

Blend cheese, mustard and mayonnaise well. Beat egg whites with salt until stiff. Gently fold in cheese mixture. Pile lightly onto toasted bread or crackers. Place on cooky sheet and bake at 350° F. until puffed and brown, baking as many at a time as needed for immediate serving. Mixture may be spread on crackers or toast about an hour before baking.

Recipe may be doubled.

CARAWAY COTTAGE CHEESE STICKS
(24 servings)

24 slices rye bread with
caraway seeds
½ cup butter or margarine,
melted

1 pound creamed cottage
cheese
Additional caraway seeds, if
desired

Toast bread lightly on both sides. Brush with melted butter and cut in strips, lengthwise, while hot. Whip cottage cheese with fork till creamy and spread in center of each strip, leave ¼-inch edge on all sides. Sprinkle with additional caraway seeds, if desired. Arrange on buttered baking sheet. Just before serving, toast in 400° F. until cheese is bubbly.

To prepare ahead: Thoroughly coat bread with soft butter, then spread cheese. Place on baking sheet and refrigerate until just before toasting.

Recipe may be doubled.

CELERY STUFFED WITH BLUE CHEESE
(48 servings)

½ pound blue cheese
1 pound cream cheese
1 pint sour cream

3 bunches long, straight
    celery

Blend both cheeses with sour cream. Wash celery thoroughly. Separate stalks. Trim off leaves. Dry with paper towels or clean cloths. Fill with cheese mixture. Cut celery into 3-inch lengths.

If pinwheels are desired, spread about ½-inch layers on uncut stalks, beginning with center pieces and replace in form of original bunch. Wrap and chill. To serve, cut in ½-inch slices.

Recipe may be doubled.

CHEESE STICKS
(24 servings)

3 cups sifted all-purpose
    flour
1½ teaspoons salt
3 teaspoons double action
    baking powder
2 tablespoons celery seed

2 tablespoons caraway seed
⅔ cup butter or margarine
1 cup creamed cottage
    cheese
2 tablespoons cream

Sift together flour, salt and baking powder. Stir in seeds. Cut in butter until mixture resembles coarse cornmeal. Blend in cottage cheese and cream with a fork to form soft dough. On lightly floured board, roll dough out into rectangle and cut in 48 strips. With hands roll into pencil-thin sticks. Bake on lightly greased cooky sheets in 425° F. oven about 10 minutes. Cool on rack.

Recipe may be doubled. Sticks are good served hot or cold. May be baked ahead and reheated.

CRAB ROLL-UPS
(48 servings)

2 pounds sliced bacon, cut in half
2 (6½-ounce) cans crab meat
1½ cups fine dry bread crumbs
½ cup catsup
2 eggs, slightly beaten

2 teaspoons dried parsley flakes
1 tablespoon minced onion
½ teaspoon salt
¼ teaspoon pepper
½ teaspoon Worcestershire sauce

Cook bacon until half done. Combine crab meat, bread crumbs, catsup, eggs, parsley, onion, salt, pepper and Worcestershire. Chill 1 hour. Shape into 48 small balls, wrapping with bacon and fastening with toothpicks. Broil 5 inches from heat for 3 minutes, turning once. Serve hot.

Recipe may be doubled.

DEVILED DECKERS
(48 servings)

3 (4½-ounce) cans deviled ham
1 tablespoon prepared mustard

72 slices cocktail rye bread
1 pound (4 cups) grated Cheddar cheese
2 tablespoons minced onion

Blend ham with mustard and spread on 24 slices of the rye bread. Blend cheese with onion and spread on another 24 slices of bread; cover with third slice of bread. Place each on a ham-spread slice to form double-decker sandwiches. Cut each sandwich in half. Bake in 450° F. oven about 5 minutes or until heated through.

Recipe may be doubled.

GOURMET CHEESE BALL
(48 servings)

*1 pound Cheddar cheese,
  grated
½ pound blue cheese
1 pound cream cheese*

*¼ cup minced onion
¼ cup minced parsley
2 cups chopped nuts
½ cup sherry or sour cream*

Grate or grind Cheddar cheese. Crumble blue cheese and blend with Cheddar cheese. Mix in cream cheese, blending on low speed with electric mixer. With wooden spoon, blend in onion, parsley, nuts and sherry or sour cream. Form into 1 large or 2 smaller balls, depending on service arrangement planned. Surround with crisp crackers, breads and/or raw vegetables.

Recipe may be doubled or divided in half.

HAM-FILLED CREAM PUFFS
(48 servings)

*¾ cup milk
⅓ cup butter or half
  margarine and half
  shortening*

*¾ cup sifted all-purpose
  flour
¼ teaspoon salt
3 eggs*

Bring milk and butter to boiling point. Add flour and salt all at once, cooking and stirring hard until batter forms a ball and leaves sides of pan. Remove from heat, and beat in 1 egg at a time, beating in each thoroughly. Drop by teaspoonfuls onto lightly greased baking sheets, using about 1-inch balls of dough for each cream puff. Bake in 400° F. oven for 20 minutes, then reduce heat to 350° F. and bake about 5 minutes longer. Test one by cutting in half to be sure center is set. Cool. Cut in half and fill with ham filling below or other preferred filling. *Do not double recipe.*

HAM FILLING

3 cups chopped cooked ham
1 cup mayonnaise or salad
* dressing*
½ cup chopped celery
½ cup chopped sweet pickle

½ cup chopped toasted
* almonds*
¼ cup minced onion
Salt and pepper to taste

Combine ham, mayonnaise, celery, pickle, nuts, onion and salt and pepper. Use to fill cream puffs, or to spread on buttered bread for canapés. Chill filled puffs until served, filling as close as possible to serving time.

HOT BACON-CHEESE CANAPES
(48 servings)

1 large (1½ pound) loaf each white and whole wheat
* bread, unsliced*
1 pound thinly sliced sharp American cheese
1 to 1¼ pounds thin-sliced bacon

Trim crusts from bread. Cut into thin lengthwise slices. Cut crosswise into small squares or rectangles. Cut cheese into slightly smaller squares or rectangles and lay on top of bread arranged on baking sheet. Top each canapé with a small piece of bacon. Broil until bacon is browned and cheese bubbly. Serve hot. Allow 3 small squares per serving, including some of both kinds of bread.

Garnish cooked canapés with pimento-stuffed olives and parsley sprigs for a festive look. These are very popular. Canapés may be baked in 425° F. oven until bacon is done, about 10 to 12 minutes. Ready sliced bread can be used. Do trim off crusts, though.

Recipe may be doubled.

MELON CUP
(24 servings)

3 cups cantaloupe balls   *3 cups seedless green grapes*
3 cups cubed watermelon   *1 pint sauterne, if desired*
3 cups pineapple cubes

Prepare fruits and combine, adding sauterne, if desired. Chill thoroughly, well covered. If omitting sauterne, additional fruit juice is not necessary. Holds well as long as 24 hours.

Recipe may be doubled or tripled.

MOLDED HAM AND LIVER PATE
(48 servings)

4 (4½-ounce) cans liver   *1 teaspoon Tabasco*
spread or 1 pound   *1 pint beer or ale*
braunschweiger   *4 envelopes (3 ounces)*
4 (4½-ounce) cans deviled   *unflavored gelatin*
ham   *1 cup cold water*
1 teaspoon dry mustard   *1 (10½-ounce) can*
½ teaspoon pepper   *condensed consommé*
1 teaspoon thyme   *1 cup finely chopped parsley*

Blend liver spread, deviled ham, seasonings and beer. Meanwhile, soften gelatin in cold water 5 minutes. Add to consommé, which has been heated to boiling. Stir until dissolved. Remove from heat. Blend into meat mixture. Pour into two 4-cup molds or one 2-quart mold. Chill until serving time. Unmold and sprinkle with finely chopped parsley.

Recipe may be doubled.

PINEAPPLE STRAWBERRY KEBABS
(48 servings)

2 quarts fresh, hulled strawberries
3 No. 2 (1-pound 4-ounce) cans pineapple chunks
2 cups granulated sugar

Arrange strawberries and pineapple chunks alternately on small skewers or toothpicks, allowing 2 of each per serving. Roll in sugar and chill until served.

Recipe may be increased as desired. If well wrapped, the kebabs may be prepared as long as 12 hours ahead of serving time.

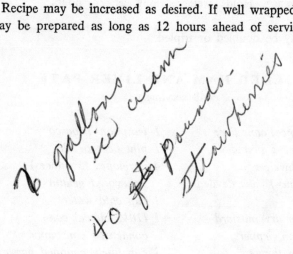

10 gallons ice cream
40 pounds strawberries

BEVERAGES

WINE REFERENCE CHART

(For reasons of ready availability and cost, domestic wines are listed. Any good wine shop can provide suitable imported counterparts, if desired.)

Course	Wine Type	Varietal Names or Recommended Type
Appetizer (Hors d'oeuvres and soup courses)	Madeira	Dry
	Marsala	Not too sweet
	Sherry	Pale and dry
	Vermouth	Dry
Red Meat Entrees (Also may be used with poultry and fish)	Burgundies:	Cabernet
		Gamay
		Pinot Noir
		Zinfandel
	Clarets:	Cabernet
		Charbono
	Rosé	Not too sweet
White Meat Entrees including Fish and Poultry (Also may be used with red meats)	Sauternes:	Dry sauterne types:
		Pinot Blanc
		Pinot Chardonay
		Chateau Beaulieu
		Dry Semillon
		Haut Sauterne

Course	Wine Type	Varietal Names or Recommended Type
	Rhine	Dry and very dry:
	Wines:	Chablis
		Folle Blanche
		Riesling
		Sauvignon Blanc
		Traminer
	Rosé	Not too sweet
Dessert	Cream	
	Sherry	Full flavored and not too sweet
	Madeiras	Full flavored and not too sweet
	Muscatel	Full flavored and not too sweet
	Tokay	Full flavored and not too sweet
	White Port	Full flavored and not too sweet
	Port	Full flavored and not too sweet

NOTE: Champagne and Sparkling Burgundy may be served correctly throughout the meal.

POINTERS

All wines are served at room temperature except white wines, sparkling wines and champagne, which are served slightly chilled, in chilled glasses.

Wineglasses are filled slightly less than two-thirds full.

The host is always served a small portion (to approve the wine), then guests served, to the right, if seated at the table.

The concept of a particular style glass for a particular wine has gone with other nonessentials of a more elaborate way of living. Any goblet is considered appropriate for any wine.

NOTE: See also wine charts, pages 354–55.

PIQUANT FLAVOR CALLS GUESTS

A lovely way to say welcome, this bright tableful of help-yourself tidbits includes, at left, multi-layer sandwiches made with Braunschweiger Filling. Fancy Sandwiches, right foreground, are cut in a variety of shapes and brightened with slices of stuffed olives and cherry tomatoes over Cheese and Olive Spread for Sandwiches. Behind these trays are crunchy Blue Cheese Balls, rolled in additional nuts before baking. Hot Tomato Juice (or cold, depending on the weather) is dressed for the party with a small spoonful of sour cream garnishing each portion. See Index for recipes.

COFFEE

Coffee makers: Party-size coffee makers require 1 pound of coffee for 2 gallons water to make 40 servings. Choose grind of coffee required by the appliance—regular, drip or fine. Follow manufacturer's directions for use.

Boiled: Bring 2½ gallons fresh, cold water to boiling in large container. Divide 1 pound regular grind coffee among four cheesecloth bags. Use several layers of cheesecloth and tie with twine loosely to allow coffee grounds to swell. Add bags to boiling water, cover and adjust heat so that water is at simmering temperature for 10 minutes. Remove bags. Clear coffee just before serving by adding ½ cup cold water. (48 servings)

Instant: Bring 2½ gallons water to full, rolling boil. Stir in 4 ounces instant coffee (2 cups). (48 servings)

TEA

Basic method:

1 cup tea leaves
2 gallons water

Tie tea leaves loosely in two cheesecloth bags made of several layers of cheesecloth tied with twine. Bring fresh water to brisk boil, then drop in tea bags. Reduce heat, cover and allow tea to steep 3 to 5 minutes. Remove tea leaves. Do not boil. (48 servings)

Tea concentrate:

1½ quarts water
¼ pound tea leaves or 16 regular tea bags or 2 1-quart-size
tea bags

Bring fresh, cold water to boiling and add tea. Stir to immerse tea leaves completely. Cover and let stand 5 minutes. Strain infusion into warmed teapot. Provide additional teapots of very hot water. At serving time, pour 2 tablespoons tea concentrate into a cup and fill with clear, hot water. (40 servings)

Iced tea:

Prepare tea concentrate as directed above. Strain into 5 quarts cold (not iced) water. At serving time, pour tea infusion over ice-filled glasses. (30 to 35 servings)

Instant tea:

> ¾ ounce instant tea
> 5 quarts water

Combine instant tea and rapidly boiling water for hot tea or cold water for iced tea in large container. Pour into cups, if hot, or over ice in glasses, if cold. (30 servings)

CHAMPAGNE PUNCH
(About 150 servings)

6 (⅘-quart) bottles
champagne
6 (⅘-quart) bottles dry
sauterne

1 (⅘-quart) bottle brandy
3 (46-ounce) cans
sweetened grapefruit juice

Chill all ingredients thoroughly. Combine in large chilled punch bowl just before serving.

Both punch cups and champagne glasses are suitable for serving this light, golden punch which is an old favorite with both hosts and guests.

This amount allows about 3 punch cup (4-ounce) servings for 48 persons.

FRUIT PUNCH
(About 65 4-ounce servings)

3 (46-ounce) cans
pineapple juice
3 (6-ounce) cans frozen
orange juice concentrate

3 (12-ounce) cans apricot
nectar
3 (28-ounce) bottles ginger
ale or dry white wine

Have juice chilled thoroughly. Mix one-third at a time in punch bowl to keep mixture fresh and cold. Serve in punch cups.

Recipe may be doubled, as needed. This punch has a color as delightful as its flavor.

FRUIT PUNCH II
(About 25 servings)

1 quart sherbet (orange, pineapple, raspberry or lime)
1 quart well chilled fruit juice (orange, pineapple, grape,
cranberry or sweetened grapefruit)
2 (28-ounce) bottles ginger ale, well chilled

Place sherbet in large chilled punch bowl. Stir to soften. Add fruit juice, blending with sherbet. Then stir in ginger ale. Bowl, fruit juice and ginger ale should all be very cold because this punch is better without ice in it to dilute fruit flavors. Makes 25 to 30 servings in 4-ounce punch cups.

Do not double ingredients. Prepare each recipe as needed separately.

HOT MULLED PUNCH
(24 servings)

2 quarts sweet cider
2 cups orange juice
1 cup lemon juice
1 (18-ounce) can pineapple
juice

1 2-inch stick cinnamon
12 whole cloves
1 (⅘-quart) bottle rum or
brandy

Simmer cider, juices and spices 15 to 20 minutes. Remove spices and add rum or brandy. Serve hot. An orange stuffed with cloves may be floated in the punch bowl.

Recipe may be doubled. Simmering may be done ahead and mixture reheated, if more convenient.

HOT SPICED TOMATO JUICE
(12 servings)

1 (46-ounce) can tomato
juice
1 (10-ounce) can beef
consommé or bouillon
½ cup lemon juice
6 whole cloves

1 tablespoon Worcestershire
sauce
¼ teaspoon Tabasco
12 thin lemon slices
or sour cream for garnish

In saucepan combine tomato juice, consommé, lemon juice, cloves, Worcestershire and Tabasco. Simmer at least 30 minutes, longer for more flavor or prepare ahead and reheat. Remove cloves. Add water if mixture becomes too thick during heating. Brands of tomato juice vary in consistency. Serve piping hot in mugs or cups with thin slice of lemon floated on top or with a dollop of sour cream as garnish.

Recipe may be doubled. Excellent cold, too, served over ice cubes in tall glasses or poured out, pre-chilled, from a pitcher.

HOT TOMATO JUICE
(24 servings)

1 No. 10 or 2 46-ounce
cans tomato juice or
vegetable juice cocktail
1 tablespoon Worcestershire
sauce
1 teaspoon salt
¼ teaspoon pepper

1 bay leaf
1 lemon, sliced thin
For garnish, if desired: fresh
quartered lemon wedges or
stiffly beaten sweet or sour
cream

Combine tomato juice, Worcestershire, salt, pepper. Add bay leaf
and lemon slices. Simmer about 5 minutes. Remove bay leaf and
lemon slices with fork. Garnish with either of suggested foods.

Cold Tomato Juice Cocktail is a fine way to open a luncheon or
dinner—especially when seasonal fruits are expensive or scarce.

Recipe may be doubled. Remove bay leaf and lemon slices before
chilling.

RUM PUNCH
(About 75 4-ounce servings)

3 fifths light rum
3 (46-ounce) cans
unsweetened grapefruit
juice

3 (28-ounce) bottles
sparkling water
3 (8-ounce) bottles
maraschino cherries with
juice

Have all ingredients thoroughly chilled. Combine just before serving.
Recipe may be mixed one-third at a time so that each batch is fresh
and sparkling water stays "sparkling."

Recipe may be increased as desired.

WASSAIL BOWL (Cold)
(About 24 4-ounce servings)

1 quart apple juice
1 quart orange juice
1 cup lemon juice
1 (20-ounce) can pineapple
    juice
Sugar to taste

1 (28-ounce) bottle
    lemon-sour soda or Tom
    Collins mix
Orange slices or twists of
    lemon rind, for garnish

Blend juices, add sugar, stirring until dissolved. Chill until serving
time. Add chilled soda just before serving. Garnish each serving
with orange slices or lemon twists or float them on top.

Recipe may be doubled.

WINE PUNCH
(About 50 4-ounce servings)

3 quarts dry sauterne
1 pint brandy
1 (6-ounce) can frozen
    concentrated pineapple
    juice
1 (6-ounce) can frozen
    concentrated lemon juice

3 28-ounce bottles sparkling
    water, chilled
For garnish, if desired:
    whole strawberries,
    pineapple slices, melon
    balls or sliced peaches

Combine wine, brandy and fruit juice concentrates. Chill thoroughly. Just before serving add sparkling water. If desired, float fresh
or canned fruits in punch bowl, such as those suggested.

Recipe may be doubled.

BAKED BREAD SPECIALTIES

CHEESE-MUSTARD FRENCH BREAD
(24 servings)

3 long loaves French bread
1 pound Cheddar cheese
  grated
¼ cup prepared mustard

½ cup mayonnaise or salad
  dressing
¼ cup minced onion, if
  desired

Cut French bread in ½-inch slices, not cutting through bottom crust. Blend together well the cheese, mustard, mayonnaise and onion. Spread between slices. This may be done ahead. Place in shallow baking pan and heat in 350° F. oven until browned and bubbly, about 15 minutes. Serve hot.

Recipe may be doubled.

PARMESAN FRENCH BREAD
(48 servings)

2 long loaves French bread, about 1½-inches in diameter
½ pound butter or margarine
½ pound grated Parmesan cheese

Cut French bread into 48 slices. If bread of 1½-inch diameter is not available, cut slices in half. Toast on baking sheet in oven at

350° F. until golden brown, about 15 minutes. Brush one side of each slice with melted butter, then dip in grated Parmesan. Toast at 350° F. until cheese is melted. Serve as garnish for onion soup or as salad accompaniment on other menus. Toast does not need to be hot when served in soup, as latter will heat it.

Recipe may be increased as needed for occasion. May be made ahead and reheated as featured hot bread.

PIMENTO CHEESE TOPPING
(24 servings)

3 (3-ounce) packages
pimento cheese
4 (3-ounce) packages
cream cheese
1 cup (½ pound) margarine
or butter

2 teaspoons Worcestershire
sauce
1 finely minced clove
garlic (more to taste)
3 long French loaves or
2 dozen crusty French rolls

Allow cheese and margarine or butter to soften at room temperature. Blend smooth with Worcestershire sauce and minced garlic. Cut French loaves or rolls lengthwise. Spread cut sides with pimento cheese topping. Heat in 450° F. oven or broil watching carefully until cheese bubbles.

Cheese topping may be formed into a roll or a ball to chill and served as a spread for cocktail crackers, melba toast or breads. For a "help-yourself" cheese tray, roll formed cheese mixture in finely minced nuts, parsley or chives.

Recipe may be doubled.

TOAST BASKETS
(24 servings)

24 slices, fresh sandwich loaf bread
½ cup (¼ pound) butter or margarine, melted
½ cup salad oil

Spread both sides of bread with combined butter and oil. Press into muffin tins or custard cups and toast in oven at 350° F. until light brown. Let stand in pans until cooled, so that baskets retain shape. Re-crisp briefly by toasting in oven at 350° to 375° F. just before filling with creamed mixtures. Baskets may be prepared several days in advance.

Recipe may be increased as needed.

BREAKFAST BREADS

BREAKFAST CREPES
(24 servings)

6 cups sifted all-purpose
flour
2 teaspoons double acting
baking powder
1 teaspoon salt
18 eggs, separated

1½ quarts milk
2 tablespoons melted butter
or margarine
⅓ cup undiluted frozen
orange juice concentrate

Sift together flour, baking powder and salt. Beat together egg yolks, milk, melted butter, orange juice. Add dry ingredients and beat just until smooth. Fold in stiffly beaten egg whites. For each crepe, pour about 2 tablespoons batter on heated, lightly greased griddle. Brown lightly on both sides. Roll or fold into quarters and keep warm on paper towels in oven at 250° F. until all crepes are baked. Serve with orange sauce or maple syrup.

Separate mixings for additional batches are recommended.

BUTTERMILK PANCAKES
(48 servings)

12 cups sifted all-purpose
   flour
4 tablespoons sugar
1½ tablespoons salt
2 tablespoons baking soda

2 tablespoons double acting
   baking powder
7½ cups buttermilk
15 eggs, beaten
2 cups oil, melted butter or
   shortening

Sift dry ingredients together. Stir buttermilk into beaten eggs. Add flour mixture, then oil. Bake on lightly greased griddle until golden brown, turning once. Allow 4 medium-size pancakes per serving.

These delicious buttermilk pancakes will bring forth calls for more from most guests—better plan on the extras needed for additional mixings and bakings!

Dry ingredients for additional batches can be measured and packaged in individual containers (paper sacks or plastic bags) for mixing quickly with fresh eggs and oil. When dry buttermilk is used, substitute water for liquid buttermilk in specified quantity. Use 1½ cups dry buttermilk to 1 quart water to equal 1 quart fresh buttermilk. Combine 6 tablespoons powdered buttermilk to 1 cup water for 1 cup. Dry milk powder may be used in place of fresh sweet milk in recipe for basic pancakes in following proportions:

⅓ cup dry milk powder plus ¾ cup water to equal 1 cup
   liquid milk
1⅓ cups dry milk powder plus 3¾ cups water to equal
   1 quart liquid milk
2⅔ cups dry milk powder plus 7½ cups water to equal
   2 quarts liquid milk

PANCAKES
(48 servings)

6 quarts plus 1 cup sifted all-purpose flour	15 eggs
	2½ cups sugar
2½ tablespoons double acting baking powder	5 quarts milk
	2 cups oil or melted
4 teaspoons salt	butter or shortening

Sift flour, baking powder and salt together. Beat eggs until light, stir in sugar. Add milk, then sifted dry ingredients. Stir in oil. Bake on lightly greased griddle until golden brown on both sides, turning once. Allow 4 medium-size pancakes per serving.

Pouring batter from pitcher onto hot griddle is an efficient way to control size of pancakes as well as providing ease of handling. Prepare additional quantities separately.

PANCAKES FROM COMMERCIAL MIX
(24 servings)

9 cups commercial pancake mix (42 ounces)	½ cup oil plus 1 tablespoon (melted shortening may be substituted)
8 cups milk	
3 eggs	

Combine pancake mix, milk, eggs and oil. Stir together until smooth. Bake on hot griddle or lightly greased skillet, turning once. Allow 4 medium-size pancakes per serving.

Separate mixings of batter as needed assure best quality of lightness in golden brown pancakes. Be generous in providing toppings of syrup, butter and jam.

FRENCH TOAST
(48 servings)

96 slices bread   10 cups milk
50 eggs   About 1 pound shortening
⅔ cup sugar   for frying
1 teaspoon salt

Cut slices of bread diagonally. Beat eggs until frothy and then beat in sugar and salt. Stir in milk until well blended. Dip bread into mixture and then brown on hot greased griddle. Turn to brown both sides. Allow 4 half slices for each serving.

Light dusting of sifted powdered sugar over browned French toast has a festive look. Small cups of fruit preserves or jellies are attractive, too, on serving plates. Increase recipe as needed, but keep to workable-size batches at all times. Dip bread slices in egg mixture immediately prior to frying.

OVEN FRENCH TOAST
(24 servings)

12 eggs   48 slices enriched white
1½ cups sugar   bread
1 cup orange juice   2 teaspoons cinnamon
2 tablespoons grated orange
  rind

Combine eggs, 1 cup sugar, orange juice and rind. Beat just until blended. Dip each slice of bread in egg mixture. Arrange on well-buttered shallow pans, 18×26×1 inch. Combine cinnamon and remaining ½ cup sugar. Sprinkle lightly over top of each slice. Toast in oven at 500° F. about 10 minutes or until golden brown.

Recipe may be doubled.

WAFFLES SUPREME
(12 servings)

6 cups sifted all-purpose
  flour
2 tablespoons double acting
  baking powder
2 teaspoons salt

8 eggs, separated
1 quart milk
1 cup melted butter or
  margarine

Sift together flour, baking powder and salt. Beat egg yolks well; then add sifted dry ingredients alternately with the milk. Stir in melted butter. Fold in stiffly beaten egg whites. Do not overbeat batter at any point. Bake on hot waffle irons. Makes 12 large waffles.

Recipe may be doubled if care is used in blending to avoid over-mixing.

QUICK BREADS AND BISCUITS

BASIC HOT BISCUITS with Orange Tea Biscuit Variation
(48 servings)

4 cups sifted all-purpose
  flour
4 teaspoons double acting
  baking powder
3 teaspoons salt

2 tablespoons sugar
½ cup butter, margarine or
  shortening
1½ cups light cream

Sift together flour, baking powder, salt and sugar. Cut in butter until mixture is the consistency of coarse cornmeal. Add cream all at once, then stir gently until dough forms. Knead lightly on lightly floured board. Roll out ½ inch thick. Cut with biscuit cutter. Bake on lightly greased baking sheet in 425° F. oven about 12 minutes. May be baked ahead, wrapped in brown paper or foil, and reheated in 400° F. oven about 10 minutes.

ORANGE TEA BISCUIT VARIATION

1 tablespoon grated orange rind
48 cubes sugar
1 cup orange juice

Add orange rind to above dough. After biscuits are cut and arranged on baking sheet, dip cubes of sugar, one at a time, into orange juice, then press gently into biscuits. Bake as directed above.

Recipe may be doubled if adequate baking facilities are available and care is taken in mixing. Cut biscuits may be refrigerated while first ovenful is being baked. Avoid overcrowding oven.

CORNMEAL BISCUITS
(12 or 48 servings)

INGREDIENTS	12 SERVINGS	48 SERVINGS
biscuit mix	3 cups	3 quarts
cornmeal	1 cup	1 quart
milk	1⅓ cups	5⅓ cups

With fork, combine biscuit mix with cornmeal. Quickly stir in milk. Turn dough onto waxed paper or board well floured with additional biscuit mix. Knead and roll out into rectangle. Flatten to ½ inch thickness. Cut into 2-inch diamonds, squares or circles with floured knife or biscuit cutter. Bake on ungreased sheet in 450° F. oven 10 to 15 minutes, until golden.

Richer biscuits result from spreading rolled rectangle of dough with melted butter or margarine. Fold dough in half evenly. Cut biscuits. Brush tops lightly with melted butter. Bake as above or use as topping on meat pie. Recipe for 12 will require ⅓ cup butter or margarine and the recipe for 48 servings will require 1 cup butter or margarine.

BOSTON BROWN BREAD
(24 servings)

2 cups graham flour	*1½ cups molasses*
1 cup rye flour	*1 cup buttermilk*
1 cup cornmeal	*2 cups water*
2 teaspoons baking soda	*1½ cups raisins*
1 teaspoon salt	

Stir together both flours, cornmeal, baking soda and salt. Add molasses, buttermilk, water and raisins, mixing until blended. Divide batter evenly into 4 greased 1-pound coffee cans, filling them about three-quarters full. Grease lids and tape on tightly. (Two layers heavy aluminum foil may be substituted for a plastic lid.) Place in pan with boiling water halfway up sides of cans. Steam for 3 hours, keeping water at halfway mark. Uncover and dry 10 minutes in oven at 350° F.

Recipe may be doubled if large size steamer is available. May be made ahead and reheated over hot water on top of range or in oven.

CHEESE STICKS
(48 servings)

½ pound (2 cups) grated
  Cheddar or Swiss cheese
½ cup (¼ pound) butter or
  margarine
2 cups sifted all-purpose
  flour

1 teaspoon seasoned salt
2 tablespoons sesame or
  other seeds
4 tablespoons cream

Cut cheese and butter into flour, using pastry blender or two knives. Add seasoned salt and seeds. Stir in cream, mixing just until dough forms. Chill 30 minutes. Roll out on lightly floured board. Cut into 48 strips with pastry wheel or into diamonds or rectangles with sharp knife. Prick in three or four places with fork. Bake on ungreased baking sheet in 400° F. oven about 10 minutes or until golden. These scorch readily so watch them closely. Serve hot or cold.

Recipe may be doubled.

May be baked ahead and reheated in moderate oven on baking sheet.

CORN BREAD
(48 servings)

4 cups sifted all-purpose
  flour
4 tablespoons double acting
  baking powder
1⅓ cups sugar

1 tablespoon salt
3 cups cornmeal
1 quart milk
4 eggs, well beaten
½ cup shortening, melted

Sift together flour, baking powder, sugar and salt. Stir in cornmeal until evenly distributed. Combine milk with beaten eggs; add with shortening to dry ingredients. Stir just until flour mixture is moistened. Spread in two well-greased 13×9×2-inch baking pans or four 8×8×2-inch pans. Bake smaller pans in 425° F. oven for 20 minutes, about 25 to 30 minutes for larger pans. When toothpick or cake tester inserted in center comes out clean, corn bread is done. Cut into squares and serve hot.

Prepare additional quantities in separate mixings, do not double recipe.

SESAME CORN BREAD
(48 servings)

⅓ cup sesame (or caraway or cumin seeds)

4 cups sifted all-purpose flour

4 cups yellow cornmeal

2 tablespoons double acting baking powder

1½ tablespoons salt

1¼ cups melted butter or margarine

4 eggs

1 quart milk

Sprinkle sesame seeds evenly over bottoms of greased shallow baking pans (two 9×13 inch or equivalent). Combine flour, cornmeal, baking powder and salt. Pour in melted butter. Beat eggs and milk together and mix with dry ingredients just until blended. Pour into prepared pans and bake in oven at 400° F. for 25 minutes or until toothpick inserted in center comes out clean. Makes 48 squares, about 1½×2 inches.

Recipe may be doubled. Overbeating makes the corn bread tough and coarse, so extra care is needed in mixing larger amounts. May be baked ahead and reheated in brown paper bags, sprinkled with water, in 350° F. oven for 15 to 20 minutes.

SCONES
(24 servings)

6 cups sifted all-purpose
   flour
¼ cup double acting baking
   powder
1 tablespoon salt
¼ cup sugar

1½ cups nonfat dry milk
¾ cup shortening
6 eggs, beaten
1½ cups water
1 cup dried currants

Sift together flour, baking powder, salt, sugar and dry milk. Cut in shortening with pastry blender. Set aside ¼ cup beaten eggs for brushing top. Combine remaining beaten eggs with water. Make well in dry ingredients and add egg mixture, blending with a few quick strokes. Blend in currants. Divide dough in three parts and pat or roll each into a circle ¾ inch thick. Place on lightly greased baking sheet. Brush with reserved egg and sprinkle lightly with sugar. Cut each circle into 8 wedges. Bake in 425° F. oven 10 to 12 minutes, until golden brown.

Recipe may be doubled if care is used in blending. Currants may be omitted and dough cut into circles for use as shortcake.

QUICK FRUIT BREADS

BANANA BREAD
(48 servings)

4 cups sifted all-purpose flour	½ cup melted butter or margarine
3 teaspoons double acting baking powder	2 eggs, slightly beaten
1 teaspoon baking soda	1½ cups mashed bananas
½ teaspoon salt	¼ cup lemon juice
1½ cups sugar	¼ cup milk
	1 cup chopped nuts

Sift together flour, baking powder, soda, salt and sugar. Add melted butter, eggs, mashed banana and lemon juice, stirring in milk as mixture is moistened. Add nuts. Pour into two greased 9×5-inch loaf pans. Bake in 350° F. oven about 1 hour. Cool on racks. Loaf slices better if made a day ahead and stored in airtight wrapping or container. Cut each loaf into 24 thin slices.

Recipe may be doubled.

CANDIED FRUIT OR APRICOT LOAF
(20 to 24 thin slices)

2 cups sifted all-purpose
   flour
½ cup granulated sugar
2½ teaspoons double acting
   baking powder
½ teaspoon salt
1 egg

1 cup milk
2 tablespoons salad oil
¾ cup chopped, mixed
   candied fruit[1]
½ cup chopped nuts
1 tablespoon grated orange
   rind

Sift together flour, sugar, baking powder and salt into mixing bowl.
Add egg, milk and salad oil, then stir just to moisten flour mixture.
Quickly stir in fruit, nuts and grated orange rind. Turn into greased
9½ × 5¼ × 2½-inch loaf pan. Bake in 350° F. oven for 55 to 60
minutes. Cool in pan 5 minutes, then turn out carefully on a rack. Let
stand 24 hours before slicing into thin slices.

Recipe may be doubled or tripled. Three loaves will require about
1 pound chopped candied fruit or 1½ pounds dried apricots.

DATE BREAD
(48 servings)

2 cups pitted dates, cut
   fine
½ cup water
3 eggs
1¼ cups sugar
1 cup milk
3 cups sifted all-purpose
   flour

3 teaspoons double acting
   baking powder
1 teaspoon baking soda
½ teaspoon salt
1 cup chopped nuts
1 teaspoon cinnamon

[1] Dried apricots (1½ pounds) may be substituted for candied fruit.

Cook dates in water until soft; cool. Beat eggs and sugar until thick. Stir in milk. Sift flour, baking powder, soda and salt together; add to egg mixture. Add dates with liquid. Stir in nuts and cinnamon. Pour into two greased 8×4×3-inch loaf pans and let stand 30 minutes. Bake in 350° F. oven for 1 hour. Cool on racks. Bread will slice better if baked a day or two before serving and aged in airtight wrapping or container. Cut each loaf into 24 thin slices.

Recipe may be doubled.

ORANGE BREAD
(About 48 thin slices)

1 cup orange peel cut in
   thin strips
1½ cups sugar
4 cups sifted all-purpose
   flour
4 teaspoons double acting
   baking powder

½ teaspoon salt
½ cup butter or margarine,
   melted
2 eggs
2 cups milk

Boil orange rind in water to cover until tender. Drain, rinse with cold water and chop. Mix with 1 cup sugar and cook until thick, about 10 minutes. Cool. Sift together ½ cup sugar, flour, baking powder and salt; combine with melted butter. Beat eggs and milk and add to flour mixture, stirring just to moisten. Add orange rind. Pour into two greased 9×5-inch loaf pans. Let stand 20 minutes. Bake in 300° F. oven 1 hour. Cool on racks. This slices better if made a day ahead and stored in airtight wrapping or container. Cut each loaf into 24 thin slices.

Recipe may be doubled. Avoid overbeating.

MUFFINS

BRAN MUFFINS I
(48 servings)

5½ cups sifted all-purpose
   flour
1 tablespoon baking soda
3 tablespoons double acting
   baking powder
1 tablespoon salt
4½ cups bran
1½ cups oil or melted
   shortening

3 cups raisins, plumped in
   hot water
1½ cups sugar
1¼ cups molasses
6 eggs, beaten
2¾ cups milk

Sift together flour, baking soda, baking powder and salt. Combin
with bran, oil, drained raisins, sugar and molasses. Mix unt
blended. Add eggs and milk, blending well, but avoid overmixing o
beating. Drop into well-greased muffin pans, filling ⅔ full. Bake i
425° F. oven about 20 minutes. Makes 48 muffins.

Recipe may be doubled. Muffins may be made ahead and reheate
in oven at 350° to 375° F. enclosed in brown paper bags.

BRAN MUFFINS II
(48 servings)

1½ quarts shredded bran
3½ cups water
3 tablespoons vinegar
5 eggs
1½ cups sugar
6 cups sifted all-purpose
  flour
2 cups nonfat dry milk

1 tablespoon salt
3¼ tablespoons double acting
  baking powder
1 tablespoon baking soda
1 cup melted shortening or
  salad oil
2 cups raisins, rinsed in hot
  water, drained

Soak bran in water and vinegar 10 minutes. Beat eggs lightly then add soaked bran. Sift together sugar, flour, dry milk, salt, baking powder and baking soda and add one-fourth at a time to egg mixture, mixing just until moistened. Add melted shortening and raisins with last addition of dry ingredients. Do not overmix. Let stand 5 minutes. Bake in greased muffin tins in 400° F. oven 20 to 25 minutes. Makes 48.

Recipe may be doubled if care is used in blending and adequate oven space is available for baking.

CORN MUFFINS
(48 servings)

6 cups sifted all-purpose
  flour
4 tablespoons double acting
  baking powder
2 teaspoons salt

½ cup sugar
2 cups yellow cornmeal
4 eggs, well beaten
1 quart milk
1⅓ cups shortening, melted

Sift flour, baking powder, salt and sugar together. Stir in cornmeal. Combine beaten eggs and milk; add with melted shortening to dry ingredients. Mix quickly just to moisten flour. Spoon into well-greased muffin pans. Bake in 425° F. oven for 20 minutes. Makes forty-eight 2-inch muffins.

Plain muffins can be made from this recipe by substituting 2 cups sifted all-purpose flour for 2 cups cornmeal. For best results prepare separate mixings of larger quantities.

Variations:

BLUEBERRY: Add 1 quart fresh blueberries (or thawed frozen blueberries) to sifted dry ingredients.

CHERRY: Add 3 cups chopped, well-drained fresh or canned pie cherries to prepared batter.

CURRANT, DATE OR RAISIN: Add 2 cups of one of these dried fruits to sifted dry ingredients. Chop dates coarsely.

NUT: Add 2 cups coarsely cut or broken nuts to sifted dry ingredients.

WHEAT MUFFINS
(48 servings)

3½ cups whole wheat flour	1 cup shortening, melted, or salad oil
3½ cups sifted all-purpose flour	1⅓ cups molasses
2 tablespoons salt	4 eggs, beaten
1 tablespoon baking soda	2½ cups milk
3 tablespoons double acting baking powder	3 cups raisins, plumped in hot water 10 minutes, then drained
1½ cups granulated sugar	

Stir together both flours, salt, baking soda and baking powder. Add sugar, shortening, molasses, eggs, milk and raisins, blending just until mixed. Fill greased muffin pans two-thirds full. Bake in oven at 425° F. about 15 to 20 minutes. Makes 48 muffins. Double recipe if you want to provide "seconds."

Recipe may be increased up to 5 times amount given, if containers are available for mixing and baking, without having batter waiting. Muffins may be made ahead and reheated in heavy brown paper or foil, about 15 minutes in moderate oven.

QUICK COFFEE CAKE

ORANGE COFFEE CAKE
(48 servings)

9 cups sifted all-purpose flour	¼ cup grated orange rind
3 tablespoons double acting baking powder	5 eggs, slightly beaten
1½ tablespoons salt	2¼ cups milk
2¼ cups sugar	2¼ cups orange juice
	1½ cups salad oil

Sift together flour, baking powder, salt and sugar into large bowl. Stir in grated orange rind with a fork. Add eggs, milk, orange juice and oil. Mix just sufficiently to dampen flour, stirring from the bottom. Batter will appear lumpy. Quickly turn into three greased 13×9×2-inch baking pans, spreading evenly with spatula. Sprinkle with Crumb Topping (below). Bake in 350° F. oven 45 to 50 minutes. Cut into bars approximately 2×3 inches. Best served warm. Make additional coffee cakes in separate mixings.

CRUMB TOPPING

2¼ cups sugar
1 cup all-purpose flour
1 tablespoon grated orange
rind

½ cup (¼ pound) margarine
or butter

Combine sugar, flour and grated orange rind. Cut in ½ cup margarine or butter to form coarse crumb mixture. Set aside at room temperature until needed. Use about 1⅔ cups to top each coffee cake.

SPICY COFFEE CAKE
(24 servings)

3½ cups sifted all-purpose
flour
5 teaspoons double acting
baking powder
1¼ teaspoons salt
1 teaspoon nutmeg, if
desired

1 teaspoon cinnamon, if
desired
¾ cup butter or margarine
1½ cups sugar
3 eggs
1¾ cups milk
2 teaspoons vanilla

Grease a 13×9×2-inch baking pan, line with waxed paper, then grease slightly. Sift flour, baking powder, salt and spices, if used, together. Cream butter or margarine and sugar. Beat in eggs one at a time. Stir in sifted dry ingredients alternately with milk. Add vanilla. Spread in baking pan. Sprinkle Topping (below) over batter. Bake in oven at 350° F. 30 to 35 minutes or until cake tester comes out clean. Cut in 24 small squares.

Separate mixings of this batter will give best results. Prepare two batches if large servings are planned. Baked coffee cake may be frozen.

TOPPING

¼ cup butter or margarine, softened	½ cup sifted all-purpose flour
½ cup brown sugar	½ teaspoon cinnamon
	Few grains salt

Blend soft butter or margarine with brown sugar. Sift flour, cinnamon and salt together and cut into sugar mixture until it resembles fine crumbs. Sprinkle over dough before baking.

YEAST DOUGHS

CINNAMON COFFEE CAKE
(24 servings)

REFRIGERATOR SWEET DOUGH

¾ cup milk, scalded	½ cup warm water
½ cup butter or margarine	1 egg
2 teaspoons salt	4 cups all-purpose flour
½ cup granulated sugar	
2 packages active dry or cake yeast	

Combine scalded milk, butter or margarine, salt and sugar, stirring to dissolve sugar and melt butter. Cool to lukewarm. Sprinkle yeast over water in large bowl and stir until dissolved. Add milk mixture, egg and 2 cups flour. Beat dough smooth. Stir in 2 cups flour additional to make a stiff dough. Cover dough tightly with aluminum foil or waxed paper and bowl cover. Chill overnight. Dough will keep in refrigerator 3 days. This dough may be used for a variety of sweet rolls, braids, coffee cakes or rings.

CINNAMON COFFEE CAKE

1 recipe Refrigerator Sweet Dough
1 cup all-purpose flour
½ cup sugar
2 teaspoons cinnamon
½ cup chopped nuts (optional)

½ cup butter or margarine
⅔ cup powdered sugar
3 tablespoons milk
¼ teaspoon vanilla

Divide prepared, chilled dough in half. Roll or pat each half to a 9-inch square and place in greased, 9-inch square baking pans. Mix flour, sugar, cinnamon, nuts and butter to a coarse crumb consistency and sprinkle over dough. Cover. Let rise until doubled in bulk, 1 hour or longer. Bake in 375° F. oven 35 minutes. Remove from pans to cool on rack. Combine powdered sugar, milk and vanilla and drizzle over crumb topping (a bit more liquid may be required). Serve warm.

Recipe may be doubled.

DINNER ROLLS
(48 rolls)

1 cup milk, scalded
2 cakes fresh yeast
⅓ cup sugar
⅓ cup shortening (part butter, if desired)

1½ teaspoons salt
2 eggs
4 to 4½ cups all-purpose flour

Cool milk to lukewarm. Stir in yeast, sugar, shortening, salt and eggs thoroughly. Stir in 2 cups flour and beat batter well. Let rise until bubbly, about 40 minutes. Stir in 2 to 2½ cups flour or enough to make a soft dough that is easily handled. Turn onto lightly floured board and knead until dough is smooth. Place in lightly greased bowl, turning to grease top of dough. Cover and let rise until doubled about 1 hour in a warm place. Shape into rolls and arrange on lightly greased baking sheets. Dough may be covered and stored in refrigerator for baking within 6 hours. Chilled rolls require 1½ hours raising time, unchilled rolls 1 hour. Keep rolls covered with warm, damp cloth while rising until doubled in bulk. Bake in 425° F. oven 12 minutes or until light golden brown. Brush tops with melted butter when taken from the oven. Makes 4 dozen small rolls.

Recipe may be doubled if heavy-duty power mixer is available. Hand-mixed batches should not be doubled.

QUICK BUTTERMILK ROLLS
(36 rolls)

1 pint buttermilk, scalded
¼ cup sugar
¼ cup butter or margarine
¼ cup shortening
1 tablespoon salt

½ teaspoon baking soda
2 packages active dry or
  cake yeast
5½ cups sifted all-purpose
  flour

Cool buttermilk to lukewarm. Add sugar, butter, shortening, salt, soda and yeast. Stir to mix well. Stir in flour to make a moderately stiff dough. When flour is completely blended into yeast mixture, turn dough out on a lightly floured board. Knead dough just enough to smooth out and round up. In large oiled bowl place ball of dough, turning so that all surfaces are oiled. Cover and let rise 45 minutes in warm place. Shape dough into 3 dozen rolls. Brush tops with melted butter and let rise until doubled, about 30 minutes. Bake in oven at 425° F. for 15 minutes.

Mix additional batter for Quick Buttermilk Rolls separately unless heavy-duty power mixer is available to blend flour-yeast mixture together.

REFRIGERATOR ROLLS
(48 rolls)

½ cup sugar	1 cup warm water
1 tablespoon salt	1 egg, well beaten
3 tablespoons shortening	6 cups sifted all-purpose
¾ cup hot water	flour (about)
2 packages active dry or	
yeast cakes	

Combine sugar, salt, shortening and hot water, stirring until shortening is dissolved. Cool to lukewarm. Combine yeast and 1 cup warm water in large bowl, stirring to dissolve yeast. Add lukewarm sugar mixture, egg and 3 cups flour. Beat until smooth. Stir in enough of remaining 3 cups sifted flour to make a soft dough. Turn out on lightly floured board and knead until dough is smooth and elastic, about 8 to 10 minutes. Place dough in oiled bowl, turning to grease all sides. Cover and store in refrigerator, holding no longer than 4 to 5 days at 40 to 45° F. When ready to use, remove dough from refrigerator and punch down, cutting off just the amount that will be needed for current baking. Shape rolls as desired and place on greased baking sheet. Cover and let rise in warm place until doubled in bulk, about 30 minutes. Baking time varies slightly according to size of rolls. Most shapes bake well at 400° F. for 12 to 15 minutes.

Recipe may be doubled only if heavy-duty power mixer is available.

If active dry yeast is substituted for fresh yeast, use very warm water (105° to 115°) to dissolve granules. First rinse cool or room temperature mixing bowl with warm water. Use dissolved yeast as recipe directs.

Fresh yeast cakes are dissolved in lukewarm water in order to preserve leavening power. Too much heat kills yeast.

DIRECTIONS FOR SHAPING
YEAST ROLL DOUGH

Cloverleaf: Divide roll dough into four portions. Shape each into 9-inch roll. Cut into nine equal pieces. From each piece form three small balls. Dip in melted butter or margarine and place three balls in each section of medium-size, greased muffin pans.

Crescents: Divide roll dough into three portions. Roll each to a circle about 12 inches in diameter. Cut into sixteen pie-shaped wedges. Beginning at wide end, roll up tightly. Seal point firmly, using a bit of milk or water, if necessary. Curve ends slightly toward each other.

Curlicues: Cut rolled dough into strips about 1 inch wide and 9 inches long. Hold one end to greased cookie sheet and wind closely to form a coil, tucking open end firmly underneath. Allow about 2 inches between rolls.

Fan Tans: Cut rolled dough into 1-inch strips. Stack 5 strips of dough and cut into 1-inch slices. Place slices with cut edges up in greased muffin pans. Dough strips may be very lightly brushed with melted butter before stacking, if desired, to make *Butterflake Rolls*.

Figure 8: Cut strips of dough ½ inch wide by about 7 inches long. Twist strip and fasten the two ends together to make an oblong ring. Turn one end of oblong over, forming a figure 8.

Knots: Cut strips of dough ½ inch wide by about 7 inches long. Tie a loose knot in center of strip of dough.

Lucky Clovers: Cut dough into three or four equal portions, shaping each into approximately a 9-inch roll. Cut each roll into nine equal pieces. Form balls and place in greased muffin pans approximately 2½ inches in diameter. With kitchen shears, cut deeply into each ball crosswise, almost to bottom. Then cut dough into quarters. Brush tops with melted butter.

Pan Rolls: Form 1-inch balls of dough into even rounds. Place in greased pans about ¼ inch apart.

Parker House Rolls: Roll dough to ¼-inch thickness. Cut into rounds with 2-inch floured biscuit cutter. Brush with melted butter or margarine. Make a crease with back of knife across each round, just off center. Fold at crease and press edges together at crease to prevent them from springing open.

STOLLEN
(24 servings)

¼ teaspoon salt
½ cup sugar
¼ cup butter or margarine
¾ cup scalded milk
¼ cup warm (not hot) water
2 packages active dry yeast
2 eggs, slightly beaten
1½ teaspoons grated lemon or orange peel
4½ cups all-purpose flour

1½ cups raisins
½ cup mixed candied fruit, chopped
⅔ cups blanched almonds, slivered
¼ cup melted butter or margarine (additional)
Glazed fruits and whole nutmeats to garnish, as desired

Combine salt, sugar, butter or margarine and scalded milk. Cool to lukewarm. Measure warm (not hot) water into a large bowl. Add yeast, stirring to dissolve. Blend in cooled milk mixture, eggs, grated peel and half the flour. Beat with spoon until smooth. Add remaining flour. Turn onto lightly floured board. Knead until dough is smooth and elastic. Round into ball and place in greased bowl, turning to grease top. Cover and let rise until doubled in bulk, about 1 hour in warm place free of drafts. Divide dough in half by cutting with sharp knife. Into each portion, knead half of measured fruits and nuts, working until well distributed through the dough. Roll each ball of dough to an oblong shape approximately ½ inch thick. Brush with half of melted butter. Fold in half lengthwise, as for Parker House rolls. Brush tops with remaining melted butter. Arrange on greased baking sheet. Cover and let rise until doubled in bulk, about 1 hour. Bake in 350° F. oven 35 to 40 minutes until deep golden brown. If desired, while warm, spread with glaze of powdered sugar and milk or dust with sifted powdered sugar before serving, if preferred. Glazed fruits and whole nuts may be placed on freshly frosted stollen as desired.

Prepare additional quantities in separate mixings.

CAKE CUTTING GUIDE

8" 2 layer cake
12 servings

9" 2 layer cake
16 servings

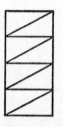

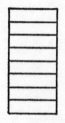

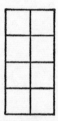

1 pound loaf cake
8 servings

1 pound loaf cake
8 servings

1 pound loaf cake
8 servings

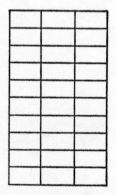

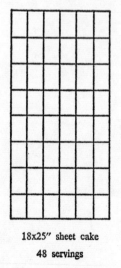

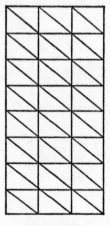

9x13" sheet cake
30 servings

18x25" sheet cake
48 servings

18x25" sheet cake
48 servings

BASIC CAKES

TROPICAL GINGERBREAD
(24 servings)

4⅔ cups sifted all-purpose
flour
3 teaspoons double acting
baking powder
1½ teaspoons baking soda
1 teaspoon salt
1 teaspoon cinnamon
1 teaspoon nutmeg
1 teaspoon ginger

½ teaspoon ground cloves
1 cup sugar
1 cup shortening
1½ cups milk
4 eggs
2 cups molasses
1 cup well-drained crushed
pineapple

Sift together flour, baking powder, soda, salt, spices and sugar. Blend in softened shortening. Add milk, stirring until dampened. Beat 2 minutes on low speed. Add eggs and molasses and beat 1 minute more. Fold in pineapple. Pour into two greased and floured 8×8×2-inch square pans or twenty-four prepared cupcake pans. Bake 20 to 25 minutes in 375° F. oven. Cover with Topping (below), if desired, or serve with Orange Sauce*.

TOPPING

4 egg whites
½ cup water
2 cups sugar
¼ cup molasses

¼ teaspoon salt
1 teaspoon vanilla
2 cups grated coconut

Combine egg whites, water, sugar, molasses and salt in top of double boiler. Beat over rapidly boiling water with rotary or electric beater until frosting stands in peaks. Remove from heat. Add vanilla and coconut. Spread on cooled cakes or cupcakes. Sufficient to frost 2 square cakes or 24 cupcakes generously.

Recipes may be doubled if large-size mixers and bowls are available and oven space is adequate.

ORANGE CAKE
(24 servings)

⅔ cup butter or margarine
⅔ cup shortening
3 cups sugar
1½ tablespoons grated orange
    rind
6 eggs

5 cups sifted cake flour
5 teaspoons double acting
    baking powder
2 teaspoons salt
2 cups fresh or reconstituted
    frozen orange juice

Cream together butter, shortening, sugar and orange rind. Add eggs one at a time. Beat well. Sift together flour, baking powder and salt, and add to butter mixture alternately with orange juice. Pour into four greased and floured 9-inch round cake pans, about 2 cups to each pan. Bake in 350° F. oven 25 to 30 minutes. Cool on racks. Fill and frost two 2-layer cakes with Orange Butter Frosting (below).

ORANGE BUTTER FROSTING

1 cup (½ pound) butter or
  margarine
2 pounds 8 ounces (2¼
  quarts) sifted powdered
  sugar

1 (6-ounce) can (¾ cup)
  undiluted frozen orange
  juice concentrate
1 tablespoon grated orange
  rind

Cream butter and sugar. Add orange juice and rind. Beat until
smooth and fluffy.

Recipes may be doubled. Cake stays fresh well for 3 or 4 days. It
also freezes well; wrap after freezing to keep icing neat.

POUND CAKE
(24 servings)

2 cups butter or 1 cup
  butter and 1 cup
  shortening
2 cups sugar
9 eggs
1 teaspoon vanilla

½ teaspoon nutmeg
4 cups sifted cake flour
½ teaspoon salt
2 teaspoons double acting
  baking powder

Cream butter very well until thick and light, like whipped cream.
Gradually add sugar, beating well. Continue to beat until sugar is
completely dissolved. Beat in eggs one at a time. Add vanilla and
nutmeg. Sift together flour, salt and baking powder. Add gradually
to butter mixture, folding in gently. Avoid overbeating when adding
flour. Bake in two greased and floured 9×5×3-inch loaf pans or in

a 10-inch tube pan in 325° F. oven for about 1 hour, or until toothpick or cake tester inserted in center comes out clean.

Recipe may be doubled if care is taken in blending. Cake is even better if baked a day or two before serving.

EASY SPICE CAKE
(12 servings)

2½ cups sifted cake flour
1 teaspoon baking soda
1 teaspoon double acting
   baking powder
1 teaspoon salt
1 teaspoon cinnamon
½ teaspoon nutmeg or mace
¼ teaspoon ground cloves
1 cup granulated sugar

½ cup vegetable shortening
⅔ cup brown sugar
1 cup plus 2 tablespoons
   buttermilk or sour milk
   or reconstituted dry
   buttermilk
⅓ to ½ cup whole eggs (2
   large)

Sift flour, baking soda, baking powder, salt, spices and white sugar together three times, the last time into a mixing bowl. Add shortening, brown sugar and buttermilk or sour milk. (Reconstituted dry buttermilk may be used, mixed according to package directions.) Mix with a spoon until flour mixture is moistened. Beat with electric mixer at low speed 2 minutes or beat vigorously with a spoon, approximately 150 strokes per minute. Add unbeaten eggs and beat 1 minute longer. Spread in two waxed-paper-lined 9-inch layer pans. Bake in oven at 375° F. for 25 to 30 minutes or until cake tester comes out clean. Cake may be baked in 13×9×2-inch baking pan at 375° F. for 40 minutes or until done.

Recipe may be doubled if powerful mixer is used and care is taken to scrape batter down from sides of bowl with spatula during beating time.

WHITE CAKE
(24 servings)

3 cups sifted cake flour
4 teaspoons double acting
  baking powder
1 teaspoon salt
¾ cup butter or margarine

1½ cups sugar
1½ teaspoons vanilla
1 cup milk
4 egg whites, beaten stiff

Sift flour, baking powder and salt together. Cream butter or margarine until fluffy. Gradually blend in sugar until smooth. Stir in vanilla. Add flour mixture and milk alternately in small portions, blending thoroughly after each. Fold in stiffly beaten egg whites. Spread in two 11×7×2-inch greased and waxed-paper-lined cake pans. Bake 375° F. oven until top springs back when touched, 30 to 35 minutes. Cool 10 minutes and then remove to racks. When thoroughly cool, frost as desired. Layers can be cut into 48 petits fours about 1½ inches in diameter; allow 2 per serving.

Separate mixings are preferable to doubling cake recipe, unless adequate power mixer is available. Batter may also be baked in three greased and floured 8- or 9-inch round layer pans, in 375° F. oven for about 25 minutes. For sheet cake, turn batter into 13×9×2-inch greased and floured pan to bake at 375° F. 35 minutes. Batter may be spread in 15×10×1-inch greased and floured jelly roll pan to bake at 375° F. about 25 to 30 minutes. Recipe will make about 30 2½-inch cupcakes. Grease cupcake pans thoroughly, fill with batter two-thirds full. Bake at 375° F. about 15 to 20 minutes or until done.

YELLOW LAYER CAKE
with Chocolate Variation
(24 servings)

2 cups shortening	1½ teaspoons salt
4 cups granulated sugar	2 cups milk
8 eggs, separated	1 tablespoon vanilla
7 cups sifted cake flour	
1½ tablespoons double acting baking powder	

Cream shortening until light and fluffy. Gradually blend in sugar, beating until very creamy. Beat in egg yolks. Sift together flour, baking powder and salt, and add in thirds alternately with milk, beginning and ending with flour mixture. Add vanilla. Beat egg whites until stiff. Gently fold into batter. Divide evenly between four greased and floured 8- or 9-inch layer cake pans. Bake in 350° F. oven about 30 minutes or until tops spring back when touched lightly with finger. Cool on rack. Frost as desired; see recipes for frosting in Index. Makes two 2-layer cakes, to be cut into 12 servings each.

For Chocolate Variation:

Melt four (1-ounce) squares unsweetened chocolate, cool and add with egg yolks to creamed shortening and sugar mixture.

Recipes may be doubled only if commercial-size mixer and ovens are available for mixing and baking. Otherwise, prepare and bake in two mixings.

CAKES FROM MIXES

LAZY-DAISY CAKE
(48 servings)

4 packages spice cake mix
1 cup chopped walnuts or pecans or slivered almonds

Prepare spice cake mix according to package directions. Bake in four
13×9×2-inch greased and floured baking pans according to package directions. Let cakes cool in pan to warm. Spread Meringue
Topping (below) carefully over cakes in baking pans and sprinkle
with nuts. Bake in 375° F. oven 20 minutes or until lightly browned.

Do not double meringue recipe. White sugar may be substituted
for brown in the Meringue Topping. Almond extract is an alternate
choice to vanilla extract when white sugar is used, especially suitable
when slivered almonds are sprinkled over top.

Do not mix more cake batter than can be baked at one time. If
separate bakings of cakes are planned, divide and mix Meringue
Topping for each cake separately, too.

MERINGUE TOPPING

8 egg whites   *1 teaspoon vanilla*
¼ teaspoon salt
2 cups brown sugar, firmly
    packed

Beat egg whites with salt until frothy. Add sugar, 2 tablespoons
at a time, beating well after each addition. Continue beating after

all is added until meringue will stand in stiff peaks. Add vanilla, beating in well.

LEMON CAKE
(24 servings)

2 packages lemon cake mix
2 (3-ounce) packages lemon-
flavored gelatin
1½ cups water
1½ cups salad oil

8 eggs
1 (6-ounce) can frozen
lemonade concentrate,
undiluted
2 cups powdered sugar

Combine cake mix and gelatin. Add water and oil and beat two minutes. Add eggs and beat 2 minutes longer. Bake in greased and floured sheet cake pans, either two 13×9×2-inch pans or one 22×13-inch pan, in 300° F. oven. Allow about 50 minutes for 13×9-inch pans, about 65 minutes for 22×13-inch pan. Cakes test done when toothpick inserted in center comes out clean, and top springs back when lightly touched with finger. Meanwhile make topping by combining frozen lemonade with powdered sugar. Pour over cake while warm, inserting cooking fork in cake so that topping will "soak in." Good warm or cold.

Recipe may be doubled only if equipment is large enough to ensure thorough mixing and proper baking. Bake only one layer of cake pans in oven at a time.

PINEAPPLE MERINGUE TORTE
(12 servings)

1 package white cake mix
¾ cup slivered almonds

Prepare cake mix according to package directions. Grease and line with waxed paper two 9-inch layer pans. Divide batter between pans and let stand in refrigerator or cool place while preparing Meringue Topping. Spread Topping lightly over cake batter. Sprinkle slivered almonds over meringue. Bake in 350° F. oven for 30 minutes or until cake tester comes out clean. Cool cake 5 minutes, loosen meringue from sides of pan. Let cool in pans 10 minutes longer then turn out of pans and cool cake on wire rack, meringue side up. When cake is completely cool, fill and serve.

MERINGUE TOPPING

4 egg whites   *1 cup sugar*
¼ teaspoon salt   *½ teaspoon almond extract*

Beat egg whites and salt until frothy. Gradually beat in sugar about 1 tablespoonful at a time. Continue beating until meringue is thick and glossy. Add extract.

PINEAPPLE FILLING

1 cup whipping cream   *1½ teaspoons sugar*
1 cup crushed pineapple,   *¼ teaspoon vanilla*
drained

Beat cream until stiff. Fold in pineapple, sugar and vanilla. Place one layer of cake with meringue side down on serving plate. Spread filling on cake. Place second layer on top of filling with meringue side up.

Recipe may be doubled for this spectacular dessert with wide flavor appeal.

DESSERT SPECIALTIES MADE WITH CAKE

CHOCOLATE WHIPPED CREAM-FILLED ANGEL LOAF CAKE
(12 servings)

1 large angel loaf cake
1 pint whipping cream
¼ cup chocolate dessert syrup

Slice cake into four layers lengthwise. Beat cream until stiff. Fold in chocolate dessert syrup. Spread chocolate mixture evenly between layers, reserving part for top and sides. Chill at least 8 hours.

Recipe may be doubled. Sponge cake may be substituted for angel cake, if desired, in preparing this popular dessert.

MINIATURE CUPCAKES
(about 72 little cakes)

1 package cake mix

Prepare according to package directions. Spoon batter carefully into 1½-inch diameter muffin tins or tiny baking paper cups set on a baking sheet. Bake in 400° F. oven until cakes are golden, approximately 10 minutes. Cool on rack. One package will make approximately 6 to 7 dozen tiny cupcakes. These may be frozen after baking. Frost with butter cream icing tinted in delicate colors and decorate with frosting in contrasting colors formed with decorating tube or with bits of glacé fruits, coconut, chocolate shot or nut halves, as preferred.

Prepare two kinds of cake mix and use contrasting frosting and decoration to add variety and attractive appearance to a tea table. If cakes are to be frozen after frosting, do not wrap until frozen hard so that decorations are not pushed out of shape. Remove wrappings carefully when brought to room temperature. Best length of storage time in a freezer is 1 week.

ORANGE LAYER CAKE
(48 servings)

4 rectangular long loaf or two 9-inch round angel cakes

Cut each cake into three layers. Fill with Orange Filling and frost with Orange Frosting.

ORANGE FILLING

1 cup granulated sugar
½ cup cornstarch
1 teaspoon salt
3 cups water
5 egg yolks

1 (12-ounce) can frozen concentrated orange juice, undiluted
2 tablespoons butter or margarine

Blend sugar, cornstarch and salt. Stir in water. Bring to boil over medium heat. Beat egg yolks with orange juice concentrate. Beat quickly into hot mixture, stirring constantly. Cook 2 minutes or until thickened. Remove from heat. Add butter and cool completely before spreading on cake.

ORANGE FROSTING

1 cup (½ pound) butter or margarine
2 pounds (2¼ quarts) sifted powdered sugar

1 (6-ounce) can frozen concentrated orange juice, undiluted
1 tablespoon grated orange rind
5 egg whites

Cream butter and sugar. Add orange juice, rind and egg whites, whipping until fluffy. Spread on top and sides of cake.

Recipe may be doubled. May be prepared 24 hours ahead.

PETITS FOURS (Cake)
(48 servings)

1 cup shortening	1 teaspoon salt
2 cups granulated sugar	1 cup milk
3½ cups sifted cake flour	1½ teaspoons vanilla
4 teaspoons double acting	6 egg whites
baking powder	¼ teaspoon cream of tartar

Cream shortening until fluffy. Gradually blend in sugar, beating until very light and fluffy like whipped cream. Sift together flour, baking powder and salt; add in thirds alternating with milk, beginning and ending with flour mixture. Add vanilla. Beat egg whites until stiff, with cream of tartar. Fold gently into batter. Pour into greased and floured 13×9×2-inch pan. Bake in 350° F. oven about 45 minutes or until top springs back when touched lightly with finger. Cool on rack. When thoroughly cooled, cut into 1- to 1½-inch squares or diamonds.

Chill cakes 1 hour or more before frosting to firm outer edges and keep crumbs from spoiling decoration. Cover each cube with Fondant Frosting*, Caramel Frosting* or Chocolate Glaze*; let stand until firm and then add flowers or piped edges formed with Decorator's Icing*, tinted in variety of colors. The latter may also be used as basic coating, with small amounts tinted in variety of colors and flavored to provide pleasing contrast.

Recipe may be doubled. This amount make 96 petits fours.

PETITS FOURS
(36 servings)

1 (13×9-inch) white cake	*White Frosting (recipe below)*
1 egg white	*Colored Decorating Icing*
1 tablespoon water	*(recipe below)*

Trim brown outside edges of cake. Cut into about 1½-inch squares, diamonds or rectangles. Combine egg white with water and brush over sides and top of cakes. Let dry. (This prevents crumbs in the frosting.) Place cakes one inch apart on wire racks set over cooky sheet or large sheet of aluminum foil or waxed paper. Spoon White Frosting over top and sides of each cake. Excess frosting which runs to sheet beneath rack may be scraped up, reheated and reused. Decorate cakes with delicate motifs using small decorating tubes or applying colored frosting with toothpicks. Candied cherries, angelica, citron and nutmeats may be used in decorating. Place each finished petit four on a small, fluted paper cup when frosting and decoration are set.

WHITE FROSTING

1½ cups granulated sugar	*½ teaspoon vanilla*
⅛ teaspoon cream of tartar	*1 pound sifted powdered*
¾ cup water	*sugar (about)*

Place granulated sugar, cream of tartar and water in saucepan over moderate heat, stirring until sugar dissolves. Boil without stirring to 226° F. on candy thermometer. Remove from heat, add vanilla and cool to lukewarm. Stir in enough sifted powdered sugar to make a good pouring consistency. A too-thick frosting is difficult to work with. Pour over cakes from tablespoon, tipping the rack so that all sides of each cake are coated evenly. All or part of this frosting may be tinted if preferred.

COLORED DECORATING ICING

1 cup sifted powdered sugar
2 to 3 tablespoons water
Food coloring

Add enough water to sugar to make mixture thick enough to force through decorating tube and hold its shape. Divide and tint delicately to form leaves and flowers or special designs on frosted cakes.

TIERED CAKE
(70 servings)

First Mixing:

1 Recipe White Cake* or 2 packages white cake mix

Prepare White Cake or mix as directed, increasing beating by 1½ times that given on package, if using mix. Divide batter evenly among well-greased and floured 12-inch, 9-inch and 6-inch pans.[1] Bake 12-inch layer in 350° F. oven for 30 to 40 minutes or until top springs back when lightly touched with finger. (Refrigerate batter in other two layer pans until first is done if only one oven is available.) Bake 9-inch layer near back of oven 30 to 35 minutes. Bake 6-inch layer near front of oven 25 to 30 minutes at same temperature. Cool on racks 10 minutes before removing from pans. Cool thoroughly before icing.

[1] If the available pan sizes vary from the ones specified, the only way to estimate the amount of batter needed for available pans is to approximate the variation as closely as possible. The first baking will be a good test for judging the amount of batter needed. Pans should be filled no more than two-thirds full nor less than one-half full.

DELICATE DESSERTS DELIGHT EYE

Pictured in foreground is light and luscious Strawberry Chiffon Pie in Graham Cracker Crust, highlighted with thoroughly drained fresh strawberries. Also shown is an assortment of Miniature Cup Cakes, frosted in an array of colors and garnished with an assortment of toppings, including walnut halves and thin wedges of fresh orange, lemon or lime. Such a variety of choices can be offered without great effort. Recipes are listed in Index.

Second Mixing:

1 Recipe White Cake* or 2 packages white cake mix

Repeat mixing and baking as directed above. When thoroughly cooled, put 12-inch layers together with frosting on the plate or tray on which cake will be served. Frost sides and top. Place 9-inch circle of light white cardboard, preferably the lightly waxed variety, on top. Put 9-inch layers together as second tier on top of 12-inch tier, frosting sides and top. Repeat with 6-inch cardboard circle and 6-inch layers of cake.

TIERED CAKE FROSTING

3 (1-pound) packages confectioners' sugar	1 cup egg whites, unbeaten (8 to 10)
2 cups sifted cake flour	½ teaspoon salt
4 cups white vegetable shortening	1 teaspoon each lemon and almond flavorings

Combine all ingredients in large bowl of electric mixer and beat until smooth and creamy. Cover sides and top of cake as directed in Tiered Cake recipe. Spoon remaining frosting into pastry bag for decorating.

CUTTING GUIDE FOR TIERED CAKE

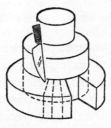

Cut vertically through bottom layer cutting even with center layer; then cut in wedge-shaped slices.

When lower layer has been served, follow same procedure with middle layer, cutting vertically along edge of top layer, then cutting in wedge-shaped slices.

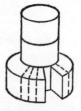

When second layer has been served, return to bottom layer and cut again even with center layer.

Remaining layers may be cut as ordinary layer cake.

14-inch layer yields approximately 40 pieces
12-inch layer yields approximately 30 pieces
10-inch layer yields approximately 20 pieces
9-inch layer yields approximately 16 pieces
8-inch layer yields approximately 12 pieces

NOTE: If cake is being served from reception table and you wish to preserve appearance of cake, follow this procedure but cut only from one side of cake, until necessary to turn and cut second half.

STRAWBERRY GLAZED CHEESECAKE
(24 servings)

3 cups vanilla wafer crumbs,
  firmly packed
½ cup melted butter or
  margarine
6 (8-ounce) packages
  cottage cheese, sieved
2 cups sugar
⅔ cup all-purpose flour

1 teaspoon salt
⅓ cup lemon juice
2 teaspoons grated lemon
  rind
2 teaspoons vanilla
6 eggs, separated
1 pint heavy cream,
  whipped

Blend together cooky crumbs and butter. Press evenly to sides and
bottoms of two 9-inch springform pans. Combine cottage cheese,
sugar, flour and salt. Stir in lemon juice and rind and vanilla. Beat
egg whites until stiff. Beat egg yolks until thick. Fold egg yolks into
cheese mixture, then fold in whipped cream and finally egg whites.
Spoon lightly into crumb-lined pans. Bake in 300° F. oven for 1
hour. Turn off heat and let cake remain in oven one hour with door
closed. Cool on cake rack. Remove sides of pans. Top with Strawberry Glaze and chill until serving time.

STRAWBERRY GLAZE

2 quarts strawberries
1 cup sugar
½ cup water
1½ tablespoons cornstarch

1 tablespoon butter or
  margarine
Red food coloring

Wash and hull strawberries. Crush enough berries to fill 1 cup.
Keep remaining berries whole and drain on paper towels. Combine crushed berries, sugar, water and cornstarch. Bring to boil and

cook until thickened, stirring constantly. Add butter and food coloring. Strain through sieve. Arrange whole berries on top of baked, cooled cheesecakes. Pour glaze evenly over berries. Chill until ready to serve.

Recipe may be doubled if oven space is available and care is taken in mixing and baking.

STRAWBERRY SHORTCAKE
(48 servings)

6 (12-ounce) packages frozen sliced strawberries or 6 quarts
    fresh, halved strawberries
48 shortcakes prepared from Basic Biscuit* or Scone Recipe*
1 quart heavy cream, whipped

If using fresh berries, sprinkle with 4 cups sugar or more to taste and chill. Arrange berries over halved shortcakes shortly before serving time. Replace top halves. Top with cream that has been whipped until stiff, flavored with 1 tablespoon vanilla and 2 cups sugar, if desired.

Recipe may be doubled.

CAKE FROSTINGS

CARAMEL FROSTING

(Frosting for about 30 petits fours, 12 cupcakes or 1 9×13-inch loaf cake)

½ cup (¼ pound) butter   *½ teaspoon salt*
* or margarine*   *1½ teaspoons vanilla*
1 cup evaporated milk   *3 cups sifted powdered*
1 cup brown sugar   *sugar*

Combine butter, evaporated milk, brown sugar and salt. Cook over low heat, stirring until sugar is melted. Cool. Stir in vanilla and sugar. To return to pouring consistency, place over bowl of hot water until thinned to proper degree.

Recipe may be increased.

CHOCOLATE GLAZE

(Frosting for about 30 petits fours, 12 cupcakes or 1 13×9-inch loaf cake)

2 (6-ounce) packages semi-sweet chocolate morsels
¼ cup butter or margarine
½ cup evaporated milk or cream

Melt chocolate morsels and butter over very low heat. Gradually add evaporated milk, stirring to blend. Cool to proper consistency for pouring or spreading, depending on manner of frosting desired.

Recipe may be doubled. Avoid overheating or overblending as grayed and grainy mixture will result.

DECORATOR'S ICING

(Rosettes, edging for 96 petits fours, 48 cupcakes or to frost two 8- or 9-inch layer cakes)

2 egg whites
⅛ teaspoon cream of tartar
2 teaspoons water

2½ to 3 cups sifted powdered sugar
Food coloring, as desired

Blend egg whites, cream of tartar and water. Beat until frothy. Gradually beat in powdered sugar, adding enough to permit mixture to hold soft peaks. Tint as desired with food coloring. Use for rosettes, piping, etc., through pastry tube or swirl on with spatula. May also be used to pour over petits fours by placing over bowl of hot water to bring to thinner consistency.

Recipe may be doubled if care is used in mixing. If mixture becomes too thick, add a little hot water to give consistency desired.

FONDANT FROSTING

(Frosting for 96 petits fours, 48 cupcakes or 2 8- to 9-inch layer cakes or angel cakes)

¼ cup butter or margarine, melted
⅓ cup cream (or fruit juice or coffee)
3½ cups (1 pound) sifted powdered sugar

½ teaspoon salt
1 teaspoon vanilla
Food coloring, as desired

Combine butter and cream and blend gradually with powdered sugar, mixing until smooth. Add salt and vanilla. Tint as desired.

Pour over chilled petits fours or swirl on top of cupcakes. If thicker frosting is desired for layer cakes, add additional powdered sugar to give consistency desired.

Recipe may be doubled, or cut in halves or thirds if variety of frosting is desired for attractive assortment of little cakes. For easy division, note that there are 4 tablespoons in ¼ cup; 5⅓ tablespoons in ⅓ cup.

COOKIES

APPLESAUCE BARS
(48 bars)

4 cups sifted all-purpose flour	¼ cup raisins, chopped
4 teaspoons baking powder	1 cup nuts, chopped
½ teaspoon baking soda	⅔ cup butter or margarine
1 teaspoon salt	1 cup brown sugar, firmly packed
½ teaspoon cloves	2 eggs
1 teaspoon cinnamon	2 cups thick applesauce

Sift together flour, baking powder, baking soda, salt and spices. Dredge raisins and nuts with 2 tablespoons of flour mixture. Cream butter until soft, then blend in brown sugar. Beat in eggs. Add dry ingredients alternately with applesauce, raisins, and nuts, mixing quickly. Spread in two greased and lightly floured 8×8×2-inch baking pans. Bake in 350° F. oven for 25 to 30 minutes. Test doneness with cake tester or toothpick. Cool in pan. Cut each baked layer into 24 small bars.

Recipe is best made in quantity suggested. Double only if institutional equipment is available.

BROWNIES
(60 bars)

1⅓ cups shortening (part   2 cups sifted cake flour
  margarine, if desired)   2 teaspoons double acting
10 squares or ounces   baking powder
  chocolate   1 teaspoon salt
8 eggs   4 cups coarsely chopped
4 cups sugar   walnuts or pecans
2 teaspoons vanilla

Melt shortening and chocolate. Cool slightly. Beat eggs until thick
and golden-colored. Beat in sugar gradually. Stir in cooled chocolate
mixture and vanilla. Sift together flour, baking powder and salt;
stir in quickly. Add nuts. Spread in four greased 8×8×2-inch pans
or two 11×15-inch pans. Bake in 350° F. oven 25 to 30 minutes.
Cool in pans, then cut into bars.

Do not double recipe. Rich and delicious, these bars do not keep
well stored at room temperature. If made in advance, package and
store in freezer. Defrost in packages.

BUTTERSCOTCH BARS (Blond Brownies)
(96 bars)

4 cups sifted cake flour
1 tablespoon salt
2 tablespoons double acting
  baking powder
1½ cups butter or
  margarine, softened
6 cups (3 pounds) brown
  sugar, firmly packed

6 eggs
2 tablespoons vanilla
3 cups broken nuts (walnuts
  or pecans)
3 cups fine shredded
  coconut

Sift together cake flour, salt and baking powder. Combine soft butter with brown sugar until creamy. Add eggs one at a time, blending well after each addition. Add dry ingredients. Add vanilla, then nuts and coconut. Spread in three greased and floured 11×15-inch baking pans. Drizzle hot Topping (below) over batter. Bake in 350° F. oven 30 minutes. Cool 30 minutes, then cut into bars and remove from pan, working carefully to avoid unnecessary crumbling. Finish cooling on racks.

TOPPING

2¼ cups brown sugar, firmly
  packed
⅓ cup butter or margarine

½ cup cream
¾ cup dark corn syrup
1 tablespoon vanilla

Mix sugar, butter, cream and syrup in saucepan. Cook over moderate heat, stirring occasionally, until mixture is 234° F. on a candy thermometer or when small portion dropped into very cold water forms a soft ball. Remove from heat and add vanilla.

Separate mixings are preferable to doubling this recipe.

CHOCOLATE CHIP COOKIES
(96 cookies)

2 cups shortening
2 cups brown sugar
2 cups granulated sugar
3 eggs
1 cup nonfat dry milk
3¾ cups sifted cake flour
1½ teaspoons salt

1¼ teaspoons baking soda
1 cup cold water
2 (6-ounce) packages
  chocolate morsels
2 cups chopped nuts
1 tablespoon vanilla

Cream shortening and sugars well. Add eggs and blend thoroughly. Blend together nonfat dry milk, flour, salt and baking soda. Add alternately with water. Stir in chocolate morsels, nuts and vanilla. Do not add more flour. Chill 1 hour or more. Drop 1 inch apart onto lightly greased baking sheet. Bake in 375° F. oven about 12 minutes. Cool on rack. Makes about 8 dozen.

Recipe may be doubled if commercial-size mixer and ovens are available, otherwise amounts are hard to handle.

DATE SQUARES
(24 servings)

1 cup (½ pound) butter or
  margarine, melted
1½ cups brown sugar
3 eggs, beaten
1½ tablespoons lemon juice
1¼ cups sifted all-purpose
  flour

1 teaspoon salt
1 teaspoon cinnamon
¼ teaspoon nutmeg
1 teaspoon baking soda
2 cups pitted, chopped dates
1 cup chopped nuts

Beat together melted butter, brown sugar and eggs. Add lemon juice. Sift together flour, salt, spices and soda; mix with dates and nuts. Add liquid mixture and mix until blended. Spread in greased 9×13-inch baking pan. Bake in 325° F. oven about 45 minutes or until toothpick tests clean. Cool; cut into squares. Serve with whipped cream, ice cream, orange or lemon sauce, if desired, or a light dusting of powdered sugar. Also delicious unadorned. May also be served warm.

Recipe may be doubled only if you have an extra-large bowl for mixing and your oven space will accommodate two baking pans without their touching each other or oven sides. Be sure to use a light hand in blending the larger batch so that the dough doesn't toughen.

GLAZED SPICE BAR COOKIES
(24 bars)

2½ cups sifted all-purpose flour	1¼ teaspoons cinnamon
1 teaspoon salt	½ cup butter or margarine
1½ teaspoons double acting baking powder	¾ cup brown sugar, firmly packed
½ teaspoon baking soda	2 eggs
1 teaspoon ginger	½ cup molasses
	¾ cup boiling water

GLAZE

2 tablespoons soft butter or margarine
1 cup sifted powdered sugar
1 tablespoon milk

Sift together flour, salt, baking powder, soda and spices. Cream butter until soft, then blend in brown sugar. Add eggs one at a time, beating after each addition until batter is smooth. Combine molasses and boiling water. Add liquid and dry ingredients alternately to creamed mixture. Bake in greased and wax-lined 13×9×2-inch baking pan in 350° F. oven 20 to 25 minutes.

Combine ingredients for Glaze and spread on warm cake. Cool. Cut into 24 bars.

Recipe may be doubled.

MATRIMONIAL BARS
(36 bars)

2½ cups quick-cooking
rolled oats
3 cups all-purpose flour
2 cups brown sugar, firmly
packed

1½ cups butter or margarine
1½ cups raspberry jam

Stir rolled oats, flour and sugar together until evenly mixed. Work in butter until mixture is crumbly. Divide into four portions of approximately equal size. Press one portion evenly into bottom of a lightly greased 8×8×2-inch baking pan. Spread ¾ cup raspberry jam over crumb layer. Sprinkle second portion of crumb mixture over jam, covering it completely. Press down lightly and evenly. Arrange remaining ingredients in layers as described in another lightly greased 8×8×2-inch baking pan. Bake both pans in 325° F. oven for 45 minutes or until golden brown. Cool in pans and cut in bars.

Prepare additional quantities in separate mixing to avoid overworking of crumbs which will make them greasy and heavy when baked. Thick, golden apricot jam is a good substitute for raspberry jam filling.

MEXICAN CINNAMON CRESCENT COOKIES
(48 cookies)

2 cups sifted all-purpose
flour
½ teaspoon cinnamon
¼ teaspoon salt

¼ teaspoon double acting
baking powder
1 cup butter or margarine
2 cups sugar
½ teaspoon vanilla

Sift together three times the flour, ½ teaspoon cinnamon, salt and baking powder. Cream butter until very soft, then gradually blend in sugar. Add vanilla, then the sifted dry ingredients in small portions, keeping batter smooth. Turn dough onto floured cloth and pat out or roll to ¼ inch thickness. Cut with crescent-shape cooky cutter. Bake in oven on ungreased cooky sheet at 400° F. 10 to 12 minutes. Dip hot cookies in cinnamon-sugar topping and cool on rack.

TOPPING

⅓ cup sugar
1 teaspoon cinnamon

Combine sugar and cinnamon.

Recipe may be doubled.

PUNCH BOWL COOKIES
(48 cookies)

¼ cup butter (do not
substitute)
¼ cup sugar
1 egg
½ cup sifted all-purpose
flour

¼ teaspoon salt
½ teaspoon vanilla
Colored Decorating Sugars*
or Chopped Candied
Fruit, if desired

Cream butter until soft, then blend in sugar. Add egg. Stir in flour, salt and vanilla. Drop by tiny spoonfuls onto ungreased baking sheet. Top with light sprinkling of Colored Decorating Sugars* or bits of Chopped Candied Fruit, if desired. Makes 4 dozen small cookies. Bake in 325° F. oven about 10 to 12 minutes.

Recipe may be increased to serve large groups. Vary appearance by using a variety of colored sugars and colorful fruit garnishes.

SPANISH STICKS
(24 servings)

1 pound butter or margarine	*1 cup orange marmalade or*
1 pound all-purpose flour	*tart jam*
(5 cups sifted)	*6 egg whites*
½ cup brown sugar	*½ teaspoon salt*
6 egg yolks	*1½ cups sugar*
1 tablespoon vanilla	*2 cups grated coconut*

Cream butter until fluffy. Blend in flour and sugar until dough forms. Blend in egg yolks and vanilla. Spread in 10×15-inch jelly roll pan. Cover with marmalade or jam. Beat egg whites and salt until stiff. Gradually beat in sugar, 2 tablespoons at a time until all is completely blended. Fold in coconut. Spread over dough. Bake in 325° F. oven about 30 minutes or until toothpick inserted in center comes out clean. Cool on rack. Cut into 48 sticks. Allow 2 per serving.

Recipe should not be doubled unless commercial-size mixer is available.

CHILLED DESSERTS

CHARLOTTE RUSSE
(48 servings)

12 envelopes (3 ounces)
   unflavored gelatin
1½ quarts cold water
1 quart scalded milk
3 cups sugar
1 teaspoon salt

2 quarts whipping cream
¼ cup vanilla
4 dozen ladyfingers, split or
   equal amount of sponge
   cake slices

Soften gelatin in cold water, then dissolve in hot milk along with sugar and salt. Chill to unbeaten egg white consistency. Beat cream until stiff. Fold into gelatin mixture along with vanilla until blended. Line forty-eight ⅔-cup molds with split ladyfingers; or line four 6-cup molds or two 12-cup molds with split ladyfingers. Spoon cream mixture into molds carefully. Chill until firm and unmold just before serving. Garnish with sweetened fresh or thawed frozen fruits or serve plain.

Charlotte Russe is rich and elegant and especially good with a bit of sweetened, fresh fruit. Do not increase this recipe.

CHOCOLATE MOUSSE
(24 servings)

3 envelopes (¾ ounce)
   unflavored gelatin
2 cups sugar
6 eggs, separated
1½ quarts milk

6 squares unsweetened
   chocolate
1 tablespoon vanilla
   extract
¾ teaspoon salt

In top of double boiler combine gelatin, 1 cup sugar, egg yolks, milk and chocolate. Cook over simmering water until chocolate melts and mixture thickens, stirring constantly. Beat until smooth. Remove from heat. Stir in vanilla. Chill until mixture mounds slightly when dropped from spoon. Beat egg whites and salt until foamy. Beat in 1 cup sugar, 1 tablespoon at a time, beating until stiff peaks form. Fold gently into chocolate mixture. Pour into 24 individual ½-cup molds or into large shallow pan. Chill until firm. Top with whipped cream and shaved chocolate, if desired.

Recipe may be doubled successfully.

CHOCOLATE MINT MOUSSE
(48 servings)

5 envelopes (1¼ ounces)   1½ teaspoons salt
  unflavored gelatin   2 tablespoons vanilla
3 cups sugar   2 (9-ounce) packages solid
12 eggs, separated   chocolate mint wafers
3 quarts milk

In top of double boiler combine gelatin, 2 cups sugar, egg yolks and milk. Cook over simmering water, stirring constantly, until mixture thickens. Remove from heat and add salt, vanilla and chocolate mint wafers. (These may be broken up before adding but having some undissolved adds to texture interest.) Beat egg whites until foamy. Add remaining 1 cup of sugar a tablespoon at a time, beating until stiff. Fold gently into chocolate mixture. Pour into molds or shallow pan, 18×12 inches. Cut into squares or unmold at serving time, topping with sweetened whipped cream or whipped topping, if desired, and grated chocolate mint wafers.

Recipe should be doubled only if large-size equipment and refrigerator space are available.

CHOCOLATE SPANISH CREAM
(48 servings)

5 envelopes (1¼ ounces)   12 squares (12 ounces)
  unflavored gelatin   unsweetened chocolate
3 cups sugar   2½ tablespoons vanilla
12 eggs, separated   1½ teaspoons salt
3 quarts milk

In top of double boiler combine gelatin, 2 cups sugar, egg yolks, milk and chocolate. Cook over hot water, stirring constantly, until chocolate melts and the custard thickens. Remove from heat; add vanilla. Chill mixture until it mounds slightly when dropped from a spoon. Beat egg whites and salt together until foamy, then beat in remaining 1 cup sugar a small amount at a time. Continue beating after all is added until stiff peaks form. Fold into cooled chocolate mixture. Pile lightly into 48 individual 4-ounce molds or 1 18×12×2-inch pan. Chill until firm. Cut into 48 squares.

Glazed red cherries and a wisp of whipped cream look attractive on this dessert.

Do not increase ingredients in this recipe. For best results, prepare separate mixings of this delicious cream.

COFFEE SOUFFLE
(48 servings)

4 cups sugar   2 quarts cold, strong
10 envelopes (2½ ounces)   coffee
  unflavored gelatin   1 teaspoon salt
12 eggs, separated   Sweetened whipped cream,
1 quart milk   for garnish

In top of large double boiler combine 2 cups sugar, gelatin, egg yolks, milk and cold coffee. Stir together. Place over simmering water and cook and stir until mixture will coat a spoon. Cool until a portion dropped from a spoon will mound slightly. Beat egg whites with salt until foamy, then gradually beat in remaining 2 cups sugar about 2 tablespoons at a time. Continue beating until stiff peaks form. Fold into thickened gelatin mixture. Spoon lightly into 48 individual serving dishes. Chill until firm. Garnish with sweetened whipped cream before serving.

Do not double recipe. Prepare increased quantities separately. Sparkling glass sherbet dishes make this good-to-eat dessert attractive at serving time.

FRUITED CALILOUPE MOLD
(48 servings)

12 cantaloupes (or 1 No. 10 can pineapple slices, see Note)

3 (7-ounce) bottles lemon-lime sparkling soda

1 pound marshmallows

4 (3-ounce) packages lemon-flavored gelatin

2 (8-ounce) packages cream cheese, room temperature

2 (1-pound 4-ounce) cans crushed pineapple (5 cups), undrained

1 quart whipping cream or 2 packages whipped topping, beaten stiff

Cut 1½-inch slice off one end of cantaloupe and scoop out all seeds and center pulp. Invert and drain thoroughly. Meanwhile, combine sparkling soda and marshmallows and cook over medium heat until marshmallows are melted. Add gelatin and stir until dissolved. Whip cream cheese until fluffy and gradually stir in hot mixture, beating until smooth. Add pineapple and chill until mixture begins to thicken. Fold in whipped cream or whipped topping prepared according to package directions. Chill until set, at least

12 hours. To serve, cut each melon into four crosswise slices; trimming off outside rind.

Double recipe only if you have equipment and chilling space to handle these large amounts.

NOTE: Salad may be molded in individual molds or two 13×22-inch pans and unmolded or cut into squares and served on cantaloupe rings or pineapple slices, instead of molding the salad in the cantaloupe.

HEAVENLY AMBROSIA
(48 servings)

4 envelopes (1 ounce)
    unflavored gelatin
1 pint cold water
1 quart orange juice
½ cup lemon juice
1 quart nonfat dry milk
    powder
2 tablespoons vanilla
    extract

1 teaspoon salt
2 cups sugar
1 quart diced oranges
2 cups finely cut
    shredded coconut
For garnish, if desired:
    1 pint whipping cream

Soften gelatin in cold water. Combine orange juice and lemon juice in very large mixing bowl. Stir in nonfat dry milk powder until dissolved. Beat with electric mixer until very thick, 8 to 10 minutes. Dissolve gelatin over boiling water. Add in thin stream to whipped milk, beating constantly. Beat in vanilla and salt. Beat in sugar, 2 tablespoons at a time, until soft peaks form. Chill until mixture mounds slightly when dropped from a spoon. Fold in oranges and coconut. Pile into 48 individual ½-cup molds, dessert dishes or large serving bowls. Chill until firm. Garnish with whipped cream, when served, if desired.

All the good flavor of traditional ambrosia, in pretty whipped form. Do not double—whipping becomes difficult.

LEMON CRUNCH PUDDING
(24 servings)

8 eggs, separated
1 cup sugar
4 lemons, grated rind
   and juice
3 (3-ounce) packages
   lemon-flavored gelatin
3 cups boiling water

1 pint whipping cream
   or 1 package whipped
   topping
1 pound graham crackers
   or vanilla wafers,
   crushed

In top of double boiler, combine egg yolks, sugar, lemon juice and rind. Beat until blended. Cook over hot water, stirring constantly, until thickened. Cool. Dissolve gelatin in boiling water and cool until mixture begins to thicken. Beat egg whites until stiff. Whip cream or prepare whipped topping. First, fold cooled custard into gelatin mixture, then fold in stiffly beaten egg whites, then whipped cream. Sprinkle half the crumbs in buttered 13×19-inch pan. Gently spoon in prepared pudding mixture and sprinkle with remaining crumbs. Chill until firm. To serve, cut into 24 squares.

Recipe may be doubled if large-scale equipment is available.

LEMON SNOW I
(24 servings)

5 envelopes (2½ ounces)
   unflavored gelatin
3 cups cold water
6 eggs, separated
2½ cups sugar

1 cup lemon juice
¼ cup grated lemon rind
½ teaspoon salt
1 pint whipping cream,
   beaten stiff

Soften gelatin in cold water. Beat egg yolks with 1½ cups sugar, lemon juice and rind. Cook over simmering water in top of double

oiler until mixture coats a metal spoon, stirring constantly. Stir in
oftened gelatin until dissolved. Chill until mixture begins to thicken.
Beat egg whites and salt until frothy. Gradually beat in remaining 1
cup sugar, a tablespoon at a time, beating until stiff peaks form.
Fold in lemon mixture just until blended. Fold in whipped cream
and pile lightly into 24 sherbet glasses. Chill until firm.

Recipe may be doubled if care is used in blending and sufficient
refrigerator space is available.

LEMON SNOW II
(48 servings)

8 envelopes (2 ounces)	1 pint lemon juice
unflavored gelatin	¼ cup grated lemon rind
2½ quarts cold water	2 teaspoons salt
6 cups sugar	16 egg whites

In top of double boiler, combine gelatin and 1 quart cold water and
let stand 10 minutes. Dissolve over boiling water. Pour into very
large mixer bowl (5-gallon size is adequate). Stir in sugar, lemon
juice, rind, salt and remaining 1½ quarts water until sugar is
dissolved. Chill to unbeaten egg white consistency. Add 16 egg
whites. Beat with electric mixer at low speed setting until light
and fluffy. Pile lemon mixture into 48 individual sherbet glasses
and chill. Mixture may be spread in one large pan, 18×12×2 inches.
Cut chilled Snow into 48 squares. Serve with a tablespoon of
Custard Sauce* or a bit of sweetened, crushed fruit.

Important to success of this recipe is very large equipment for
mixing. Do not double recipe.

MOCHA SOUFFLE
(48 servings)

8 envelopes (2 ounces)
unflavored gelatin
2 quarts cold strong
coffee
½ pound pure cocoa
powder
2 quarts sugar

18 eggs, separated
2 tablespoons rum
1 tablespoon vanilla
1 teaspoon salt
Whipping cream and
semi-sweet chocolate,
shaved, for garnish

Soften gelatin in 1 quart cold coffee. Combine cocoa, 1 quart sugar and remaining 1 quart cold coffee. Bring to boil and boil gently 3 minutes, stirring constantly. Beat egg yolks. Add a little of the hot cocoa mixture to yolks, stirring constantly. Combine with remaining cocoa mixture and cook over low heat 3 to 5 minutes, stirring constantly, until mixture coats a silver spoon. Stir in softened gelatin until it dissolves. Add rum and vanilla. Chill until mixture mounds slightly when dropped from spoon. Beat egg whites and salt until foamy. Beat in remaining 1 quart sugar, 2 tablespoons at a time, until stiff peaks form. Fold into chilled mixture. Pile into individual or large molds. To serve, unmold and garnish with whipped cream and shaved semi-sweet chocolate curls.

Recipe may be doubled if adequate molds and refrigerator space are available.

ORANGE RUM BAVARIAN
(24 servings)

8 envelopes (2 ounces)
unflavored gelatin
2 quarts water
4½ cups nonfat dry
milk
2 cups sugar
8 eggs, separated
5 cups orange juice
3 tablespoons grated
orange rind

½ teaspoon salt
1 tablespoon rum
flavoring
1 quart heavy cream,
whipped
For garnish, if desired:
fresh orange segments,
canned mandarin
orange segments or
grated coconut

In top of double boiler sprinkle gelatin on water and let stand
5 minutes. Add nonfat dry milk and blend with whip. Add half the
sugar and well-beaten egg yolks. Cook over hot water until mixture
coats metal spoon. Remove from heat at once. Add orange juice,
rind, salt and rum flavoring. Beat egg whites with remaining half of
sugar until very stiff. Fold into orange mixture. Fold in whipped
cream and pile into 24 sherbet glasses. Chill until ready to serve.
Garnish with suggested foods, if desired.

Recipe may be doubled if large double boiler is available and
care is used in blending.

PEARS A LA CUMBERLAND
(12 servings)

1 quart pear syrup
1 No. 10 can (3 quarts) pear
halves, drained,
reserving syrup
1 cup orange juice
4 cups sugar

1 (2-inch) stick
cinnamon
2 cups rosé wine or
cranberry juice
For garnish, if desired:
whipped cream or
ice cream

Drain syrup from pears. Allow 2 pear halves per serving. Combine pear syrup, orange juice, sugar and stick cinnamon. Stir until sugar is dissolved. Boil 5 minutes. Remove from heat, add wine and pour over pears. Cool until served. Remove cinnamon before serving. Garnish as suggested, if desired.

Recipe may be doubled and may be prepared several days in advance.

SHERRIED PEARS WITH CUSTARD SAUCE
(24 servings)

1 No. 10 can (3 quarts) pear
halves, drained,
reserving syrup
2 oranges, sliced
2 lemons, sliced
2 cups brown sugar

2 cups sherry or
pineapple juice
2 teaspoons ground
nutmeg or freshly
grated orange rind

Drain syrup from pear halves into saucepan. Add orange and lemon slices to syrup. Stir in brown sugar until dissolved. Simmer 20 minutes. Add sherry or pineapple juice and pour over pear halves. Let stand at least 6 hours. Prepare Custard Sauce* (see below).

To serve, arrange 1 large pear half or 2 small pear halves for each serving, cut side up, with some of the sherry-flavored syrup. Spoon Custard Sauce* into pear centers. Sprinkle with nutmeg or grated orange rind. This may be done several hours in advance if refrigerator space is available. Dessert may also be served buffet-style with pears in large serving bowl and sauce in nearby sauce bowl with ladle.

CUSTARD SAUCE

8 whole eggs, beaten   2 quarts milk, scalded
1½ cups sugar   1 tablespoon vanilla
½ teaspoon salt   extract

In top of double boiler combine eggs, sugar and salt. Slowly add scalded milk, stirring constantly. Cook, stirring constantly, over simmering water, not touching top pan of double boiler, until mixture coats a metal spoon. Remove from heat. Add vanilla and chill.

Recipe may be doubled if careful with the sauce. Use large double boiler.

STRAWBERRY MELON MOLD
(24 servings)

6 cantaloupes   1 tablespoon vanilla
4 envelopes (1 ounce)   1 quart fresh strawberries,
  unflavored gelatin   sliced
2 cups cold water   Whipped cream and
1½ pints whipping cream   whole strawberries,
1 cup sugar   for garnish
¼ teaspoon salt

Cut slice off end of melon, scoop out seeds and center pulp. Invert and drain well. Soften gelatin in cold water. Dissolve over boiling water. Whip cream until stiff, gradually adding sugar, salt and vanilla. Fold in gelatin mixture and strawberries. Spoon into hollowed out melon, being careful to avoid air bubbles. Chill until firm, at least 12 hours. To serve, cut melon in quarters. Garnish with additional whipped cream and whole strawberries on each serving.

Recipe may be doubled, if you have adequate refrigerator space. Whole upright melons need room!

TROPICAL ORANGE PUFF
(24 servings)

4 (3-ounce) packages
orange-flavored gelatin
1 quart boiling water
4 (6-ounce) cans
frozen orange juice
concentrate, undiluted
1 quart whipping cream

3 cups grated coconut
2 cups crushed pineapple,
well-drained
For garnish, if desired:
whipped cream,
sprinkled with coconut
or chopped nuts

Dissolve gelatin in boiling water. Add orange juice concentrate and chill until mixture begins to thicken. Whip cream stiff and fold into chilled gelatin mixture. Add coconut and pineapple. Pile into 24 sherbet glasses and chill until firm. If desired, garnish as suggested.

Recipe may be doubled.

FROZEN DESSERTS

BISCUIT TORTONI
(24 servings)

1 quart finely rolled
Italian-style macaroon
crumbs
1 pint rich milk (5%
butterfat)
2 cups sugar

Few grains salt
2 quarts whipping cream
1 tablespoon vanilla
1½ teaspoons almond
flavoring

Mix 2 cups macaroon crumbs with milk, sugar and salt. Beat cream until fluffy, add flavorings and beat stiff. Fold into macaroon mixture. Spoon into 24 decorative paper cups or into freezing trays. Sprinkle tops with reserved macaroon crumbs. Freeze until firm.

Recipe may be doubled. Whole glacé cherries or colorful cocktail cherries with stems make attractive garnish for individual servings of Biscuit Tortoni. Add cherries before freezing so that they remain securely in place.

CHERRIES JUBILEE
(24 servings)

3 (1-pound) cans pitted dark cherries	½ cup lemon juice
	1 cup Cointreau
4 teaspoons grated lemon peel	1 cup brandy or light rum
3 cups sugar	1 gallon vanilla ice cream

Combine cherries with syrup, lemon peel, sugar and bring to boil. Boil gently 15 minutes. Add lemon juice and Cointreau. Let stand until serving time. Heat cherry mixture in chafing dish if desired. Float brandy over surface in chafing dish and let warm, then ignite and ladle, still flaming over individual servings of ice cream.

Recipe may be doubled but do not attempt to flame more than the chafing dish will accommodate well.

FROZEN LEMON CREAM
(about 12 to 16 servings)

½ cup fresh lemon juice	2 cups sugar
4 teaspoons grated lemon rind	1 quart whipping cream, stiffly beaten

Combine lemon juice, rind and sugar and let stand 30 minutes. Stir well and fold in whipped cream. Freeze in refrigerator trays until firm. Cover with foil. Use No. 12 or No. 16 ice cream scoop for each serving.

Recipe may be doubled. Simple ingredients combine for fresh flavor in this frozen dessert.

ICE CREAM BALLS

Allow commercially made ice cream of desired flavor to soften very slightly. Form balls of ice cream with No. 12 ice cream scoop. Roll in toasted, grated coconut or in a mixture of chocolate drink powder and granulated sugar (3 tablespoons chocolate drink powder to ½ cup sugar) or finely ground nuts (almonds, walnuts or pecans). Place on trays. Return to freezer. When coatings are set, wrap ice cream balls with freezer-weight foil or transparent freezer wrap. One gallon of ice cream makes approximately 24 ample servings.

PEACH-BLUEBERRY PARFAIT
(48 servings)

1½ cups sugar
½ cup cornstarch
1 teaspoon salt
1 teaspoon cinnamon
1 teaspoon nutmeg
1 No. 10 can (3 quarts)
blueberries, drained,
reserving syrup
1 No. 10 can sliced
peaches, drained,
reserving syrup

¼ cup lemon juice
¼ cup lemon juice,
additional
2 cups sugar, additional
3 tall cans (14½-ounce)
evaporated milk, well
chilled
1 teaspoon nutmeg

Combine 1½ cups sugar, cornstarch, salt, cinnamon and nutmeg. Measure syrup from blueberries and peaches to make 1 quart; blend into cornstarch mixture. Cook until thick and clear over medium heat, stirring constantly. Add ¼ cup lemon juice and blueberries and chill. Be sure peaches are thoroughly drained. Cut into small pieces. Meanwhile, beat remaining lemon juice and 2 cups sugar gradually into chilled evaporated milk until very thick. Fold in drained peaches. Spoon alternate layers of peach mixture and blueberry sauce into parfait glasses or deep freezing trays. Freeze until time to serve.

Recipe may be doubled only if large enough containers are available to handle these mixtures.

PEACHES MELBA
(48 servings)

24 fresh, large freestone
   peaches or 2 No. 10 cans
   (6 quarts) peach halves
1½ quarts raspberry juice
   (strained from fresh
   or frozen berries)
2 (8-ounce) glasses
   currant jelly

½ cup cornstarch
1 cup sugar
1½ gallons vanilla ice
   cream
1½ cups slivered, toasted
   almonds

Place peaches, cut side up, in individual dessert dishes. If using fresh peaches, sprinkle with lemon juice. Combine raspberry juice and currant jelly, mashing jelly with fork. Blend cornstarch and sugar and add to juice mixture, blending smooth. Cook until clear and slightly thickened, about 15 minutes. Cool. At serving time, place scoop of ice cream in each peach half. Top with Melba sauce and sprinkle with toasted almonds.

Recipe may be doubled.

PEPPERMINT CHOCOLATE ICEBOX LOG
(48 servings)

*12 envelopes (3 ounces)
unflavored gelatin
1½ quarts cold water
1 quart light cream,
scalded
4 cups crushed peppermint
stick candy
1 teaspoon salt*

*Red food coloring, as
desired
2 quarts chilled whipping
cream, beaten stiff
5 pounds chocolate wafer-
type cookies (or 4
dozen ladyfingers, split)*

Soften gelatin in cold water. Meanwhile, scald cream with candy and salt. Stir until candy is dissolved. Add gelatin and stir until dissolved. Tint as desired with food coloring. Cool until mixture begins to thicken. Fold in whipped cream. Stack cookies with filling of peppermint cream mixture between each cookie, to form four "logs." When stacks are completed, place on squares of aluminum foil and frost each with remaining cream mixture. Freeze until serving time. Cut each log diagonally into 12 slices. If using ladyfingers, split them in same manner or line molds with ladyfingers and spoon peppermint mixture into center.

Recipe may be doubled if containers of adequate size for beating and blending are available.

WATERMELON-CANTALOUPE BALLS
WITH SHERBET
(24 servings)

*1½ quarts watermelon balls
1½ quarts cantaloupe balls
2 cups apricot nectar*

*2 quarts lime, lemon or
pineapple sherbet*

Prepare balls and cover with apricot nectar, chilling until ready to serve. Arrange in sherbet glasses and top with No. 12 scoop of sherbet.

Recipe may be increased as required.

PINEAPPLE ICEBOX CAKE
(12 to 16 servings)

2 envelopes (½ ounce)
   unflavored gelatin
⅔ cup sugar
¼ teaspoon salt
6 eggs, separated
2½ cups (1-pound-4-ounce
   can) crushed pineapple and
   juice

¼ cup lemon juice
2 cups whipping cream
1 pound thin chocolate
   wafers (cookies)
For garnish, if desired:
   whipped cream

Mix gelatin, 4 tablespoons of the sugar and salt together thoroughly in top of double boiler. Beat egg yolks slightly. Stir in crushed pineapple and juice. Add egg-pineapple to gelatin and cook over boiling water, stirring constantly, until gelatin is dissolved. Remove from heat and stir in lemon juice. Chill mixture until thickened but not set. Beat egg whites until stiff, then beat in remaining sugar. Fold into gelatin mixture. Beat cream until stiff and fold into mixture. Line two 9×5×3-inch loaf pans with waxed paper, allowing paper to extend above pan 1 inch. Spread a layer of gelatin mixture in prepared pans; add a layer of thin chocolate wafers. Repeat three times ending with gelatin. Chill in refrigerator until firm. Unmold icebox cake on serving platter and slice. Cake may be topped with additional whipped cream, if desired.

Recipe may be doubled. Do-ahead versatility distinguishes this icebox cake.

PEPPERMINT PARFAIT
(24 servings)

2 eggs

1½ cups sugar

½ teaspoon salt

6 cups evaporated milk,
   undiluted, well chilled

2 teaspoons mint extract

Few drops red food
   coloring

Beat eggs. Gradually beat in sugar and salt. Whip milk until thick. Fold in egg mixture and flavoring gently. Tint delicately with food coloring. Spoon into freezer trays; chill while preparing Chocolate Sauce below. When Sauce is cool, scoop peppermint mixture, 1 tray at a time, into bowl and beat smooth. Spoon into chilled parfait glasses, beginning with layers of peppermint, adding layer of Sauce and continuing until glasses are full. Make at least three layers of each, ending with sauce. Store in freezer section until ½ hour before serving.

CHOCOLATE SAUCE

1½ cups sugar

⅔ cup cocoa

½ cup water

⅓ cup corn syrup

1 cup evaporated milk,
   undiluted

1½ teaspoons vanilla

Combine sugar, cocoa, water and corn syrup. Boil to soft-ball stage. Stir in evaporated milk and vanilla. Cool and use as directed above.

MISCELLANEOUS DESSERTS

APPLE CRISP
(48 servings)

2 No. 10 cans (6 quarts)
sliced apples
2 (4/5 quart) bottles
California chablis or
other white dinner wine
6 quarts sifted all-purpose
flour

2 pounds brown sugar
3 tablespoons cinnamon
1 tablespoon nutmeg
2 pounds butter or
margarine

Drain apple slices and arrange in two lightly buttered pans, approximately 20×12×2 inches. Pour wine over apples. Stir flour, brown sugar and spices together. Cut in butter or margarine until coarse crumbs form. Sprinkle topping over apples and press down lightly. Bake in 375° F. oven until golden brown and crisp on top, about 45 minutes. Best served warm rather than hot. Apple Crisp may be served chilled, too.

Fresh Apples may be substituted for canned apples. Use 6 quarts tart apples cut in thin, uniform slices and increase baking time to 1 hour or until fruit is tender when pierced with a fork.

APPLE CRUNCH A LA MODE
(48 servings)

1 No. 10 can (3 quarts)
sliced apples
1 teaspoon salt
¼ cup lemon juice
2 cups sugar, granulated
or brown
1 cup (½ pound) butter
or margarine

2 cups sifted all-purpose
flour
1½ cups crushed cornflakes
or other cereal crumbs
1 tablespoon cinnamon
2 cups (additional) brown
sugar
2 gallons ice cream

If apples are in thick slices, cut into thinner slices or bite-size pieces. Combine apples and syrup with salt, lemon juice and 2 cups sugar. Place in forty-eight individual baking dishes or two $16 \times 10 \times 2$-inch pans. Cut together butter and flour until in coarse crumbs. Mix with cereal crumbs, cinnamon and brown sugar. Sprinkle on top of apples. Bake individual servings in 350° F. oven for 20 minutes, large pans at 400° F. 30 to 40 minutes. Serve warm or cold topped with ice cream.

Recipe may be doubled. Apple Crunch may be made ahead and reheated in 350° F. oven 15 minutes for individual servings, 30 minutes for large pans. This permits heating while main course is being served.

BAKED APPLES IN PORT
(12 or 48 servings)

INGREDIENTS	12 SERVINGS	48 SERVINGS
apples	12	48
sugar	1 cup	1 quart
boiling water	1½ cups	1½ quarts
California port	1½ cups	1½ quarts

Prepare apples for baking by washing, removing core and top ⅓ of outer peel of each. Place in 2-inch deep baking pans. Dissolve sugar in boiling water. Pour syrup over apples, then cover pans and bake at 375° F. 30 to 40 minutes. Remove tender fruit to serving dishes. Pour 2 tablespoons California port into each. Boil baking syrup down until fairly thick. Cool slightly and pour over apples to glaze fruit.

Spicy glaze for apples is a pleasant flavor variation. Let a whole cinnamon stick and 2 or 3 whole allspice and whole cloves simmer in sauce while it thickens. Strain out before spooning glaze over apples. Omit port flavoring.

BAKED FRUITS
(24 servings)

2 (1-pound-13-ounce)
cans peach halves
2 (1-pound-13-ounce)
cans pear halves
3 (1 pound) cans
pineapple chunks
2 cups currant or other
tart red jelly

1 (6-ounce) can frozen
orange juice concentrate,
undiluted
For garnish, if desired: ice
cream or whipped cream

Combine peaches, pears and pineapple, with syrup, in shallow baking pan. Bring jelly and orange juice to boil. Pour over fruits. Bake in 350° F. oven 30 minutes. Serve warm or cold, plain or topped with ice cream or whipped cream.

Recipe may be doubled. Even better if made ahead.

BANANAS A L'ORANGE
(24 servings)

24 small bananas (about
6 pounds)
1 cup lemon juice
1 quart crushed corn
cereal crumbs or
graham cracker crumbs
1 cup butter or margarine
2 cups sugar

½ cup cornstarch
1 quart water
1 quart orange juice
½ cup grated orange rind
For garnish, if desired:
whipped cream or ice
cream

Peel bananas and slice. Sprinkle thoroughly with lemon juice. Combine cereal crumbs and margarine and toast in oven at 350° F. for 10 minutes or until golden. Set aside. Combine sugar and cornstarch.

Gradually blend in water, orange juice and rind. Cook over low heat until thick and clear. In individual serving dishes or shallow pans arrange layer of banana slices. Cover with orange sauce and crumbs in alternate layers, ending with crumbs. Chill until serving time. Top with whipped cream or ice cream, if desired.

Recipe may be increased as needed, but is best made the same day it is to be served. Holds well up to 8 hours.

BLUEBERRY CRISP
(24 servings)

1 cup sugar
6 tablespoons cornstarch
½ teaspoon salt
½ teaspoon cinnamon
½ teaspoon nutmeg
3 tablespoons lemon juice
1 No. 10 can (3 quarts) or 5 (14-ounce) cans blueberries

2 cups butter or margarine
2 cups brown sugar, firmly packed
2 cups all-purpose flour
2 cups cereal or graham cracker crumbs
1 cup chopped nuts

Combine 1 cup sugar, cornstarch, salt, cinnamon and nutmeg. Add lemon juice and 3 cups blueberry syrup. Stir smooth and cook over medium heat until thickened, stirring constantly. Add blueberries and pour into 13×18-inch pan. Blend together butter, brown sugar and flour until mixture is like coarse crumbs. Add cereal or graham cracker crumbs and nuts. Sprinkle over top of blueberries. Bake at 375° F. for 30 minutes. Serve warm or cold, with whipped cream or ice cream, if desired.

Recipe may be doubled.

CHERRY UPSIDE-DOWN PUDDING
(24 servings)

2 quarts or 3 (1-pound 4-ounce) cans pitted water-pack red pie cherries
6 cups cherry juice and water, combined

2 cups sugar
¼ cup butter or margarine
Whipped cream or ice cream, if desired

Drain and measure juice from cherries and add water to make 6 cups. Add cherries, bring to boil, add sugar and butter and stir until dissolved. Let stand while preparing following batter:

6 cups sifted all-purpose flour
8 teaspoons double acting baking powder

1 teaspoon salt
4 cups sugar
½ cup butter or margarine
3 cups milk

Combine flour, baking powder, salt and sugar. Cut in butter until mixture is like coarse cornmeal. Stir in milk, mixing just until blended. Pour into well-greased 15×10×3-inch pan. Pour cherry mixture over top. Bake in 375° F. oven about 1 hour or until cake mixture which comes to the top is well done. Serve hot or cold, with whipped cream or ice cream, if desired.

Recipe may be doubled, but use care in blending the batter.

CHOCOLATE UPSIDE-DOWN PUDDING
(24 servings)

3 cups sifted all-purpose
  flour
2 tablespoons double
  acting baking powder
2 teaspoons salt
2¼ cups granulated sugar
1½ cups cocoa, divided

1½ cups milk
½ cup melted shortening
1 tablespoon vanilla
1½ cups chopped nuts
3 cups brown sugar,
  firmly packed
1 quart boiling water

Sift together flour, baking powder, salt, granulated sugar and ½ cup cocoa. Add milk, melted shortening and vanilla. Mix just until smooth. Add nuts. Pour into two greased 9-inch square pans or one 18×12-inch pan. Combine brown sugar and 1 cup cocoa. Sprinkle evenly over batter. Divide boiling water evenly if using two pans. Pour over top. (This makes a chocolate sauce on bottom of pans after pudding is baked.) Bake in 350° F. oven 30 to 45 minutes. Cut in squares. Best served warm. Top with sauce from bottom of pans. May be baked ahead and reheated at 350° F. for 10 minutes.

Recipe may be doubled.

GLAZED ORANGE PEACHES
(24 servings)

1 No. 10 can (3 quarts)
  peach halves, drained,
  reserving syrup
3 cups sugar
⅔ cup cornstarch
½ cup butter or margarine
½ cup grated orange rind

1 quart orange juice
½ cup lemon juice
For garnish, if desired:
  2 quarts grated coconut
  or crushed cereal
  crumbs

Drain peach halves and arrange in shallow baking pans. In saucepan, combine sugar and cornstarch. Measure peach syrup and add water to make 1½ quarts; blend into cornstarch and cook until thick and clear, stirring constantly. Add butter, orange rind and juice and lemon juice. Pour over peaches. Serve warm or cold, sprinkled with coconut or cereal crumbs, if desired. If serving warm, brown under broiler to toast coconut or crumbs lightly.

Recipe may be doubled, and may be prepared ahead.

PEACH CRISP
(24 servings)

4 quarts sliced sweetened
peaches or 4 (1-pound
13-ounce) cans, drained
¼ cup all-purpose flour
½ teaspoon salt

1 teaspoon freshly grated
nutmeg
2 tablespoons granulated
sugar
2 tablespoons lemon juice

Place peaches in large container. Mix flour, salt, nutmeg and sugar. Sprinkle lemon juice over fruit. Turn into two 13×10-inch greased baking pans. Prepare Topping (below). Sprinkle over peaches. Bake in 350° F. oven for 25 minutes.

TOPPING

3 cups all-purpose flour
1½ cups brown sugar
¾ cup granulated sugar

½ teaspoon salt
½ cup butter or margarine

Combine flour, both sugars and salt; then cut in butter until like coarse crumbs.

Fruit crisps may be served plain or topped with ice cream, whipping cream or slightly sweetened sour cream or with a fluffy prepared dessert topping made according to package directions.

MELON BALLS IN WATERMELON SHELL
(48 servings)

2 *large watermelons*
3 *or 4 varieties of melons (Cranshaw, Persian, honeydew*
  or cantaloupe, for example)
1½ *pounds powdered sugar*
2 *(⅘ quart) bottles California port*

Cut 600 melon balls from watermelon and other melons, being careful to avoid seeds of watermelon. Combine sugar and wine and stir to dissolve sugar. Pour over melon balls. Watermelons to be used as containers should be well chilled. Fill with melon balls and wine sauce just before serving. Top edge of melon may be cut in scallop pattern, sawtooth edge or plain. Small individual cantaloupe halves may be used as container for a mixture of kinds of melon balls. Allow ¼ to ⅓ cup per serving.

Recipe may be doubled. Dramatic centerpiece for a party table, watermelons filled with melon balls are a delight to view as well as partake of at dessert time.

PEARS ROSE
(48 servings)

96 *canned pear halves,*
  approximately 2 No. 10
  cans (6 quarts), drained,
  reserving syrup (see note at
  end of recipe for fresh
  pears)

2 *quarts rosé wine*
1 *cup lemon juice*
5 *pounds sugar*
3 *(3-inch) sticks cinnamon*
1 *tablespoon whole cloves*

Combine 2 quarts pear syrup, rosé wine, lemon juice, sugar and spices, which have been tied in a bag. Stir until sugar dissolves and mixture comes to a boil. Slip pear halves carefully into boiling syrup and simmer 5 minutes. Remove from heat, remove spice bag and let pears cool in syrup. Flavor is improved if pears stand overnight. Chill.

When whole fresh pears are prepared for this dessert, leave on stems. Peel or not, as desired, depending upon variety used. For 48 fresh pears, prepare light syrup of 4 cups sugar and 2 quarts water. Proceed as with canned pears, simmering pears just until tender, to preserve shape. Avoid too many pieces of fruit in one container for the same reason.

Do not double recipe. Prepare additional batches in separate containers to avoid spoiling shape and appearance of pears.

DESSERT SAUCES

CUSTARD SAUCE I
(24 servings)

2½ quarts (10 cups) rich
  milk
6 tablespoons cornstarch
½ teaspoon salt
4½ cups sugar

¾ cup cold milk,
  additional
2 teaspoons vanilla
½ cup butter or margarine

Heat 2½ quarts milk to boiling. Mix cornstarch, salt, and sugar with ¾ cup cold milk. Stir into hot milk, cook and stir until mixture thickens and boils. Remove from heat. Add vanilla and butter. Serve warm or chilled. Makes about 15 cups.

Do not double recipe. Best results are obtained in separate mixings of this sauce. Warm custard sauce is a welcome addition to apple desserts such as Apple Crisp*, Baked Apples*, Apple Pie* or Apple

Dumplings*. Add 1 teaspoon cinnamon and ½ teaspoon nutmeg to cold milk-sugar combination for a spiced sauce.

CUSTARD SAUCE II
(24 servings)

6 eggs or 12 egg yolks,   ½ teaspoon salt
    slightly beaten   5 cups milk, scalded
¾ cup sugar   2¼ teaspoons vanilla

Combine eggs, sugar and salt in top of double boiler. Slowly stir in scalded milk. Cook and stir over simmering water, being sure water level does not touch top part of double boiler. When custard will coat a metal spoon, remove from heat and stir in vanilla. Serve chilled.

Recipe may be doubled. This amount makes 24 rounded tablespoon servings. Yields about 6 cups of sauce.

ORANGE SAUCE
(24 servings)

2 cups sugar   2 tablespoons grated
1 cup cornstarch   orange rind
1½ teaspoons salt   1 teaspoon nutmeg
1½ quarts water
2 (12-ounce) cans frozen
    orange juice concentrate,
    undiluted

Combine sugar, cornstarch and salt in saucepan. Add water gradually. Bring to boil over medium heat, stirring constantly. Cook until thick and clear. Add orange juice, rind and nutmeg. Serve warm or cold over puddings or cakes. Makes 8 cups or about ⅓ cup serving for 24 desserts.

Recipe may be doubled. Sauce may be made ahead and reheated if desired to be served warm, heating over low heat, stirring occasionally. Delicious on Tropical Gingerbread*.

SHERRY SPICE SAUCE
(48 servings)

½ cup cornstarch	½ teaspoon salt
4½ cups sugar	¾ cup California sherry
1 teaspoon cinnamon	2½ quarts rich milk, scalded
½ teaspoon nutmeg	½ cup butter or margarine

Combine cornstarch, sugar, spices and salt, then add wine. Stir mixture into hot milk, beating with whisk. Cook over low heat stirring until sauce boils. Boil 3 minutes. Take off heat and add butter, blending well. Serve sauce warm over Apple Crisp*, Baked Apples* or Apple Pie*. This makes 48 1½-tablespoons servings.

Double recipe for larger servings or to provide small servings for additional persons. Enrich flavor with a teaspoon of freshly grated lemon rind, if desired. Add with butter and mix through sauce well.

PASTRY AND PIE CRUSTS

GRAHAM CRACKER CRUST
(for eight 9-inch pies or 48 servings)

2½ quarts finely rolled
   graham cracker crumbs
2 cups sugar

2 tablespoons cinnamon
1 pound soft butter or
   margarine

Blend crumbs, sugar and cinnamon with butter. Place about 1½ cups of crumb mixture in each of 8 (9-inch) pie pans. Press firmly to sides and bottoms of pans. Bake in 350° F. oven about 5 minutes. Cool before filling.

Recipe may be doubled. All crusts do not need to be baked immediately. There is no harm in mixture waiting. Crumb crusts also may be made out of finely rolled dry chocolate cookie or vanilla wafer crumbs.

PASTRY (Basic)
(for 4 double crust or 8 single crust 9-inch pies)
(24 or 48 servings)

8 cups sifted all-purpose
   flour
2 tablespoons double
   acting baking powder

2 teaspoons salt
1¾ cups pure lard or
   2¼ cups shortening
½ to ⅔ cup ice water

Sift together flour, baking powder and salt. Cut in shortening until mixture resembles coarse cornmeal. Add ice water very gradually, a tablespoon at a time, to form dough. Divide dough into eighths; roll out each portion on lightly floured board and fit into pie pans;

trim. If baking as single crusts, be sure to prick sides and bottom every ¼ inch with tines of fork. Do not stretch when fitting into pans. Bake single crusts in 425° F. oven about 15 minutes. Follow double crust pie recipe for baking time and temperature.

Do not increase recipe unless you have equipment to handle large amounts well. Rather than dividing for smaller amounts, double a standard pastry recipe. Baked pies and pie shells may be frozen, wrapped carefully in airtight materials after cooling.

NUT PASTRY CRUST

To Basic Pastry* recipe, combine ½ cup finely chopped pecans with each 1 pound of all-purpose flour (4 cups) after cutting in shortening and before adding water. Roll and form as usual. Follow baking directions for basic pastry for a shell or filled pie.

PUFF SHELLS (Petits Choux)
(12 or 48 servings)

Best results will be obtained if 2 mixings of each of these two sizes of recipes are made to obtain desired number of servings. As written, smaller recipe is sufficient quantity for 6 servings and the larger recipe will make 24 servings. It is not advisable to attempt to hold unbaked portion of mixed dough while another part is baking— therefore separate mixings will give superior results.

INGREDIENTS	12 SERVINGS	48 SERVINGS
shortening or margarine	*½ cup*	*1½ cups*
water	*1 cup*	*3 cups*
all-purpose flour, sifted	*1 cup*	*3 cups*
salt	*¼ teaspoon*	*½ teaspoon*
eggs, medium size	*4*	*12*

Combine shortening and water in saucepan, bring to boil over high heat. Reduce heat, add flour and salt all at once. Stir vigorously until thick, compact mass of dough forms. Add whole eggs one at a time. Beat egg into dough completely before another is added. Continue beating until dough is free of lumps and velvety in appearance. Drop scant teaspoonfuls of dough on ungreased baking sheet, leaving room between for doubling in size. Bake in 400° F. oven 30 to 35 minutes or until golden and firm to touch. Test doneness by removing one puff from oven. It is done if cold air out of oven does not cause an immediate collapse. Cool puffs on rack. Do not cover tightly to store or they will lose their crispness.

PIE FILLINGS

BLACK BOTTOM PIE
(eight 9-inch pies or 48 servings)

8 envelopes (2 ounces)
  unflavored gelatin
1 quart cold water
1 quart sugar
2 teaspoons salt
⅔ cup (3 ounces)
  cornstarch
32 eggs, separated
3 quarts milk, scalded
12 squares (12 ounces)
  unsweetened chocolate,
  melted

3 tablespoons vanilla
8 (9-inch) baked Pastry*
  or Crumb Crusts*
1 teaspoon salt
2 teaspoons cream of
  tartar
1 quart sugar, additional
2 tablespoons imitation
  rum flavoring
2 teaspoons vanilla
4 ounces semi-sweet
  chocolate, grated

Soften gelatin in cold water. In top of large double boiler, combine 1 quart sugar, 2 teaspoons salt and cornstarch. Stir in egg yolks. Slowly add hot scalded milk, stirring constantly. Cook over hot water, stirring constantly, until thickened and smooth, about 20 minutes. Remove from heat. Measure 2½ quarts of this custard and add melted chocolate, stirring to blend smooth. Allow to cool. Add vanilla to cooled chocolate mixture and turn into 8 pie shells (allow about 1¼ cups to each shell). Chill.

To remaining hot custard, add softened gelatin and stir until dissolved. Chill mixture until it will just begin to mound slightly when dropped from a spoon.

Beat egg whites with 1 teaspoon salt and cream of tartar until foamy, then beat in 1 quart sugar gradually, approximately 2 tablespoons at a time. Add rum extract and 2 teaspoons vanilla. Beat until thick peaks form. Fold meringue into plain custard and blend well. Spread over chilled chocolate mixture in shells. Garnish with grated chocolate. Cut each pie into 6 wedges.

Recipe should not be increased. Prepare additional quantities in separate mixings.

CHOCOLATE CHIFFON PIE
(eight 9-inch pies or 48 servings)

8 envelopes (2 ounces)
   unflavored gelatin
6 cups sugar
2 dozen eggs, separated
3 quarts milk
20 squares (1¼ pounds)
   unsweetened chocolate
2 tablespoons vanilla
   extract

2 teaspoons salt
8 (9-inch) baked Pastry*
   or Crumb Crust* shells
2 quarts chilled whipping
   cream
1½ cups sugar, additional
4 squares unsweetened
   chocolate, additional

Combine gelatin, 4 cups sugar, egg yolks and milk in top of large double boiler. Add 20 squares unsweetened chocolate. Cook over simmering water until chocolate is melted and mixture is thick and smooth, stirring constantly. Remove from heat. Beat smooth. Stir in vanilla. Chill until mixture begins to thicken. Beat egg whites with salt until foamy. Gradually beat in 2 cups sugar, 1 tablespoon

at a time, until stiff. Fold gently into chocolate mixture. Pile into 8
pie shells. Chill until firm. About 3 hours before serving, whip
cream stiff and sweeten with 1½ cups sugar. Pile cream on top of
pies, garnish with chocolate curls made by slowly scraping 4 squares
unsweetened chocolate warmed in the hand, with vegetable peeler or
sharp knife.

Recipe should not be doubled unless large-scale mixing equipment and adequate refrigeration facilities are available.

DEEP-DISH FRUIT PIE
(Proportions for one 9-inch pie)

*4 to 6 cups fruit (fresh,
  frozen or canned)
1 to 1½ cups sugar
2 to 4 tablespoons all-
  purpose flour (optional)
Cinnamon or nutmeg,
  if desired*

*1 to 2 tablespoons butter
  or margarine, if desired
¼ teaspoon salt
Basic Pastry* for one
  9-inch pie shell*

Place prepared fruit in deep 9-inch baking dish. Adjust amount of
sugar to quantity and tartness of fruit and mix sugar and flour with
fruit. On apples, peaches or purple plums combine well with light
sprinkling of cinnamon or nutmeg, if liked. One to 2 tablespoons
butter may be dotted over top of fruit, if desired. Sprinkle lightly
with salt. Moisten top edge of baking dish. Roll pastry ⅛ inch thick
and place over top of fruit, allowing crust to extend ½ inch beyond
rim of dish. Fold overhanging pastry under, sealing to wet edge of
dish. Cut slits in center of pastry for steam vents. Bake in 450° F.
oven for 10 minutes, then reduce heat to 350° F. baking until fruit
is tender, about 25 to 45 minutes. Serve warm, spooning juice from
dish with each serving.

Quantities of fruit needed for large pies may be determined by
consulting Quantity Serving Charts and Purchase Guide, Chapter IV.

EGG NOG CHIFFON PIE
(eight 9-inch pies or 48 servings)

8 envelopes (2 ounces)
unflavored gelatin
4 cups sugar
2 dozen eggs, separated
3 quarts milk
2 teaspoons vanilla extract

2 tablespoons imitation
rum extract
2 teaspoons salt
8 (9-inch) baked Pastry*
shells
Grated nutmeg

In top of large double boiler combine gelatin, 2 cups sugar, egg yolks and milk. Cook and stir over simmering water until custard coats a metal spoon. Remove from heat. Add flavoring. Chill until mixture mounds slightly when dropped from a spoon, stirring frequently. Beat until just smooth. Beat egg whites with salt until foamy, then gradually beat in remaining 2 cups sugar, about 1 tablespoon at a time. Continue beating until stiff peaks form. Fold this meringue into cooled custard being careful not to overmix. Spoon into baked pastry shells. Chill. Lightly dust tops with freshly grated nutmeg.

Recipe should not be doubled. Good at any season, Egg Nog Chiffon Pie has a flavor that is popular with many—a delicate rum accented by nutmeg.

LEMON CHIFFON PIE
(eight 9-inch pies or 48 servings)

8 envelopes (2 ounces)
unflavored gelatin
4 cups cold water
2 dozen eggs, separated
5 cups sugar
2 cups lemon juice

½ cup grated lemon rind
1 teaspoon salt
8 (9-inch) baked Pastry*
or Graham Cracker
Crust* shells

Soften gelatin in cold water. Mix egg yolks with 3 cups sugar, lemon juice and lemon rind in top of large double boiler. Cook, stirring constantly, over simmering water until mixture coats a metal spoon. Stir in softened gelatin mixture until dissolved. Chill until mixture will mound slightly when dropped from a spoon. Beat egg whites and salt until frothy. Beat in remaining 2 cups sugar gradually, about 1 tablespoon at a time; continue beating after all is added until stiff peaks form. Fold in gelatin-egg mixture, being careful just to blend and not overmix. Divide among cooled, baked Pastry* or Crumb Crusts*. Chill until firm.

Recipe should not be doubled for best flavor and smoothness in custard. Chiffon mixture above has a fresh, delicate flavor. If put into Graham Cracker Crusts*, pies may be topped with a light sprinkle of fine graham cracker crumbs. Allow just 2 tablespoons crumbs for each pie and add before pies are chilled.

MOCHA CHIFFON PIE
(eight 9-inch pies or 48 servings)

8 envelopes (2 ounces)
unflavored gelatin
2 quarts cold, strong
coffee
2 cups (½ pound) dry
cocoa
2 quarts sugar, divided
18 eggs, separated

2 tablespoons vanilla
1 teaspoon salt
8 (9-inch) baked Pastry*
shells (plain or Nut*)
Whipped cream and
grated chocolate or
chocolate shot, for
garnish

Soften gelatin in 1 quart cold coffee. In large, heavy saucepan combine cocoa, 1 quart sugar and remaining 1 quart cold coffee. Cook over medium heat stirring constantly; bring to boil and cook until slightly thickened and smooth, about 3 to 5 minutes. Beat egg yolks slightly. Stir some of the hot cocoa mixture into egg yolks, then blend this mixture into remaining cocoa mixture. Return to heat and cook at low temperature 3 to 5 minutes stirring constantly until mixture coats metal spoon. Stir in coffee-gelatin mixture until gelatin dissolves. Add vanilla. Chill until mixture mounds slightly when dropped from a spoon.

Whip egg whites and salt together until foamy. Gradually beat in remaining 1 quart sugar, 2 tablespoons at a time, beating until stiff peaks form. Fold into cooled cocoa mixture. Divide among baked pie shells. Chill until firm. Garnish Mocha Chiffon Pie with sweetened whipped cream and grated chocolate or chocolate shot for a party look.

Do not increase this recipe. Prepare separate mixings for additional servings.

MOCHA CHOCOLATE CHIFFON PIE
(four 9-inch pies or 24 servings)

5 envelopes (1¼ ounces)
  unflavored gelatin
2 cups sugar, divided
6 eggs, separated
1 quart cold strong coffee
1 pint milk
4 squares (¼ pound)
  unsweetened chocolate

1 teaspoon salt
2 teaspoons vanilla extract
4 baked 9-inch Pastry* or
  crumb shells
For garnish, if desired:
  whipped cream and
  shaved semi-sweet
  chocolate

In top of double boiler, combine gelatin, 1 cup sugar, egg yolks, coffee, milk, chocolate and salt. Cook over simmering water stirring constantly, until mixture coats metal spoon. Remove from heat. Add vanilla. Chill until mixture mounds slightly when dropped from a spoon. Beat egg whites until foamy. Beat in 1 cup sugar, 1 tablespoon at a time, until stiff peaks form. Fold gently into gelatin mixture. Pile into cooled pie shells. Refrigerate until ready to serve. If desired, garnish with sweetened whipped cream and shaved semi-sweet chocolate.

Recipe may be doubled. Pies may be prepared ahead, hold up well 12 hours or a little longer.

OLD-FASHIONED PUMPKIN PIE
(eight 9-inch pies or 48 to 64 servings)

3 (1-pound 13-ounce) cans pumpkin (2½ quarts)	3 tablespoons salt
2½ cups molasses	¼ cup all-purpose flour
1 quart granulated or brown sugar	10 eggs
2 tablespoons ginger	1¼ quarts evaporated milk, undiluted
2 tablespoons cinnamon	Pastry* for eight 9-inch single crust pies
2 teaspoons ground cloves	

Combine pumpkin and molasses, add sugar and mix until dissolved. Combine spices, salt and flour. Add to pumpkin, then add eggs and milk, blending well. Pour into unbaked pie shells. Bake in 425° F. oven about 40 minutes or until set. Pies should be baked immediately after filling. If oven space will not accommodate all eight pies, keep pastry-lined pans in refrigerator until they can be filled and baked. Bake only one shelf full of pies at a time. Cool on racks.

Recipe can be doubled only if ovens can accommodate this large baking.

PUMPKIN CHIFFON PIE
(eight 9-inch pies or 48 servings)

6 envelopes (1½ ounces)
unflavored gelatin
3 cups cold water
18 eggs, separated
3 cups firmly packed
brown sugar
2 (1-pound-13-ounce)
cans pumpkin
1 quart milk
1 tablespoon ginger
2 tablespoons cinnamon

2 teaspoons ground cloves
2 tablespoons salt
3 cups granulated sugar
1 quart whipping cream
or chilled evaporated
milk, beaten stiff
8 (9-inch) Crumb Crusts*
or baked Pastry* shells
For garnish, if desired:
whipped cream and
chopped nuts

Soften gelatin in cold water. Combine egg yolks, brown sugar, pumpkin, milk, and spices in heavy, broad saucepan. Cook over low heat, stirring constantly, until thick and smooth. Remove from heat and stir in gelatin mixture until dissolved. Chill until mixture begins to thicken. Beat egg whites with salt until soft peaks form. Beat in sugar, 2 tablespoons at a time, to form stiff peaks. Fold egg whites and whipped cream gently into pumpkin mixture. Pile into cooled Crumb Crusts* or baked Pastry* shells. Chill until firm. If desired, garnish with additional whipped cream and chopped nuts.

Recipe can be doubled only if institutional-size equipment is available.

RUM CHOCOLATE CHIFFON PIE
(eight 9-inch pies or 48 servings)

8 envelopes (2 ounces)
unflavored gelatin
2 quarts strong cold coffee
½ pound pure cocoa
powder
2 quarts sugar
18 eggs, separated
2 tablespoons vanilla
extract
1 teaspoon salt

½ cup rum or 2
tablespoons rum
flavoring
8 (9-inch) baked Pastry*
shells or Crumb Crusts*
1 pint whipping cream,
for garnish
1 bar (8 ounces) semi-
sweet chocolate to
shave, for garnish

Soften gelatin in 1 quart cold coffee. In large saucepan, combine cocoa, 1 quart of the sugar and remaining 1 quart cold coffee. Bring to boil and boil gently 3 to 5 minutes, stirring constantly. Beat egg yolks. Pour a little of the hot cocoa mixture over egg slowly, stirring constantly. Add egg yolks to remaining cocoa mixture and cook over very low heat 3 to 5 minutes, stirring constantly. Remove from heat. Add softened gelatin and stir until dissolved. Add vanilla. Cool until mixture will mound slightly when dropped from spoon. Beat egg whites with salt until foamy. Beat in remaining sugar 2 tablespoons at a time, beating until stiff peaks form. Fold into cooled cocoa mixture with rum. Pile into baked pie shells. Chill until firm. Several hours before serving time, spread with whipped cream and garnish with curls of shaved chocolate.

Recipe may be cut in half safely, but doubling makes too large an amount to handle readily. Pies hold up well up to 24 hours.

SCHAUM TORTE
(two 9-inch pies or 12 servings)

8 egg whites
1 teaspoon cream of tartar
2 cups sugar

Beat whites until frothy. Add cream of tartar, beat until stiff enough
to hold a point. Beat in sugar gradually. When all is added, continue
beating meringue until it is very stiff and glossy. Divide batter between two well-greased and floured 9-inch glass pie pans. Bake in
275° F. oven for 20 minutes, increase heat to 300° F. and continue
baking until done about 1 hour. Cool on rack.

FILLING

8 egg yolks   *1 tablespoon grated*
1 cup sugar   *lemon rind*
⅓ cup lemon juice   *Few grains salt*

Beat yolks until thickened, then gradually add sugar. Stir in lemon
juice and rind and salt. In top of double boiler cook, stirring constantly, over hot water until thick, approximately 5 minutes. Cool.
    When both meringue shells and filling are cool, prepare Schaum
Torte as follows:
Beat 2 cups whipping cream with 4 teaspoons sugar. Spread a thin
layer of whipping cream over baked, cooled meringue using about
one-quarter of whipped cream on each pie. Spread cooled custard
over top of whipped cream layer. Top pies with remaining whipped
cream. Chill at least 8 hours, preferably overnight.

    Recipe should not be increased. Prepare additional quantities in
separate mixings for best results. Meringue may be baked in a
13×9×2-inch glass baking dish to be cut into rectangular servings
if preferred over pie-shaped wedges as above.

SHERRY CHIFFON PIE
(12 or 48 servings)

INGREDIENTS	12 SERVINGS	48 SERVINGS
unflavored gelatin	2 envelopes	8 envelopes
	(½ ounce)	(2 ounces)
cold water	½ cup	2 cups
eggs, separated	4	16
sugar	¾ cup	3 cups
hot milk	3 cups	3 quarts
almond extract	1 teaspoon	4 teaspoons
California sherry	½ cup	2 cups
salt	few grains	½ teaspoon
baked 9-inch pie Pastry*		
shells or Crumb Crusts*	2	8
Freshly grated nutmeg	few grains	1 teaspoon

Soak gelatin in cold water 5 minutes. Beat egg yolks with one-third of sugar, stir into hot milk. Cook and stir over hot water or very low heat until mixture coats a metal spoon. Remove from heat. Stir in softened gelatin, almond extract and sherry until smooth and gelatin is dissolved. Cool until slightly thickened. Add salt to egg whites, beat until stiff, then beat in gradually the remaining sugar. Fold into cooled gelatin mixture. Mound blended mixture lightly into baked, cool Pastry* shells or Crumb Crusts*. Sprinkle top with freshly grated nutmeg. Chill until firm.

Recipe may be enriched, if desired, by spreading with slightly sweetened, stiffly beaten heavy cream before serving. A half pint heavy cream, whipped, will top 2 pies; 1 quart is sufficient for 8 pies.

STRAWBERRY CHIFFON PIE
(eight 9-inch pies or 48 servings)

4 quarts fresh strawberries
(see below for frozen
berries)
1½ quarts sugar
½ cup lemon juice
8 envelopes (2 ounces)
unflavored gelatin
1 quart cold water

16 egg whites
2 teaspoons salt
2 cups sugar, additional
1 quart whipping cream
8 (9-inch) baked Pastry*
shells or Crumb Crusts*
Whipped cream, for
garnish

Reserve 32 large, perfect berries for use as garnish. Prepare fruit and slice into large container. Crush. Stir in 1½ quarts sugar. Let stand until sugar dissolves, about 1 hour. To sweetened berries, fresh or thawed frozen, add lemon juice. Soften gelatin in cold water. Dissolve over boiling water. Stir into strawberries, blending well. Chill until mixture will mound slightly when dropped from a spoon. Beat egg whites and salt until foamy. Beat in 2 cups of sugar gradually until stiff peaks are formed. Beat cream until stiff. Fold beaten cream and egg whites into berry mixture, blending thoroughly. Pile lightly into 8 baked shells. Chill until firm. Garnish with additional sweetened whipped cream and reserved whole strawberries.

Recipe may be doubled. To substitute frozen, sweetened, sliced strawberries, thaw berries and drain well. Use 1¼ quarts drained fruit and 2 quarts drained syrup. Add 3 cups sugar only.

EGG AND CHEESE ENTREES

CHEESE BLINTZES WITH SOUR CREAM
(24 servings)

4 cups sifted all-purpose
flour
1 tablespoon salt
1 quart milk

16 eggs, well beaten
3 quarts cottage cheese
2 quarts sour cream

Sift together flour and salt and add with milk alternately to eggs, avoiding overbeating. Heat 6-inch skillets to medium heat, greasing lightly. Pour only about ¼ cup batter in skillet at a time, tipping pan so that batter covers bottom in very thin layer. Cook only until fine blisters appear on top and edges are somewhat dry. Bake on one side only. As blintzes are baked, invert pan to turn out, fried side up, on paper towels or bread boards. Place spoonful of cottage cheese in center of each and fold into squares, folding edges in from both sides. All this may be done ahead. Just before serving fry both sides in hot shortening until golden brown. Blintzes may be kept warm in oven as fried so that all do not have to be fried at once. Serve hot with sour cream and jams. Makes about 48 blintzes.

Recipe may be doubled but be assured that frying, filling and folding this many blintzes is time-consuming.

CHEESE SOUFFLE
(24 servings)

1 cup butter or margarine	1/4 teaspoon pepper
1½ cups all-purpose flour	2 tablespoons prepared
2 quarts milk	mustard
2½ teaspoons salt	1 pound sharp Cheddar
1/4 teaspoon Tabasco	cheese, grated
1/4 teaspoon nutmeg	2 dozen eggs, separated

Melt butter. Blend in flour and cook until bubbly. Stir in milk and cook until thick and smooth, stirring constantly. Add seasonings and mustard. Remove from heat and stir in cheese, blending until melted. In large bowl, beat egg yolks until thick and mix a little of the hot sauce with yolks, continuing to add sauce to yolks until all is blended. Beat egg whites until very stiff. Fold gently into cheese mixture. Spoon into two lightly greased 18×12×2-inch baking pans. Bake in 300° F. oven 1½ hours or until knife inserted in center comes out clean. This method makes soufflé firm enough to stand up during serving.

Not recommended to double recipe.

EGGS FLORENTINE
(24 servings)

5 pounds fresh or	1 quart milk
4½ pounds frozen	2½ quarts mayonnaise
spinach, cooked	1 cup lemon juice
4 dozen eggs	1½ teaspoons cayenne
1 cup butter or margarine	pepper
1 cup all-purpose flour	2 teaspoons monosodium
1 tablespoon salt	glutamate
1 cup water	

Arrange cooked spinach, well drained, in individual casseroles, ramekins or on slices of toast. Poach 2 eggs per person and place on hot spinach. Cover with mock hollandaise sauce made by blending melted butter, flour and salt in skillet and cooking until bubbly. Add water and milk and cook until thickened, stirring constantly. Cool but do not chill. Blend in mayonnaise and lemon juice, then cayenne and monosodium glutamate. Spoon sauce over eggs and brown under broiler just a few seconds, to color sauce lightly and have piping hot.

Doubling recipe is not recommended unless you have an able crew at hand. By placing ramekins where they keep warm while assembly is going on, this dish is not as difficult to produce as it may seem.

CURRIED EGGS
(48 servings)

1½ pounds butter or margarine
2 cups chopped green pepper
2 cups chopped onions
1 quart chopped celery
1 quart fresh mushrooms or 4 (8-ounce) cans, drained
4 cups (1 pound) flour
¼ cup salt
¼ cup curry powder
1 tablespoon powdered ginger

¼ cup paprika
1 teaspoon Tabasco
3 quarts cold chicken broth or bouillon
3 quarts milk or evaporated milk
2 dozen hard-cooked eggs, diced
Hot cooked rice accompaniments as below

In large skillet, melt butter and sauté green pepper, onions, celery and mushrooms. Blend in flour, salt, curry powder, ginger and paprika. Cook until bubbly. Add Tabasco and chicken broth, then milk, blending smooth. Cook until thickened, stirring frequently, thinning with additional liquid, as necessary. Gently stir in diced, hard-cooked eggs and heat through. Serve over rice, in rice nests or over toast, accompanied by condiment tray, including any or all of the following: chutney, crisp bacon bits, grated coconut, chopped nuts, chopped green onion, pickled fruits, cucumber slices or beets.

Recipe may be doubled. Curry is good made ahead and reheated, tightly covered, over moderately low heat. Thin as necessary.

HIGH-HAT MACARONI AND CHEESE
(24 servings)

2 pounds uncooked elbow macaroni	6 egg whites
1 gallon water	1½ cups mayonnaise or salad dressing
Salt	1½ cups fine dry bread crumbs
1 cup butter or margarine	
1 cup all-purpose flour	1½ cups grated cheese, additional
1½ quarts milk	
1 pound sharp Cheddar cheese, grated	1 tablespoon prepared mustard

Cook macaroni in boiling water with 2 tablespoons salt just until tender. Meanwhile, make sauce by melting butter and blending with flour and 1½ teaspoons salt. Cook until bubbly. Add milk and cook until thickened, stirring constantly. Add 1 pound grated cheese and stir until melted. Drain macaroni. Mix well with sauce and pour into a greased 20×13×2-inch pan or two 13×9×2-inch pans, or equivalent. Beat egg whites until stiff. Fold in mayonnaise, bread crumbs, remaining 1½ cups grated cheese and mustard. Pile over macaroni. Bake in 375° F. oven for 15 to 20 minutes, until top is browned and puffed.

Recipe may be doubled. Macaroni and sauce may be made ahead with topping added just before baking. Allow 10 minutes additional baking time when mixture is cold.

LENTEN DINNER CASSEROLE
(12 servings)

1 pound (2 8-ounce
packages) broad egg
noodles
1 tablespoon cooking oil
or shortening
1 pint thick sour cream
1½ pints cream-style (large
curd) cottage cheese
1 teaspoon Worcestershire
sauce

½ teaspoon salt
¼ teaspoon paprika
¼ teaspoon white pepper
1 cup thinly sliced green
onions (including tops)
½ cup fine cracker or
bread crumbs
½ cup grated Parmesan
cheese
Paprika, if desired

Drop noodles into boiling salted water, adding oil to keep noodles separated. When tender, drain well. Combine sour cream, cottage cheese, seasonings and green onions. Mix with cooked noodles. Turn into lightly greased 20×13×2-inch pan or two 13×9×2-inch baking pans. Mix crumbs with grated Parmesan cheese. Sprinkle lightly and evenly over noodle mixture. Dust lightly with paprika, if desired. Bake in 350° F. oven 20 to 30 minutes or until heated through. (Use longer time for chilled casserole).

Recipe may be doubled, although boiling noodles in separate batches is advisable. Prepare ahead, cover and chill until baking time. Chilled casserole may safely be brought to room temperature 30 minutes before baking.

SCRAMBLED EGGS
(48 servings)

8 dozen eggs
2 quarts milk or light cream
2 tablespoons salt

1 teaspoon white pepper
1 pound butter or
margarine

Combine eggs, milk, salt and pepper. Beat to blend. Melt 1 cup (½ lb.) butter in large skillet or top of double boiler and add half of egg mixture. Cook over low heat, stirring constantly, until creamy, scraping sides and bottom often. Do not overcook for best texture. Repeat with remaining egg mixture.

Recipe should not be doubled unless very large equipment is available. Double boiler method of cooking is a slow one, but gives excellent results—particularly with suggested size batches.

MUSHROOM NOODLE KUGEL SUPREME
(24 servings)

12 cups cooked noodles,
  3 (8-ounce) packages
6 eggs, beaten
3 teaspoons salt
¼ teaspoon pepper
1 pint sour cream
1 quart cottage cheese
2 tablespoons caraway
  seed (optional)
24 large mushroom caps
1 pound grated Cheddar
  cheese
3 cups fine, buttered
  bread crumbs

Arrange noodles in shallow, buttered 20×13×2-inch baking pan. Beat eggs, seasonings and sour cream together. Pour over noodles. Spoon on cottage cheese, pressing into noodles. Sprinkle with caraway seeds, if desired. Bake in 350° F. oven for 45 minutes. Remove from oven. Arrange mushroom caps so that each will center a serving when kugel is cut in squares, i.e., 4 rows of 3 squares. Combine grated cheese and bread crumbs. Sprinkle evenly over kugel. Bake at 350° F. for 15 minutes longer or until top is well browned. Cut into squares to serve.

Recipe may be increased for a larger number of servings, but do not bake more than this amount in one pan. This may be prepared ahead of baking time and stored in refrigerator. The kugel "waits well." When done, remove from oven and keep in warm place or leave in oven with door ajar.

CRAB SUZETTES
(12 servings)

2 cups sifted all-purpose
  flour
2 teaspoons salt
12 eggs

1 quart light cream
½ cup (¼ pound) butter
  or margarine

Sift together flour and salt. Add eggs and cream and beat until blended. Stir in melted butter. Bake batter as for pancakes on lightly greased griddle or individual skillets, making "crepes" about 6 inches in diameter. Brown very lightly and place on paper towels as done. When all are done, place spoonful of Filling (below) in center of each and roll up like jelly rolls. Place in buttered baking dish, dot with butter and bake in 425° F. oven until heated through, about 20 minutes. Makes 12 crepes.

FILLING

4 cans (5½ to 7½ ounces
  each) flaked crabmeat
2 cups (packed) grated
  Cheddar cheese
2 tablespoons prepared
  mustard

2 cups chopped onion
1 cup chopped green
  pepper
½ cup minced parsley
¼ cup lemon juice

Combine crabmeat, cheese, mustard, onion, green pepper, parsley and lemon juice and use to fill "suzettes" as directed above.

Recipe can be doubled satisfactorily if you allow advance preparation time for baking and rolling the crepes.

FLOUNDER ROLLS RAREBIT
(24 servings)

8 pounds flounder fillets, rolled and tied	2 teaspoons dry mustard
	2 teaspoons paprika
8 tablespoons (¼ pound) butter	½ cup milk
	2 quarts medium white sauce
1 quart beer or ale	1 teaspoon Tabasco
1 pound sharp Cheddar cheese, grated	1 teaspoon Worcestershire sauce

Place rolled fillets in shallow baking pan, dotting with butter. Add beer or ale and bake in 400° F. oven for 15 minutes. Meanwhile, combine cheese, mustard, paprika and milk with ½ cup white sauce. Heat over low heat until cheese is melted. Add remaining white sauce, Tabasco and Worcestershire. Strain beer in which fish has been poached and add to sauce. Pour over fish fillets and bake 10 minutes longer at 350° F. Sprinkle with additional paprika just before serving.

Recipe may be doubled.

BAKED FISH STROGANOFF
(24 servings)

6 pounds halibut or sole
   filet or other lean white
   fish cut in strips ½ inch
   thick
1 cup butter or margarine
1 cup finely chopped onion
2 pounds sliced
   mushrooms

½ cup all-purpose flour
1 cup dry white wine
1 cup water
¼ cup lemon juice
2 tablespoons salt
½ teaspoon Tabasco
1 quart sour cream

Sauté fish strips in butter with onion and mushrooms. Sprinkle with flour and blend lightly to mix flour and butter. Gently stir in wine, water and lemon juice. Add salt and Tabasco. Bake in 350° F. oven for 30 minutes. Just before serving, stir in sour cream, which should be at room temperature. Serve over pimento rice, fluffy rice or buttered noodles, immediately after adding sour cream.

Recipe may be increased as desired.

BAKED PRAWNS (Shrimp)
(48 servings)

28 to 30 pounds fresh, raw
   prawns (prawns or jumbo
   shrimp range from 10
   to 12 per pound)
5 quarts fine dry bread
   crumbs

3 cups butter or
   margarine, melted
3 cups minced onions
3 (⅘ quart) bottles
   California Rhine wine

Peel prawns and arrange 6 prawns in each of 48 individual baking dishes that have been lightly buttered. Stir bread crumbs, melted butter and minced onions together lightly. Sprinkle crumb mixture over prawns. Drizzle California Rhine wine evenly over crumb mixture, allowing approximately 2 to 3 tablespoons per serving. Bake in 350° F. oven for 20 to 30 minutes or until prawns are tender and crumbs are golden brown.

Recipe may be doubled. Prawns may be baked in large flat open baking pans in place of individual ramekins. This entree has great elegance of flavor and appearance.

BAKED SALMON STEAKS
(24 servings)

*8 to 12 pounds fresh
  salmon steaks
1 cup (½ pound) melted
  butter or margarine*

*½ cup fresh lemon juice
Salt and pepper to taste
1 cup chopped parsley*

Arrange steaks in shallow baking pans. (Jelly roll pans are ideal.) Combine butter and lemon juice. Brush generously on steaks. Sprinkle with salt and pepper. Bake in 500° F. oven for 10 to 15 minutes, depending on thickness of steaks, until fish flakes easily. Avoid overbaking. Fish does not require turning. Sprinkle with chopped parsley when served.

Recipe may be increased as desired as long as cooking facilities permit.

BAKED WHOLE SALMON
(24 servings)

1 whole salmon 8 to 10
*   pounds or 2 small*
*   salmon 4 to 6 pounds*
Salt
Pepper

2 lemons, sliced thin
2 onions, sliced thin
Melted butter
Parsley and lemon slices,
*   for garnish*

Pat clean salmon dry. Season cavity with salt and pepper and lay slices of lemon and onion inside. Place fish on large piece of heavy duty aluminum foil. Brush top with melted butter and lay additional onion slices on skin from head to tail. Cover tightly with foil. Wrap 2 or more fish individually. Place on flat baking pan and bake in 500° F. oven for 10 minutes per pound for large salmon, 12 minutes per pound for 4- to 6-pound size. Place hot salmon on large platter and garnish with parsley and lemon slices.

High heat of a quick oven will cook salmon rapidly and keep most of its natural flavor and oil to add to its savory goodness. Do not bake ahead or let stand when salmon is to be served hot—long standing will dry out fish. Baked ahead for serving well chilled is satisfactory method for preparing a warm weather treat.

COLD SPICED SALMON
(24 servings)

10 to 12 pounds salmon
*   (half or whole fish)*
2 quarts chicken or fish
*   stock or water*
1 cup lemon juice
3 stalks celery
3 large carrots, sliced

1 cup parsley
3 onions sliced
¼ cup salt
1 teaspoon pepper
2 cups dry white wine
Lemon slices and parsley
*   sprigs, for garnish*

Place salmon (skin on) in large covered pan. Add stock, lemon juice, celery, carrots, parsley and onions with seasonings. Simmer gently until tender, 30 to 60 minutes, depending on thickness of fish. Cool. Add wine and chill thoroughly. To serve, remove from marinade, remove skin and cut into serving-size slices. (This is most readily done, slicing first one half of fish to the bone, then turning over and slicing the other side.) Garnish with thin slices of lemon and sprigs of parsley.

Recipe may be doubled. May be made as long as 3 days ahead. If you wish to serve whole on platter, spread with softened cream cheese and garnish with slices of olives, pickles, lemons, green pepper and pimento.

SHRIMP CREAMED WITH OYSTERS
(24 servings)

3 pints oysters
1 cup chopped green pepper
1 quart sliced fresh
  mushrooms or 4
  (8-ounce) cans
½ cup butter or margarine
1 cup cornstarch or
  2 cups all-purpose flour
3 quarts cold chicken
  broth or bouillon
1 tablespoon salt
¼ teaspoon pepper

1 tablespoon onion salt
1 teaspoon Tabasco
¾ teaspoon nutmeg
1 pint milk or evaporated
  milk, undiluted
2 (10-ounce) packages
  frozen shrimp or 4
  (5-ounce) cans, drained
¼ cup chopped pimento
Toast Baskets*, toast,
  rusks or Biscuits*

Sauté oysters (chopped if large ones), green pepper and mushrooms in butter. In saucepan, combine cornstarch with chicken broth, mixing until smooth. Cook over low heat, stirring constantly until sauce is thickened and smooth. Combine salt, pepper, onion salt,

Tabasco and nutmeg with milk and add to sauce. Sauté frozen shrimp until heated through in the vegetable mixture. If using canned shrimp, add with sautéed vegetables to sauce. Heat thoroughly, adding pimento just before serving. Serve in Toast Baskets* or over crisp toast, rusks or hot Biscuits*.

Recipe may be doubled. Complete mixture may be prepared ahead and reheated in double boiler or over very low heat, stirring gently to avoid scorching.

SHRIMP CREOLE WITH RICE
(48 servings)

1/4 cup salad oil
2 cups coarsely chopped onion
3 cups coarsely chopped celery
2 cups coarsely chopped green peppers
1/2 cup finely cut parsley
3 tablespoons all-purpose flour
3 1/4 quarts tomato juice
3 (6-ounce) cans tomato paste (1 1/2 cups approximately)

1/4 cup vinegar or lemon juice
1/4 cup firmly packed brown sugar
2 tablespoons salt
1/8 teaspoon cayenne pepper
1 teaspoon black pepper
1 teaspoon cinnamon
1/2 teaspoon nutmeg
3 1/2 to 4 pounds cooked, cleaned shrimp (7 pounds raw shrimp)
5 pounds raw rice, steamed or boiled

Heat oil in large skillet. Add onion, celery and green pepper. Cook and stir until softened but not browned. Add parsley. Sprinkle flour over vegetables and blend. Combine tomato juice and paste with lemon juice, sugar and seasonings. Add to vegetables in skillet. Cook and stir until mixture boils. Allow to simmer over very low heat 30 minutes. Add shrimp to tomato sauce and cook about 12 to 15 minutes longer until shrimp are well heated through.

Serve Shrimp Creole over mounds of hot rice.

Recipe may be doubled. To prepare raw shrimp, drop fresh shrimp (peeled or unpeeled) into a large kettle of briskly boiling water (2 or more quarts). When water returns to boil, boil shrimp until tender about 3 to 5 minutes. Salt may be added to cooking water, 1 tablespoon salt to 1 gallon water. Drain. Peel shell from shrimp.

DEEP FRIED SHRIMP
(24 servings)

7 pounds fresh shrimp
or frozen shelled,
deveined shrimp
6 eggs, separated
2 cups beer, ale or milk
3 cups flour

1½ teaspoons salt
1 tablespoon paprika
¼ teaspoon pepper
⅓ cup melted butter or
margarine
Deep fat for frying

Shell and devein shrimp, if necessary. Beat egg yolks until light. Stir in beer. Sift flour with seasonings. Stir into beer mixture. Add melted butter. Let batter stand at room temperature 1½ hours. Beat egg whites until stiff but not dry. Fold into batter. Pat shrimp dry. Dip into batter. Place in fry basket a few at a time. Fry at 370° F. for 2 to 3 minutes. Drain and keep hot in 300° F. oven until ready to serve.

Recipe may be doubled if facilities for frying larger amounts are available.

FILLET OF SOLE WITH WHITE WINE

INGREDIENTS	12 SERVINGS	48 SERVINGS
fillet of sole or other white fish	12 large or 24 small fillets (3 pounds)	48 large fillets (12 pounds)
salt and pepper		
oil	3 tablespoons	¾ cup
onion, chopped	1 tablespoon	¼ cup
parsley, minced	1 tablespoon	¼ cup
mushrooms, chopped	6	½ pound
celery, chopped fine	1 cup	1 quart
bay leaf	1 large	6 large
California sauterne or Rhine wine	3 cups	2½ quarts
water	1½ cups	1¼ quarts
bouillon cubes	3	1 dozen
rich cream	⅓ cup	1 cup
Parmesan cheese, grated		

Season fillets with salt and pepper. In a large frying pan, combine oil, onion, parsley, mushrooms, celery, bay leaf, wine, water and bouillon cubes. Lay fillets, a few at a time, in hot liquid and simmer until barely tender (about 5 to 10 minutes). Remove with slotted spatula to shallow baking pans. Boil down liquid in which fish has simmered, reducing to half original quantity. Taste and add additional seasoning, if required. Add cream. Strain liquid over fish arranged in baking pans. Sprinkle grated Parmesan cheese over top. Bake in 450° F. oven until top is lightly brown and sauce bubbles, about 10 minutes.

Make this recipe economically by choosing a white fish in season of plenty. Frozen fish fillets may be substituted for fresh. Thaw frozen fillets just before cooking.

SHRIMP TALLYHO
(24 servings)

1 cup chopped onion
1 cup chopped green pepper
2 cups chopped celery
½ cup butter or margarine
½ cup all-purpose flour
1 quart chicken broth or
   bouillon, cold
1 quart dry white wine

1 (6-ounce) can tomato paste
1 teaspoon Tabasco
1 tablespoon minced parsley
1 pound Cheddar cheese,
   grated
2 pounds cooked, cleaned
   shrimp
Toast or Toast Baskets*

Sauté onion, green pepper and celery in butter; set aside. In large saucepan, blend flour with chicken broth, mixing until smooth. Blend in wine and tomato paste and heat until thickened, stirring constantly. Add Tabasco and parsley. Stir in sautéed vegetables, cheese and shrimp and heat over moderately low heat until cheese is melted. Serve over toast or in Toast Baskets*.

Recipe may be doubled as needed. Sauce may be prepared ahead; add vegetables, cheese and shrimp just before serving when reheating sauce over low heat.

BAKED TUNA CASSEROLE
(24 servings)

¼ cup butter or
   margarine
1½ cups chopped onion
1 cup finely diced green
   pepper
¼ cup finely cut parsley
6 (7-ounce) cans tuna,
   drained
Juice 1 lemon

2 cups mayonnaise
1½ teaspoons salt
½ teaspoon pepper
3 cups dry bread crumbs
1 cup milk
2 (8-ounce) cans tomato
   sauce
Additional bread crumbs,
   for garnish

Melt butter and simmer onion and green pepper until tender but not brown. Combine with parsley, flaked tuna, lemon juice, mayonnaise, salt, pepper, bread crumbs and milk. Spread mixture evenly in two greased 9×9-inch pans or casseroles. Spread tomato sauce over mixture and garnish with a light layer of additional bread crumbs. Bake in 350° F. oven until edges are browned and bubbly, about 30 minutes.

Finely minced fresh chives or parsley add a company look to this fish loaf when sprinkled over top just before cutting and serving.

MEAT ENTREES

CARVING TECHNIQUES

The first rule of carving is cut across the grain. Cutting with the grain gives long string texture to slices.

Behind scenes and beforehand is where virtually all carving should be done for any sizable group. Usually it is too slow and, unless the carver is an expert, too risky a procedure to carve leisurely at the table. However, there may be exceptions, such as a leisurely sit-down dinner when time is abundant and the carving part of the drama. The techniques are the same regardless of where the carving is done.

A dull knife complicates carving and makes it impossible to do a good job.

Avoid changing the angle of the blade of the knife while slicing. Uniform slices not only look better, the meat goes farther.

Plan the servings before carving so that portions are even and choicer cuts may be divided among all.

Carving is easier if large roast or poultry is allowed to stand about 30 minutes before slicing.

Be sure the platter is large enough or if carving in the kitchen, a cutting board may be used, but space in which to work is essential.

Slices carved ahead may be arranged on serving platters or oven-proof trays, loosely covered with foil and kept warm in 250° F. oven.

Boned, rolled roasts, of course, provide very easy carving. Available in addition to the familiar hams, are boned, rolled turkey, pork, veal, leg of lamb or rolled beef rib roasts. Both rump and sirloin tip roasts of beef are boneless, though they are more triangular than round.

Ham and other leg roasts with bone in, such as leg of veal and fresh leg of pork, are all carved in similar manner.

Before starting to carve, find out where the bones are, both by studying the following charts and by investigating as you carve. Knowing where they are will enable you to carve with finesse.

ROLLED ROAST

Push fork firmly into roast on left side an inch or two from top. Slice across grain, starting from far right, cutting even slices ⅛ to ⅜ inch thick.

Lift slices as cut to serving platter. Remove each cord only as it is approached in making slice. Cut it with tip of blade, loosen it with fork.

NOTE: Boned shoulder and loin roasts that are long and narrow are carved more easily with roast lying horizontally instead of standing upright.

STANDING RIB ROAST

Insert fork firmly between two top ribs. From far outside edge, slice across grain toward ribs, making slices ⅛ to ⅜ inch thick.

Release each slice by cutting close along the rib with knife tip.

Lift each slice as it is cut to serving platter.

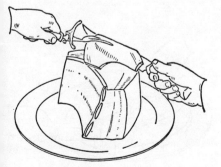

POT ROAST

The long cooking process makes it easy to slip out the large bones. Hold pot roast firmly with fork at left and separate section by running knife between the two muscles and bone.

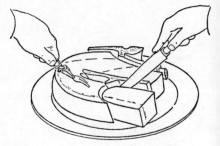

Turn section removed so that grain of meat is parallel with platter so that meat may be cut across grain.

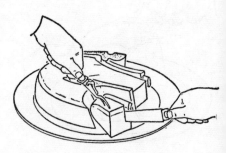

Holding piece with fork, cut slices ¼ to ⅜ inch thick. Separate and slice remaining sections, removing each slice to serving platter as cut.

WHOLE HAM

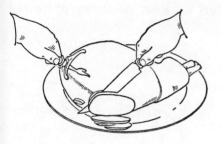

Place on platter with fat side up and shank end at carver's right. Cut first slices from the thin side, which will be side nearest carver if ham is from a left side of pork. These will be on far side if ham is from a right leg of pork and may be cut last.

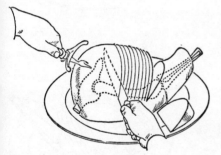

Insert fork and cut slices from thin side. Turn ham so that it rests on surface just cut. Hold ham firmly and cut small wedge from shank end, which makes it easier to cut and release other slices as cut.

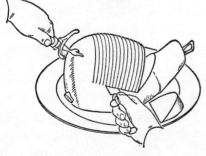

Turn ham back to original position and slice at right angles to bone, cutting meat from which first few slices were made to make flat base.

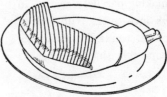

LEG OF LAMB

Different roasts will vary in shape because of difference in right and left legs. However, this does not affect the method of carving, which is very similar to ham.

Place so that shank bone is to right of carver and thick meaty section is on far side of platter. Insert fork firmly in large end of leg and cut two or three slices from the thin side.

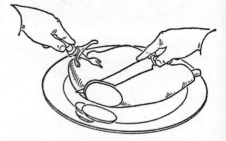

Turn roast so that it rests on surface just cut. Shank bone now points up.

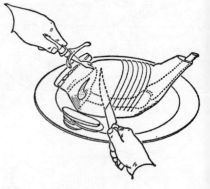

Insert fork in left side and starting at shank end, slice down to leg bone, making parallel slices ¼ to ⅜ inch thick. With fork in place, run knife along leg bone releasing all slices.

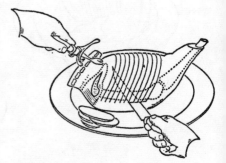

LOIN ROAST

Loin roasts are more easily carved if backbone is separated from ribs at the market, so that it loosens during roasting.

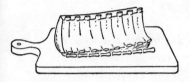

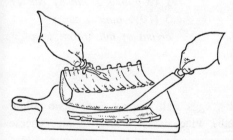

It then is easily cut away before carving. Place roast so that rib side faces carver. Use rib bones as guides for slicing. Check slant before cutting for all are not perpendicular to platter.

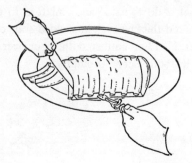

Cut slice close to each rib and fairly thin. In small loin, each slice may contain a rib. In large loin, it is possible to cut two boneless slices between ribs.

BEEF

BEEF BALLS EPICUREAN
(24 servings)

6 pound ground beef
3 cups fine dry bread crumbs
4 eggs
1 tablespoon salt
1 teaspoon pepper
2 teaspoons monosodium
  glutamate
1 pound blue cheese
2 quarts tomato sauce
1 tablespoon Worcestershire
  sauce

1 cup dry red wine or
  tarragon vinegar
1 cup chopped onion
¼ cup butter, or oil or
  other fat to sauté onion
2 quarts sour cream or
  1 (3-pound 3-ounce) can or
  5 (10½-ounce) cans
  cream of mushroom soup

Combine beef, bread crumbs, eggs, salt, pepper and monosodium glutamate. Shape into 48 balls. Place tablespoonful of blue cheese in center of 24 balls. Press remaining balls on top, being sure cheese is enclosed in center. Combine tomato sauce, Worcestershire and wine. Pour over balls and let stand 1 hour or longer, turning once or twice. Drain meat balls. Brown in hot greased skillet, rolling to brown evenly. When browned, arrange in serving pans and keep warm. Sauté onion in butter in skillet. Add tomato sauce mixture to onion and cook until reduced to desired thickness. Add scalded sour cream or hot soup undiluted to skillet, blending until smooth. Pour over meat balls. Keep hot but do not let boil. Serve promptly.

Recipe may be doubled.

BEEF BALLS ORIENTAL
(48 servings)

6 pounds ground beef
1 quart diced onion
6 cloves minced garlic
6 quarts celery, sliced
    diagonally
5 pounds carrots, pared,
    sliced diagonally
3 quarts beef bouillon
½ cup salt

2½ tablespoons monsodium
    glutamate
¼ cup powdered ginger
½ cup Kitchen Bouquet
1½ cups cornstarch
1 cup water
6 quarts or 12 No. 303 cans
    or 2 No. 10 cans bean
    sprouts

Shape ground beef into ¾-inch balls. Brown in shallow pan in oven at 350° F., shaking to brown on all sides. When meat balls are browned, add onion, garlic and celery and cook until clear in 350° F. oven about 15 minutes. In saucepan, cook carrots in bouillon until tender. Blend salt, monosodium glutamate, ginger, Kitchen Bouquet and cornstarch with water. Add to hot bouillon and carrots and bring to boil, stirring constantly. Add meat balls and vegetables, including bean sprouts. Heat thoroughly and serve over hot rice.

Double the recipe only if you have large-quantity equipment. The meat balls may be made ahead and kept refrigerated until time to reheat for serving. Avoid overcooking so that vegetables stay crisp and colors bright.

Chinese cabbage shredded and cooked last 5 minutes with carrots in bouillon makes a pleasant switch from the bean sprouts, where it is available.

BEEF STROGANOFF
(24 servings)

6 pounds boneless beef
steak (tenderloin, rib,
sirloin, chuck or round)
¾ cup salad oil
1 cup sliced onions
2 cloves garlic, minced
1 cup dry red wine or
beef bouillon

2 tablespoons salt
1 teaspoon Tabasco
2 pounds sliced fresh
mushrooms or 2 (4-ounce)
cans sliced mushrooms
½ cup all-purpose flour
1 quart sour cream, at
room temperature

Cut beef in thin strips, ½ inch thick or less. Sauté in oil over high heat, stirring frequently until brown. Add onions and garlic and cook until clear. Add wine or bouillon, salt and Tabasco. If using tenderloin or high grade sirloin, bring liquid to boil and complete recipe immediately. If using less tender cuts, such as rib, chuck or round steak, simmer meat until tender, 30 to 60 minutes. When meat is tender, add mushrooms and cook 5 minutes. Sprinkle flour over mixture and blend in gradually, until smooth, cooking until thickened. Gradually stir in sour cream. Heat but do not boil. Serve immediately.

Recipe may be doubled. Recipe may be prepared ahead up to point of adding sour cream.

BOILED TONGUE
(48 servings)

12 pounds fresh beef tongue   4 lemons, sliced
Water to cover   4 bay leaves
2 tablespoons salt   1 teaspoon peppercorns
3 cloves garlic

Cook tongue in water, adding salt, garlic, lemons, bay leaf and peppercorns. Simmer slowly until tongue is tender, about 3 hours. Cool slightly and remove skin. If to be served cold, chill tongue in broth, then slice. If serving warm, slice and keep warm in broth. If tongue is only meat to be served, portions may be increased accordingly. This amount allows about 4 ounces per person.

Recipe may be increased. Tongue may be cooked ahead and reheated in broth.

BURGUNDY BEEF BALLS
(12 or 48 servings)

INGREDIENTS	12 SERVINGS	48 SERVINGS
eggs	2	8
California burgundy	1½ cups	5 cups
dry bread crumbs	3 cups	3 quarts
salt	1 tablespoon	3 tablespoons
black pepper	½ teaspoon freshly ground	1½ teaspoons
ground beef	2 pounds	8 pounds
dry onions, minced	2	6

Beat eggs until frothy, stir in wine and then bread crumbs. Let stand until crumbs absorb liquid. If mixture seems too dry, a small amount more wine may be added. Stir in salt and pepper, then ground beef and finely minced dry onions. Shape into small balls, brown in hot fat on all sides, shaking pan to keep them round. Do a few at a time and remove to a large covered casserole as they are browned. Place covered casserole in 350° F. oven and bake 25 to 30 minutes or until balls are cooked enough.

Same mixture may be shaped into patties for serving on a bun or with a mushroom sauce with vegetables or plain with French fried potatoes. Cook patties for 2 or 3 minutes on each side, depending on degree of doneness desired.

Lean lamb may be substituted for beef in above mixture. A combination of veal and beef is excellent in flavor.

BURGUNDY SIRLOIN TIPS
(12 or 48 servings)

INGREDIENTS	12 SERVINGS	48 SERVINGS
sirloin tips	3 pounds	12 pounds
flour, salt and pepper		
shortening	½ cup	2 cups
fresh garlic	2 buds	4 to 6 buds
sweet basil, dry	¼ teaspoon	1 teaspoon
bay leaf	2	6
water	1 quart	4 quarts
California burgundy or claret	2 cups	2 quarts
small onions (1 inch diameter)	16 (1 pound)	3 quarts (4 pounds)
celery, sliced	1 cup	1 quart
carrots, diced	1½ quarts	6 quarts
fresh mushrooms	12 large or 24 small	48 large
mushroom caps, for garnish	12	48

Cut meat into small pieces, roll in seasoned flour. Heat shortening and add garlic buds, then brown meat on both sides in the fat. Remove garlic, add sweet basil, bay leaf, water and wine. Simmer, covered, until meat is very tender, adding more water as required to maintain ample stock. Cooking time will be about 2 to 3 hours. Add onions, celery, carrots and mushrooms. Cook 30 to 45 minutes or until vegetables are tender. Drain off stock, thicken with flour and water paste. (Two tablespoons flour to 1 cup liquid is medium sauce consistency). Taste and add salt and pepper, if required. Return meat and vegetables to thickened gravy. Reheat. Serve garnished with large mushroom caps that have been browned in butter in saucepan or brushed with melted butter and browned under the broiler.

Economical Oxtail Stew* may be prepared using the above recipe by substituting 4 to 5 pounds of oxtails for sirloin tips in small recipe and 16 pounds oxtails for sirloin tips in larger recipe. Cut joints apart and brown oxtails in hot fat on all sides. Add seasonings, water and wine and proceed as above. Cooking time is approximately 3 to 4 hours before adding vegetables.

CHILI CON CARNE
(48 servings)

6 pounds ground beef	5 quarts tomatoes
1 pound ground pork	2½ tablespoons chili powder
2 cups chopped onions	1 teaspoon cumin powder
½ cup shortening or	3 to 4 tablespoons salt
bacon drippings	1 teaspoon pepper
3 quarts cooked kidney	3 tablespoons sugar
beans (4 cups dried	
beans or 1 No. 10 can or	
6 No. 303 cans)	

Sauté beef, pork and onions in shortening until meat loses raw look and onions are transparent, stirring frequently. Meat may be browned in large, flat pan in 425° F. oven, stirring often, if preferred. Combine browned meat, onions and cooked beans with tomatoes, seasonings, and sugar. Bring to simmering temperature and cook, stirring occasionally, for 1 hour or longer. Chili may be baked in 350° F. oven in covered pan for 1 hour or longer, stirring frequently. If sauce is thinner than desired, stir in flour-water paste and bring to boiling, stirring constantly. (Two tablespoons flour will thicken 1 cup liquid to medium sauce consistency.) Taste and adjust seasoning after mixture has cooked for 30 minutes.

Recipe may be doubled. Chili takes well to making ahead and being reheated at serving time.

NOTE: To prepare dry beans for use, soak overnight in water to cover after washing in several clear waters. Drain. Combine soaked beans with 3 quarts boiling water and simmer until tender. Drain and discard cooking liquor.

CORNED BEEF
(12 servings)

6 to 8 pounds corned beef, 2 (3- to 4-pound) pieces
Water to cover

Cover corned beef with cold water, bring to boil, then adjust heat so that water simmers gently. Continue cooking until meat is fork-tender, approximately 1 hour per pound. (Two 4-pound pieces will require about 4 hours cooking). If beef seems excessively salty, drain cooking liquor after 1 hour of cooking and replace with fresh hot water. At serving time, slice corned beef thinly across grain of meat. May be served hot or cold.

Favorite accompaniments for corned beef and its close flavor rival—pastrami—are fresh horseradish sauce and hot English mustard. Buy pastrami ready to heat and serve from a fine delicatessen. This, too, may be served cold on rye bread slices or crusty, poppy seed rolls.

CREAMED CHIPPED BEEF
WITH MUSHROOMS
(48 servings)

4 cups butter or margarine
1 quart chopped onion
1 quart chopped green
pepper
1 quart fresh mushrooms
or 4 (8-ounce) cans,
drained
2 pounds dried beef, cut
into bite-size pieces
4 cups all-purpose flour

1 tablespoon Tabasco
2 tablespoons salt
½ teaspoon nutmeg
1½ gallons beef broth
or consommé
1 quart undiluted
evaporated milk
1 cup chopped pimento
Rice or melba toast

In skillet, melt butter and sauté onion, green pepper and mushrooms. Add dried beef and cook until heated through. Blend in flour and seasonings. Add beef broth and evaporated milk and cook until thickened, stirring constantly. Add pimento and heat through. Serve in rice nests, on rice or melba toast.

Recipe may be doubled successfully. It also may be made ahead and reheated over low heat, well covered, thinning with canned mushroom liquid or water, if necessary.

HUNGARIAN GOULASH
(24 servings)

5 to 7 pounds boneless
beef chuck
Salt and pepper
Paprika
3 cloves minced garlic

Water
Bouillon cubes or granules
(4 cubes or teaspoons
per quart water)
Flour

Cut meat in 1-inch cubes. Season meat with salt, pepper and paprika. Let stand while rendering some fat for browning the meat.

Add garlic to fat. Brown meat on all sides. Add water, 1 quart at a time until meat is covered generously. Add sufficient bouillon cubes or granules to make a good stock. Bring to simmer and cook covered until meat is very tender, about 4 hours. Thicken stock with flour. Taste gravy and add additional seasoning, as needed.

Recipe may be doubled. Bay leaf is a seasoning some good cooks use in this dish. Drop 2 or 3 whole bay leaves into simmering stock, then remove them before thickening gravy.

ITALIAN MEAT SAUCE
(24 servings)

½ cup oil
4 pounds ground beef
2 cups minced onion
4 cloves minced garlic
5 (6-ounce) cans
    tomato paste
5 tomato paste cans water
5 (1-pound 13-ounce)
    cans tomatoes

2 tablespoons salt
1 teaspoon pepper
1 teaspoon sugar
1 bay leaf
1 teaspoon dried oregano
1 teaspoon dried basil
1 teaspoon dried thyme
    leaves

In large sauce pot, heat oil and sauté ground beef, onion and garlic until meat loses red look, stirring often. Add tomato paste and water, tomatoes that have been forced through a sieve, seasonings, sugar and herbs. Simmer slowly 2 hours or longer, stirring occasionally. Taste and add additional seasonings, if required. Add more water as necessary. Makes 8 quarts.

Meat sauce recipe may be doubled. Grated cheese for topping spaghetti sauce is available ready grated or may be prepared from a wedge of Romano or Parmesan cheese. Freshly grated cheese gives superior flavor.

ITALIAN PIZZA
(24 servings)

Dough:

4 cups sifted all-purpose
  flour
1 egg
1½ teaspoons sugar
½ teaspoon salt
2 tablespoons olive oil
1 package dry or
  compressed yeast

¼ cup lukewarm water
3 tablespoons salad oil
1 clove garlic, crushed
½ teaspoon rosemary
¼ teaspoon oregano

To sifted flour, add egg, sugar, salt, olive oil and yeast, which has been dissolved in lukewarm water. Add just enough additional water to make a stiff dough. Knead well. Combine salad oil, garlic, rosemary and oregano. Use to brush baking sheet or pizza pans.

Divide dough into 6 pieces. Roll each piece into a circle about 10 inches in diameter and place on prepared baking sheet or pizza pan. Let stand while preparing sauce and filling.

Topping:

3 (8-ounce) packages
  mozzarella or pizza
  cheese
1 cup chopped onion
2 cloves garlic, crushed
½ teaspoon oregano
6 (8-ounce) cans tomato
  sauce

½ pound chopped salami
  or other sausage or
  cooked meat or seafood
2 (4-ounce) cans sliced
  mushrooms, drained
1 cup grated Parmesan
  cheese

Arrange slices of mozzarella cheese on pizza dough. Combine onion, garlic, oregano and tomato sauce. Spoon over mozzarella. Sprinkle salami and mushrooms on pizza, then top with Parmesan. Bake in 425° F. oven until crust is brown and filling bubbly, about 15 minutes. Pizza may be made ahead and frozen before baking. Allow 20 minutes for baking from frozen state.

Recipe may be doubled if dough is kneaded in amounts easily handled.

LASAGNE
(24 servings)

4 pounds ground beef
6 (8-ounce) cans tomato
    sauce
1 (6-ounce) can tomato paste
1½ quarts water
2 cups dry red wine or
    beef bouillon
1 tablespoon garlic purée
1 quart chopped onion
1 cup chopped parsley

2 tablespoons salt
1 tablespoon oregano
1 tablespoon rosemary
4 pounds lasagne noodles,
    cooked
½ cup olive or salad oil
2 pounds mozzarella or
    pizza cheese, sliced
1 pound Parmesan or
    Romano cheese, grated

Break ground beef into bite-size pieces and brown in heavy skillets or in hot oven. Add tomato sauce and paste, water, wine, garlic, onion, parsley, salt and herbs. Cover and simmer slowly 1 hour. This may be done ahead. Drain cooked noodles and toss with olive oil. Arrange in layers in oiled two 3-quart baking pans about 3 inches deep, alternating layers of noodles, sauce, mozzarella and Parmesan cheese, sprinkling cheese generously over tops. Bake in 350° F. oven, covered, for 30 minutes. Uncover and bake 15 minutes longer or until bubbling and browned.

Recipe may be doubled. Casseroles may be assembled ready for baking and refrigerated. Allow about 5 minutes longer for baking from cold state.

MEAT LOAF
(48 servings)

8 pounds ground beef
1 pound ground pork
3 quarts dry bread crumbs
6 cups milk or tomato
 juice
1 cup finely chopped
 onion
8 eggs, beaten
3 tablespoons salt
1 teaspoon pepper

½ teaspoon dry savory,
 if desired
½ teaspoon thyme,
 if desired
½ teaspoon sweet basil,
 if desired
1½ to 2 quarts tomato
 purée or tomato soup,
 if desired

Place ground beef and pork into large mixing bowl. Combine bread crumbs, milk or tomato juice, onion, beaten eggs, and seasonings in separate bowl. When crumbs are completely moistened, add to meat mixture. Lightly blend the two mixtures together until evenly mixed. Form four uniform loaves in 9×5×3-inch loaf pans. Pour tomato purée or soup over top of loaves, if desired. Place in 325° F. oven and bake 1¼ hours or until done. Let loaves stand about 20 minutes in warm place before slicing. Cut each loaf into 12 slices.

Recipe may be doubled. Two versions of meat loaf are given above: One is plain, the other rich with herb and tomato seasoning.

POT ROAST OF BEEF WITH BROWN GRAVY
(24 servings)

10 to 13 pounds (6 to
 8 pounds if meat is
 boneless) chuck beef
Salt and pepper

Shortening or other fat
All-purpose flour
Stock or water

Season meat with salt and pepper; then sear until well browned on all sides in hot fat in heavy kettles. Cover tightly and cook over low heat until tender, turning ocasionally so that meat cooks uniformly. When done (about 3 hours for 4- to 6-pound pieces), remove meat and keep warm. Measure fat and juice in pans. For 1 gallon of gravy, combine 2 cups browned fat drippings, 2 to 2½ cups flour and 1 gallon (4 quarts) hot stock or water. Stir constantly with wire whip until mixture is thickened and free of lumps. Taste and season. From 1 to 2 tablespoons salt and pepper to taste may be required. Seasoned stock may be prepared with bouillon cubes or granules.

Recipe may be doubled if large containers are available. Keep gravy warm over hot water after preparation, and stir occasionally to keep mixture free of lumps and prevent skin forming on top.

POT ROAST WITH WINE
(24 servings)

6 to 8 pounds boneless beef chuck or round roast	1 tablespoon salt
	½ teaspoon Tabasco
¼ cup salad oil	2 bay leaves
1 cup chopped onions	2 cups beef broth, for gravy
1 cup diced carrots	½ cup cornstarch
¼ cup chopped parsley	1 cup cold water
1 cup tomato juice	
1 cup dry red wine or beef broth	

Brown meat well in hot salad oil. Add onions, carrots and parsley and sauté lightly. Add tomato juice, wine, salt, Tabasco and bay leaves. Cover tightly and cook over low heat or in 300° F. oven until tender, about 3 hours. Keep meat warm. Strain pan liquid. Combine with beef broth. Blend cornstarch with cold water and stir into broth mixture. Cook, stirring constantly, until thickened and mixture boils. Correct seasoning to taste.

Recipe may be increased as required.

SWEDISH MEAT BALLS I
(24 servings)

2 pounds ground pork

2 pounds ground veal

6 pounds ground beef

8 cups fine dry bread crumbs

8 eggs, well beaten

1 cup cold stock or water

3 tablespoons salt

1½ teaspoons pepper

½ teaspoon allspice, if
desired

½ teaspoon nutmeg, if
desired

Sauce:

6 cups brown sugar

2 tablespoons dry mustard

6 cups vinegar

6 cups stock or water,
additional

Have meat ground very fine or put through grinder twice. Combine bread crumbs, eggs, 1 cup stock or water and seasonings; add to meats. Mix lightly but thoroughly. Shape into small balls. Place in very lightly greased baking pan. Combine sugar, mustard, vinegar and 6 cups stock; pour over meat balls. Bake in 325° F. oven 3 hours, basting frequently.

Recipe may be doubled. Meat balls may be prepared without sauce, if desired. Bake in 350° F. oven until done through, about 25 minutes for small 1-inch diameter balls. Cool, package and freeze plain balls for later use as desired. Precooked balls could be heated in separately cooked sauce or plain in covered casseroles.

SWEDISH MEAT BALLS II
(24 servings)

4 pounds ground beef
1 pound ground lean pork
1 pound ground veal
4 eggs
2 cups milk
2 cups fine dry bread
  crumbs
2 tablespoons minced
  onion
1 teaspoon Tabasco
1 teaspoon nutmeg

2 tablespoons salt
1 cup butter or margarine
  (may be part pan
  drippings)
1 cup all-purpose flour
1 tablespoon salt
3 pints water
1 pint light cream or sour
  cream
¼ cup minced parsley

Combine meats, add eggs, milk, bread crumbs and seasonings. Mix thoroughly, using mixer if available. Form into small balls. Brown on cooky sheet or other shallow pan with edges, in 400° F. oven about 15 minutes, rolling around pan to brown evenly and keep balls round. For gravy: melt butter, using pan drippings for part of amount, if desired. Blend in flour and 1 tablespoon salt. Add water and cream and cook until thickened, stirring constantly. Add parsley and meat balls. Keep warm but do not boil. Both meat balls and sauce may be made ahead and reheated.

Recipe may be increased, as needed.

PARTY-PRETTY BUFFET EASY TO PREPARE

A sumptuous buffet can be deceivingly uncomplicated to prepare with the kind of planning that features this menu: Ready-prepared chilled canned marinated artichokes in Tomato Aspic ring to be accompanied by Sour Cream Dressing as shown at left; Shrimp Creamed with Oysters to spoon over Parsleyed Rice; glamorous pineapple cubes to top with mayonnaise thinned lightly with cream as an alternate salad or garnish, making only three items requiring detailed preparation. Recipes for those are listed in Index.

TAMALE PIE
(24 servings)

1 quart cornmeal
2 quarts boiling water
1 tablespoon salt
½ cup bacon drippings or
  margarine
2 cups chopped onion
1 cup chopped green pepper
¼ cup chopped celery
3 pounds ground beef or
  combination of beef and
  pork, as desired

3 cups tomato sauce or
  purée
1 cup sliced ripe olives
1 cup pimento, diced
¼ cup minced parsley
2 teaspoons salt
½ teaspoon pepper
1 tablespoon Worcestershire
  sauce
1 tablespoon chili powder
  (more to taste)

Stir cornmeal into boiling water and salt, cooking until mixture thickens, according to package directions. Spread half into bottom and sides of greased baking pan, reserving half for topping. Melt bacon drippings or margarine and simmer onion, green pepper and celery until soft but not brown. Drain excess fat. Brown meat, breaking into bits with fork while stirring. Combine sautéed vegetables, meat, tomato sauce, olives, pimento, parsley, salt, pepper, Worcestershire sauce and chili powder and pour over bottom layer of mush. Top with remaining cornmeal mush. Bake in 300° F. oven 1 hour.

Meat mixture may be doubled in making twice this recipe, but prepare separate batches of cornmeal mush in order to ensure smooth consistency.

TERIYAKI BEEF
(24 servings)

8 pounds boneless lean beef
½ cup molasses
1 cup lemon juice or vinegar
2 cups soy or shoyu sauce
1½ teaspoons monosodium
   glutamate

2 cloves garlic, crushed
¼ cup chopped fresh
   ginger root or 1¼
   teaspoons ground ginger

Cut meat in 1-inch cubes and place on twenty-four 8-inch skewers. Combine molasses, lemon juice, soy sauce, and seasonings in shallow dish. Place meat in marinade so it is half covered. Turn after 1 hour. Let marinate 6 to 12 hours. Broil 3 inches from heat, turning to brown evenly. May also be broiled over charcoal.

Recipe may be doubled. Marinade tenderizes meat so less tender cuts may be used.

CURED MEATS

FRANKFURTERS IN BEER
(48 servings)

48 (about 8 pounds) old-fashioned frankfurters
4 quarts beer

Cover frankfurters with beer, instead of water, and simmer slowly or 30 minutes or longer.

Recipe may be doubled. This recipe allows only 1 frank per person. Depending on other meats and/or main dishes and the occasions, the amount may be increased accordingly. To serve as "appetizer," cut franks in fourths before heating.

BAKED HAM SLICES WITH BROILED PEACHES
(48 servings)

10 pounds precooked ham, cut into ¼-inch slices
2 No. 10 cans (6 quarts) sliced or halved peaches, drained, reserving syrup
1 cup all-purpose flour
2 (6-ounce) cans tomato paste
2 cups brown sugar
1 teaspoon Tabasco
2 teaspoons dry mustard
¼ cup vinegar

Arrange ham slices in shallow pan, topping with peach slices or halves. Combine 3 cups syrup from peaches, flour, tomato paste, brown sugar, Tabasco, mustard and vinegar, blending until smooth. Spoon over peaches and ham slices. Broil about 5 inches from heat about 10 minutes, until ham is hot through and surface is bubbly and light browned.

Recipe may be doubled. Pineapple slices may be substituted for peaches, if desired.

BROCCOLI AND HAM OR
TURKEY EN CASSEROLE
(48 servings)

10 pounds broccoli spears	5 quarts milk, scalded
48 slices (approximately	1½ tablespoons dry mustard
3 to 4 pounds)	1 quart California sauterne
(ready-to-eat) ham	2 tablespoons
or turkey	Worcestershire sauce
2½ cups butter or	2 pounds Cheddar
margarine	cheese, grated
2½ cups all-purpose flour	Paprika

Cook broccoli until tender in boiling, salted water. Drain and keep hot. Slice ham or turkey thin. Prepare cheese sauce: Melt butter or margarine and blend in flour. Stir into hot milk with whisk, beating constantly until sauce is smooth and thickened. Combine mustard, wine and Worcestershire sauce. Stir into sauce. Add grated cheese and stir until melted. Do not boil. Keep warm over hot water. At serving time, place thin slice of ham or turkey on a hot plate. Arrange 3 small or 2 large broccoli spears over meat. Spoon about ¼ cup sauce over vegetable. Dust with paprika.

Recipe should not be increased. Separate mixings of this cheese sauce are better than making one large batch.

HAM-VEAL POT PIE
(48 servings)

8 pounds boneless veal
  shoulder, cubed
4 pounds boned ham, cubed
1½ gallons water
3 tablespoons salt
20 small onions
3 quarts sliced carrots

5 (10-ounce) packages
  frozen peas
4 (8-ounce) cans sliced
  mushrooms with liquid
2 quarts milk
4 cups all-purpose flour
48 Biscuits* or pie crust
  rounds for topping

Cook veal and ham in boiling salted water until tender, about 1 hour. Add onions and carrots and cook until they are tender, adding peas when carrots are almost tender. Drain off broth, arranging cooked meat and vegetables including mushrooms, in 48 individual casseroles or shallow baking pans. Blend flour with milk, mixing smooth. Add to hot broth. Cook until thickened, stirring constantly. Pour over meat and vegetables. Serve topped with baked Biscuits* or baked circles of pie crust, use raw Biscuit* or pie dough to form a top crust over hot ingredients in casseroles or baking pans. Baking time for Biscuit* topping is 450° F. for 10 to 12 minutes. Bake pie dough at 425° F. for 12 to 15 minutes approximately.

Recipe may be doubled.

ORANGE HAM LOAF
(24 servings)

4 eggs
½ teaspoon Tabasco
2 teaspoons dry mustard
1 (12-ounce) can frozen
   orange juice concentrate,
   undiluted

1 cup water
6 cups fine dry bread crumbs
4 pounds (3 quarts)
   ground cooked ham
12 slices canned pineapple
¼ cup brown sugar

Beat eggs with Tabasco and mustard, orange juice and water. Mix
well with crumbs and ham. Shape into two loaves. Bake in 350° F.
oven 1¼ hours or until browned. Twenty minutes before end of baking time, arrange pineapple slices on top of loaves, sprinkling with
brown sugar. Return to brown in oven. Remove and let stand 10
minutes before slicing.

Loaves may be mixed and refrigerated before baking. Allow an
extra 10 minutes to offset the chilling. The ham loaf may also be
baked, cooled, sliced and arranged on sheets of aluminum foil to
reheat and serve easily. Allow 30 minutes in 350° F. oven to heat
through.

LAMB

LAMB, BEEF OR VEAL PIE TOPPED WITH CORNMEAL BISCUITS
(12 or 48 servings)

INGREDIENTS	12 SERVINGS	48 SERVINGS
potatoes, coarsely diced	6	24
carrots, coarsely diced	6	24
onions		
1 inch diameter	12	3 pounds
water		
salt	1½ teaspoons	1 tablespoon
solid pack tomatoes	1 (1-pound 12-ounce) can (3½ cups)	1 No. 10 can (3 quarts)
California burgundy	1 cup	1 quart
flour	½ cup	2 cups
oil	⅓ cup	1⅓ cups
cooked, coarsely diced lamb, beef or veal or a mixture of these	1 quart	4 quarts
Cornmeal Biscuits*		

Cover potatoes, carrots and whole onions with boiling water; add salt, cook until tender. Do not drain. Add tomatoes and wine to vegetables. Blend flour with oil and stir into hot stock, cooking until smoothly thickened. Add cooked, diced meat. Taste and add seasoning if needed. Reheat to boiling. Pour into a 12×9×2-inch baking pan for 12 servings or 4 pans for 48 servings. Top with Cornmeal Biscuits* and bake in oven until Biscuits* are golden brown and light at 400° F. about 20 minutes. Bake additional Biscuits* separately.

Colorful appearance as well as fine flavor makes this meat pie popular. It is made with economical cuts of meat, precooked to fork tenderness before combining with vegetables and wine-seasoned sauce.

SKEWERED LAMB OR BEEF CUBES WITH MUSHROOMS
(12 or 48 servings)

INGREDIENTS	12 SERVINGS	48 SERVINGS
lamb leg or shoulder or tender beef roast or steak	4 pounds	16 pounds
onions, thinly sliced	4	8
salt	1 tablespoon	3 tablespoons
pepper	½ teaspoon	1 teaspoon
oregano	1 teaspoon	1 tablespoon
rosemary	¼ teaspoon	1 teaspoon
California sherry	1 cup	3 cups
oil	¼ cup	¾ cup
fresh mushrooms	24 to 36 medium	96 medium

Cut meat into uniform 1-inch cubes. Mix with onions, seasonings, wine and oil. Let stand overnight, or at least several hours, in refrigerator, turning mixture occasionally to allow flavors to blend. Thread meat on metal skewers, alternating with mushrooms. Do not push meat and vegetables tightly together. Brush with marinade. Broil over hot charcoal or in broiling oven, turning to brown all sides.

Bacon squares threaded on skewers next to mushrooms will flavor them nicely and aid in browning process.

SHISH KEBABS
(24 servings)

6 pounds boneless, cubed
  lamb, shoulder or leg
1 cup salad oil
1 cup beer, ale or dry wine
¼ cup lemon juice
2 cloves crushed garlic
1½ tablespoons salt
2 bay leaves
1 teaspoon pepper

1 teaspoon basil
1 teaspoon thyme
8 large green peppers, cut
  in 1-inch squares
24 small onions, canned or
  parboiled
12 carrots, cut in 1-inch
  slices, parboiled
24 fresh mushroom caps

Marinate lamb overnight in oil, beer, lemon juice, seasonings and herbs. Alternate lamb cubes with vegetables, capping each kebab with mushroom. Broil 3 inches from heat 10 to 15 minutes until well browned, turning to cook evenly.

Recipe may be increased as desired.

STUFFED SHOULDER OF LAMB
(48 servings)

15 pound shoulder of lamb,
boned

1 quart chopped onions

3 tablespoons butter or
margarine

1¾ pounds ground lamb

1¾ pounds ground pork
(not sausage)

4 teaspoons thyme

4 teaspoons rosemary

1¼ teaspoons nutmeg

5 cups coarse dry bread
crumbs

5 eggs, beaten slightly

1 tablespoon salt

1 teaspoon pepper

1 cup coarsely cut onions

1½ cups chopped celery

1½ cups grated carrots

1 quart California burgundy

2½ quarts stock

Have meatman bone lamb shoulder. Sauté 1 quart onions in butter and mix into stuffing with ground lamb, pork, herbs, nutmeg, bread crumbs, eggs, salt and pepper. Stuff lamb shoulder, roll and tie securely with heavy white twine. Season lightly with salt and pepper on outside. Sprinkle coarsely cut onions, chopped celery and grated carrots in bottom of roasting pan with stuffed shoulder over them. Bake in 375° F. oven for 1 hour, until well browned. Pour burgundy over meat into baking pan, cover and continue baking until tender, about 30 to 45 minutes longer. Remove meat from pan and keep warm. Skim off excess fat. Add stock to pan drippings, bring to boil and let cook 10 minutes. Strain liquid and thicken, if desired, with cornstarch for gravy. Taste and add salt and pepper, if needed.

Stuffing recipe may be doubled for two large shoulder roasts.

One tablespoon cornstarch thickens 1 cup stock to cream sauce consistency—or ¼ cup cornstarch to 1 quart liquid. Moisten cornstarch with a small amount of cold water, then stir briskly into hot stock. Bring to boil while stirring constantly.

Or omit stock and use pan drippings after straining if only small amount of unthickened meat sauce is desired.

SHERRIED LAMB FRICASSEE OR BURGUNDY BEEF STEW
(48 servings)

18 pounds boneless lamb or
  beef
3 tablespoons salt
1¼ teaspoons pepper
1½ cups all-purpose flour
3 cloves garlic, chopped fine
1½ pints California sherry or
  burgundy
2 quarts beef stock,
  consommé or water
1½ cups tomato purée
200 carrot balls, parboiled,
  cut from 8 to 10 pounds
  raw carrots

100 turnip balls, parboiled,
  cut from 8 to 10 pounds
  raw turnips
250 potato balls, parboiled,
  cut from 8 to 10 pounds
  raw potatoes
1 No. 10 can (3 quarts)
  pearl onions, drained well
Butter or margarine
Granulated sugar

Season meat with salt and pepper. Brown on all sides in heavy skillet or in roasting pan in 425° F. oven. Dredge with flour and mix with pan drippings. Brown flour a few minutes in oven or skillet. Add garlic, wine, stock and tomato purée. Bring to boil and mix well with browned mixture on bottom of skillet or roasting pan. Cover and bake or simmer until meat is tender, about 1 hour. If baking, use 325° F. oven. Add parboiled vegetables 5 minutes before meat is removed from heat. Sauté canned onions in butter, sprinkling with a little white sugar to glaze them and add just before serving or use as garnish.

Recipe may be doubled, and other vegetables may be used. Vegetables may be cut in 1½-inch chunks, if preferred. Meat may be cooked ahead and reheated with vegetables.

PORK

PORK CHOP SUEY AMANDINE
(48 servings)

*1 pound butter or
margarine
15 pounds pork loin
2 quarts coarsely cut
onions
4 quarts celery, cut in
1-inch strips
8 (1-pound 4-ounce) cans
mixed Chinese vegetables,
drained, reserving
liquid*

*4 teaspoons salt
½ teaspoon pepper
1 cup cornstarch
1 cup cold water
⅓ cup soy sauce
11 quarts hot, cooked rice
or crisp, fried noodles
1 pound whole toasted
almonds (2½ cups), for
garnish*

Melt butter or margarine in several large, heavy skillets. Trim meat from bone and fat. Cut in thin strips about 2 inches long. Brown quickly without crowding for 2 minutes. Add onions and cook 5 minutes, stirring often. Measure vegetable liquid and add water to make 3 quarts; heat and add to onions with celery, salt and pepper. Cover and boil 5 minutes. Add Chinese vegetables. Return to boil. Combine cornstarch, 1 cup cold water and soy sauce. Add to vegetable-meat mixture, stirring constantly and thoroughly from the bottom. Cook 1 minute. Serve at once over hot rice or with crisp, fried noodles. Garnish with whole toasted almonds.

Recipe may be doubled. Goodness of Chop Suey depends on tender crispness of sautéed, but not overcooked, vegetables. Texture, color and flavor are preserved by accurate timing of cooking.

PORK CHOPS HAWAIIAN
(24 servings)

1 cup finely chopped onions
½ cup shredded carrots
½ cup finely chopped celery
¼ cup butter or margarine
2 cups canned crushed
  pineapple, drained,
  reserving liquid
½ cup raisins

1 cup fine dry bread crumbs
1 teaspoon salt
¼ teaspoon pepper
½ teaspoon Tabasco
24 pork chops, 1 inch or
  more thick, with pocket
  in each

Sauté onions, carrots and celery in butter. Add drained pineapple, raisins, bread crumbs and seasonings. Toss lightly to blend. Place stuffing in pocket of each chop. Fasten pockets with toothpicks or small poultry pins. Bake in shallow baking pans in 350° F. until chops are done, about 1½ hours. Turn chops once during baking. Serve with following sauce:

1 quart pineapple juice
¼ cup lemon juice
¼ teaspoon Tabasco

¼ cup cornstarch
½ cup cold water

Pour pan drippings off chops into large skillet. Add pineapple juice, lemon juice and Tabasco. Blend cornstarch and cold water. Add to pan liquids. Cook until thick, stirring constantly.

PORK CHOP SPAGHETTI
(24 servings)

24 (about 10 pounds)
  pork chops
1 quart chopped onion
2 cups chopped green
  pepper
2 tablespoons butter or
  margarine
1 (3-pound 3-ounce) or
  5 (10½-ounce)
  cans condensed tomato
  soup

Sufficient water to equal
  quantity of condensed soup
1 tablespoon garlic purée or
  finely minced garlic
1 cup minced parsley
1 tablespoon oregano
5 pounds spaghetti, cooked
1 pound grated Parmesan
  cheese

Brown pork chops in large skillets or shallow baking pans. When second sides are nearly browned, add onion, green pepper and butter and sauté until clear. Add tomato soup, water, garlic, parsley and oregano. Cover and cook 2 hours over low heat, adding water if sauce becomes too thick. Serve sauce and chops with fresh-cooked spaghetti, sprinkling with grated cheese.

Double recipe as needed. Chops and sauce may be cooked ahead and reheated but have spaghetti freshly cooked.

BARBECUED SPARERIBS
(48 servings)

25 pounds spareribs, cut in
  serving-size pieces
1 quart chopped onions
6 cloves garlic, minced
6 cups tomato purée
1½ cups vinegar

1½ cups brown sugar
1½ tablespoons salt
2 tablespoons dry mustard
2 tablespoons Worcestershire
  sauce

Arrange spareribs in open shallow baking pans. Bake in 350° F. oven 1 hour. Pour off fat. Meanwhile, combine onions, garlic, tomato puree, vinegar, sugar, salt, mustard and Worcestershire; simmer 30 minutes. Pour sauce over browned ribs and bake 2 hours longer, turning ribs and basting with sauce to brown evenly.

Recipe may be doubled. Ribs may be baked ahead and reheated in sauce in 350° F. oven about 30 minutes.

SWEET-SOUR PORK
(48 servings)

25 pounds boneless pork
cubes (shoulder or leg)
or 50 pounds spareribs,
cut in serving-size pieces
1 quart onions, diced
1 quart celery, sliced
diagonally
1 quart green pepper, cut
in strips
2 tablespoons salt
1 teaspoon pepper

1 tablespoon Tabasco
¼ cup Worcestershire sauce
1 cup brown sugar
1 cup cornstarch
1 cup vinegar
2 cups water
2 quarts beef bouillon
1 No. 10 can (3 quarts)
pineapple chunks, with
syrup

Brown pork in 350° F. oven in shallow pans 1 hour. Add vegetables and cook until clear. Combine seasonings, brown sugar, cornstarch, vinegar and water, blending until smooth. Add bouillon and pineapple syrup, bring to boil and cook until thickened, stirring constantly. Add pineapple cubes. Pour over meat and vegetables and keep hot until serving time. Avoid overcooking, which will cause vegetables to lose their appeal.

Recipe may be doubled. Advance preparation works fine. Completely finish, then store in refrigerator until ready to reheat.

VEAL

VEAL PAPRIKA
(24 servings)

6 *pounds boneless veal*
 cubes
2 *cups sliced onions*
6 *tablespoons butter or*
 margarine
5 *teaspoons paprika*
5 *teaspoons salt*

1 *quart boiling water*
½ *cup sherry or lemon*
 juice
2 *(10½-ounce) cans*
 condensed mushroom
 soup

Sauté veal and onions in butter, until onions are clear but not brown. Add paprika and salt and toss well until meat is coated. Add water and sherry or lemon juice. Cover and simmer until meat is tender, about 1¼ hours. Just before serving, add soup and heat through. Sprinkle with additional paprika when served.

Recipe may be increased. This is even better made ahead and re-heated.

VEAL SCALLOPINI
(12 or 48 servings)

INGREDIENTS	12 SERVINGS	48 SERVINGS
veal round steak,		
sliced ¼ inch thick	3 pounds	12 pounds
flour, salt and pepper		
oil	½ cup	2 cups
fresh garlic	3 cloves	6 to 8 cloves
California sauterne		
or Rhine wine	1½ cups	1 quart
water	1½ cups	1 quart

Cut veal into small pieces, roll in seasoned flour. Add garlic to oil in heavy skillets, then brown meat on both sides. Remove garlic, add wine and water. Reduce heat and cook covered until meat is very tender, about 30 minutes.

Zesty flavor may be achieved by adding a small quantity of thyme to veal as it simmers. Use ½ teaspoon for 12 servings and about 1½ teaspoons for the larger recipe.

POULTRY ENTREES

POULTRY CARVING GUIDE

Cut thigh away from body, slashing through skin to joint. Separate the entire leg from the body by pressing the leg outward with the knife during cutting, bending leg away from body with fork or left hand holding leg bone. Cut slices of dark meat from leg across grain of meat.

Insert fork firmly into upper wing. Cut above wing joint to body so that slices of breast will fall free as carved. Entire wing may be cut away from body, pressing away with fork while cutting, as done for leg.

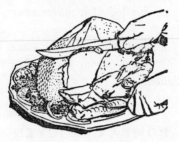

Beginning halfway up breast, slice downward with straight even strokes to incision just above wing. Slices should fall free if cut has gone through to body. Continue slicing breast, beginning at a higher point with each slice.

ALOHA BARBECUED CHICKEN
(24 servings)

12 (2½-pound) broiler-
    fryers, split
½ cup salad oil
3 (1-pound) cans crushed
    pineapple
2 cups brown sugar
2 (8-ounce) cans
    tomato sauce

1 cup lemon juice
2 cups pineapple or
    orange juice
1½ teaspoons ground ginger
1 teaspoon Tabasco
1 teaspoon onion salt
1 cup chopped green pepper

Place broilers skin side down on broiler pan and brush with oil. Bake in 425° F. oven for 15 minutes. Meanwhile, combine pineapple, sugar, tomato sauce, fruit juices, ginger, Tabasco, salt and pepper; bring to boil. Turn chickens skin side up and pour barbecue sauce over chicken. Bake at 350° F. for 30 minutes longer, or until chicken is tender. (Test by moving leg. If it moves easily, chicken is done.)

Recipe may be doubled. Chicken and sauce may be prepared ahead, before baking. Allow about 10 minutes more baking time when chicken is chilled.

BOMBAY CHICKEN
(24 servings)

*6 to 8 pounds broiler-fryers,
  cut in serving pieces*
1 cup shortening
1½ cups chopped onion
1½ cups chopped celery
1½ cups light raisins
*12 cups cooked rice
  (4 cups raw)*

1½ cups flaked coconut
*1½ cups chopped salted
  cashews, filberts or
  peanuts*
1½ tablespoons curry powder
½ teaspoon ginger
3 teaspoons salt
¼ teaspoon pepper

Brown chicken pieces in shortening in one or more skillets, avoiding overcrowding pan. Remove from skillet as browned. Cook onion and celery in drippings remaining in skillets after all chicken pieces are browned. Cook until clear but do not let brown. Add raisins and heat until puffed. Stir in rice, coconut and nuts to permit them to absorb flavor of drippings. Sprinkle with seasonings and mix thoroughly but gently. Spoon into oblong shallow baking pan or pans. Top with chicken pieces, placing skin side up. Bake in 325° F. oven about 45 minutes or until chicken is done.

Preparation of this dish up to the final baking may be done a day ahead. Refrigerate carefully if you choose to prepare it in advance. The combination gives the equivalent of chicken curry but in baked form. Chutney is traditional accompaniment.

CHARCOAL OR OVEN-BARBECUED CHICKEN
(12 or 48 servings)

INGREDIENTS	12 SERVINGS	48 SERVINGS
broiler-fryers	6 (1½-pound)	24 (1½-pound)
onions, chopped	2 large	1 quart
parsley	4 sprigs	12 sprigs
cold water	1 quart	3 quarts
California sauterne	2 cups	1½ quarts
fresh garlic	2 cloves	4 cloves
fresh lemon juice	⅓ cup	1 cup
salt, pepper		
oil	¼ cup	1 cup
flour	3 tablespoons	¾ cup
margarine	3 tablespoons	¾ cup

Split fryers in half for broiling. Cut off necks; place all of these in heavy saucepan with giblets, onions and parsley. Cover with cold water and bring to boil. Simmer covered until tender. Strain and add wine to stock. Part is needed for basting chickens during broiling; use remainder for gravy. Chop cooked giblets fine and reserve for use in gravy later. Crush garlic cloves and rub over fryer halves; sprinkle them with lemon juice, salt and pepper. Brush with oil and place, skin side down, in shallow pans. Place pans under broiler at lowest position. Baste chickens frequently with wine sauce, turning occasionally. Cook until chickens are well browned, thoroughly cooked (leg and thigh joint will move easily) and fork-tender, about 40 minutes to 1 hour. Then remove chicken from broiling pans, keep warm. Thicken remaining wine sauce with flour and margarine, which have been mixed together until smooth, beating briskly with a whisk until gravy is smoothly blended. Stir in chopped giblets. Spoon some of wine-flavored gravy over each serving of chicken.

Charcoal broiling chicken requires about 30 minutes longer cooking over very low heat. Baste chickens and turn frequently. Thicken reserved sauce with flour-margarine mixture as above, adding chopped giblets to thickened gravy. Serve spooned over each serving.

Lemon juice and garlic combine in this recipe to produce broiled chicken of exceptionally pleasing flavor. There is a slight tenderizing action from the acid of the lemon juice as well. Thorough cooking will ensure tenderness—do not hurry cooking, but do remove halves from heat as they become done.

CHICKEN ALEXANDRIA
(48 servings)

1 pound butter or margarine
2 cups all-purpose flour
2½ quarts hot chicken stock
2 quarts warm milk
2 teaspoons Worcestershire sauce
3 tablespoons salt
½ teaspoon pepper
3 quarts diced, cooked chicken (meat from 4 [5-pound] dressed weight chickens)

1½ quarts (8 [4-ounce] cans) sliced mushrooms
1½ cups (4 [4-ounce] cans) pimento, chopped
1 cup parsley, finely chopped
½ cup onion, minced
2½ pounds rice, steamed or boiled
1½ to 2 cups buttered bread crumbs

Melt butter in top of double boiler. Blend in flour. Stir in hot stock and warm milk. Beat with whisk, cooking until sauce is smooth and thickened. Add Worcestershire sauce, salt and pepper. Taste and correct seasoning. Stir in chicken, mushrooms, pimento, parsley, onion and rice. Spread mixture evenly in greased shallow baking pans and top with buttered crumbs. Bake 10 minutes in 450° F. oven to brown crumbs and heat through. (If prepared in advance and warmed in oven at serving time, allow additional time for heating mixture through.)

Recipe may be doubled. Filling and flavorful, Chicken Alexandria is a popular dish with hostesses because it may be readied well in advance of serving. Store in baking pans in refrigerator.

CHICKEN EN CASSEROLE
(12 or 48 servings)

INGREDIENTS	12 SERVINGS	48 SERVINGS
broiler-fryers, cut up	12 to 16 pounds	25 to 32 pounds
flour	2 cups	4 cups
salt	2 teaspoons	1 tablespoon
pepper	½ teaspoon	1 teaspoon
paprika	1½ teaspoons	2½ teaspoons
cooking oil	½ cup	2 cups
celery, sliced	2 cups	1 quart
onion, chopped	¼ cup	1 cup
all-purpose flour	2 tablespoons	½ cup
California sherry	½ cup	2 cups
milk	1 cup	3 cups
water	½ cup	2½ cups

Roll pan-ready chicken pieces in flour seasoned with salt, pepper and paprika. Brown on all sides in cooking oil. Place in casseroles or baking pans that can be covered with lids or heavy duty foil. Add celery, onion and measured flour to hot oil in frying pan, allowing mixture to cook while stirring for 2 minutes. Season lightly with a sprinkling of salt and pepper. Add to chicken in casserole. Add wine, milk and water to chicken. Cover and bake in 350° F. oven until chicken is fork-tender.

Be sure to scrape casserole free of all sauce in serving this chicken because the flavor is delectable and just right for serving with Mock Wild Rice* or Steamed White Rice*.

CHICKEN-HAM SUPREME
(24 servings)

12 (about 8 pounds)   4 teaspoons paprika
   chicken breasts   4 teaspoons garlic salt
12 slices boneless ham,   4 teaspoons celery salt
   about ½ inch thick   1 teaspoon pepper
1 quart dairy sour cream   3½ cups dry bread crumbs
½ cup lemon juice   1 pound butter or margarine
4 teaspoons Worcestershire   Additional melted butter
   sauce   for basting

Cut chicken breasts and ham slices in half. Combine sour cream,
lemon juice, Worcestershire sauce and seasonings. Coat chicken with
sour cream mixture and let stand overnight. Roll chicken breasts in
crumbs. Place chicken breasts on half ham slices and arrange in
single layer in shallow baking pan. Melt butter and pour over chicken.
Bake in 350° F. oven for 30 minutes. Baste with additional melted
butter and bake 10 to 15 minutes longer, until chicken is tender and
well browned.

Recipe may be increased as needed. Mushroom caps may be
baked with the chicken, stuffed with any leftover bread crumbs, if
desired.

CHICKEN LIVERS SAUTE
(24 servings)

6 pounds chicken livers   ¼ teaspoon pepper
1 cup minced onion   1 tablespoon paprika
1 pound fresh button   1 cup dry red wine or
   mushroom caps   bouillon
1 cup butter or margarine   Toast points, if desired
   (or ½ butter and   ½ cup finely chopped
   ½ chicken fat)   parsley, for garnish
1 teaspoon salt

Cut livers in half. Sauté with onion and mushroom caps in butter over moderate heat, sprinkling with seasonings. When browned evenly, add wine or bouillon and cook over low heat 15 minutes. Serve on toast, if desired. Sprinkle with parsley as served.

Recipe may be doubled, if desired. May be made ahead and reheated if great care is taken to avoid overcooking. Livers cook quickly and dry out and scorch easily.

CHICKEN POLYNESIAN
(24 servings)

12 chicken breasts, split
   or 8 pounds chicken
   thighs, legs or quarters
Salt and pepper
1 No. 10 can (3 quarts)
   orange sections, drained,
   reserving 1½ cups juice
1½ cups light corn syrup
½ cup dry mustard
¾ cup cider vinegar

1 teaspoon Tabasco
2 teaspoons salt
1 teaspoon powdered ginger
2 tablespoons cornstarch
2½ cups canned crushed
   pineapple
2 cups light raisins
1 cup slivered toasted
   almonds, for garnish

Sprinkle chicken with salt and pepper. Place in shallow baking pan, skin side down. Bake in 350° F. oven for 30 minutes. Combine orange juice, corn syrup, dry mustard, vinegar, Tabasco, 2 teaspoons salt and ginger. Blend cornstarch with a little of this cold liquid. Combine thoroughly. Bring to boil, stirring constantly. Pour over chicken, turning pieces skin side up. Bake at 350° F. 30 minutes longer. Add orange sections, pineapple and raisins in the last 10 minutes, mixing into sauce. Heat through. Garnish with almonds when served.

Recipe may be doubled. May be prepared in advance for reheating at serving time. Though this may sound "sticky sweet," vinegar and seasonings give it real piquancy that makes the combination exotic and unusually delicious.

CHICKEN SAUTE
(48 servings)

24 (2-pound) broiler-fryers, split
4 cups flour
3 teaspoons salt
1 teaspoon white pepper
1 teaspoon paprika
1 pound margarine or shortening

Additional paprika for dusting
2 pounds mushrooms, sliced
2 cups onions, finely chopped
2 (⅘ quart) bottles California chablis
2½ quarts chicken stock, heated
Noodles or rice

Shake chicken halves in bag of flour seasoned with salt, pepper and paprika. Brown on both sides in margarine or shortening until golden brown. Transfer to casseroles or large baking pans. Sprinkle lightly with additional paprika. Sauté mushrooms and onions in same browning skillet until tender, then spoon over chicken halves. Pour wine into browning skillet and reduce by half. Pour over chicken and place in 400° F. oven. Bake 10 minutes. Add heated chicken stock, cover and continue cooking until chicken is tender, 25 to 35 minutes. Serve chicken and sauce over hot noodles or rice.

Recipe may be doubled. Large whole mushrooms browned in butter are a fitting garnish for Chicken Sauté. Favorite pieces of disjointed chicken (thighs, legs or halved breasts) may be substituted for halves.

COQ AU VIN ROUGE
(48 servings)

24 (2-pound) broiler-fryers,
  split or 48 pounds
  preferred chicken parts
  (thighs, legs and breasts)
4 cups flour
1 tablespoon salt
1 teaspoon pepper
2 cups bacon drippings
144 small mushrooms

1 cup onions, minced
2 (⅘ quart) bottles
  California burgundy
96 small, whole cooked or
  canned potatoes
144 small, whole cooked or
  canned onions
1 cup butter

Shake chicken pieces in bag of flour seasoned with salt and pepper. Brown on all sides in bacon drippings. Add mushrooms and onions and cook until vegetables are very lightly browned. Pour wine over chicken and bring to boil. Cover and bake in 350° F. oven, 25 to 35 minutes or until chicken is fork-tender. Brown cooked potatoes and onions in butter until well heated. Arrange a chicken breast, 3 mushrooms, 2 potatoes and 3 onions in each individual casserole.

Recipe may be doubled. Minced parsley gives an extra fillip of color to this richly flavored chicken.

OVEN-FRIED CHICKEN
(48 servings)

20 to 25 pounds broiler-
  fryers, cut-up
1 pound butter or margarine

2 tablespoons salt
1 teaspoon pepper
2 tablespoons paprika

Arrange chicken pieces in single layer in shallow pans with skin side down. Dot well with butter or margarine. Bake in 400° F. oven 20 to 30 minutes until pieces are browned. Turn chicken skin side up. Baste well with drippings. Sprinkle with seasonings. Bake 20 to 30 minutes longer, until tender. Chicken may be kept warm at low temperature in oven but avoid letting it dry out. It also may be cooked ahead, using shortest browning times, and reheated at 400° F. for about 15 minutes.

Recipe may be increased or decreased. Use of larger amount of chicken enables discard of necks and allows more generous servings.

CHICKEN OR TURKEY A LA KING
(12 or 48 servings)

INGREDIENTS	12 SERVINGS	48 SERVINGS
mushrooms, sliced	1½ cups	1½ quarts
green pepper, diced	½ cup	2 cups
butter or margarine	½ cup	2 cups
all-purpose flour	½ cup	2 cups
milk or combined milk		
and stock	1 quart	4 quarts
salt, pepper and paprika		
diced, cooked chicken		
or turkey	1 quart	4 quarts
pimento	½ cup	1 cup
California sherry	½ cup	2 cups
Toast points, Biscuits* or		
patty shells		

Cook mushrooms and green pepper in butter or margarine until soft but not brown. Blend in flour. Add measured liquid and cook, stirring, until sauce thickens. Season with salt, pepper and paprika to taste. Stir in chicken, pimento and wine; heat to boiling. Serve at once over toast points or Biscuits* or in patty shells.

Keep this creamy dish warm over hot water, if necessary, for 1 hour before serving. It is attractive on a buffet table when served in a handsome chafing dish, which will allow guests to serve themselves as well as keep it warm.

WILD ROAST DUCK OR GOOSE

INGREDIENTS	12 SERVINGS	48 SERVINGS
wild duck or goose	6 pounds	48 pounds
California burgundy	1½ cups	1 quart
oil	½ cup	1½ cups
celery stalks and onion		
slices, if desired		

Place oven-ready poultry breast side up on rack in open roasting pans. Bake in 350° F. oven, 25 to 30 minutes per pound. Combine wine and oil and warm slightly. Use to baste poultry frequently. Stalk of celery and a slice of onion may be placed in body cavity for seasoning if desired.

Salt is omitted on the poultry so that skin will not be toughened during roasting. Frequent basting gives fine flavor and tends to produce slight glazed appearance. Poultry is done when leg joint moves readily.

RELISHES AND ACCOMPANIMENTS

CINNAMON APPLES
(24 servings)

12 large cooking apples, such as Rome Beauties	2 cups water
4 cups sugar	1 cup red cinnamon candies
2 cups cider vinegar	1 2-inch stick cinnamon
	Red food coloring, as desired

Halve and core apples but do not peel. Combine sugar, vinegar, water, cinnamon candies and stick and food coloring, if desired, in broad pan. Blend well and cook until syrupy. Place apples in boiling syrup, cut side down. Simmer gently until barely tender. Cool in pan. Remove to shallow pans, arranging cut side up. Cover with syrup and chill until served.

Recipe may be increased as needed, but avoid overcrowding apples in pan. A delicious Cinnamon Apple Salad with Cream Cheese Balls* using these colorful apple pieces is located in the section "Accompaniment Salads (Mixed Fruit)."

CRANBERRY HORSERADISH RELISH
(48 servings)

3 envelopes (¾ ounce) unflavored gelatin	1½ cups sugar
1½ cups cold water	4 cups raw cranberries
2 cups boiling water	⅓ cup prepared horseradish

Allow gelatin to soften in cold water. Add boiling water and sugar, then stir until gelatin and sugar dissolve. Put cranberries through fine grinder, then combine with gelatin and horseradish. Divide mixture among 48 (1-ounce) paper cups arranged in shallow pans. Chill until firm.

Recipe may be doubled. Relish is taste delight with both hot and cold ham and chicken and turkey entrees. The ruby-red color pleases, too.

MAPLE SYRUP
(24 servings)

1 quart water	*2 cups corn syrup*
1 pound brown sugar	*1 tablespoon maple flavoring*
1 quart granulated sugar	*½ teaspoon salt*

Combine water, both sugars and corn syrup. Stir until sugar is dissolved over medium heat, then boil 3 minutes. Add flavoring and salt. Serve warm. May be reheated in pitchers set in pans of hot water.

Recipe may be doubled.

MUSTARD SAUCE SUPREME
(24 servings)

3 cups heavy cream or powdered whipped topping	*3 tablespoons prepared mustard*
1 cup powdered sugar	*1 tablespoon or more horseradish to taste*
1 pint sour cream	
3 teaspoons salt	

Whip cream until thick. If using powdered whipped topping, prepare according to package directions. Whip together powdered sugar and sour cream. Fold into whipped cream. Gradually beat in salt, mustard and horseradish. Chill until served. Made with whipped cream, sauce holds well for several hours. With whipped topping, it holds indefinitely.

Recipe may be doubled. This pale golden sauce is the crowning touch for rare roast beef, baked ham or tender slices of boiled tongue, fresh or cured. Another meat with which it is a delight is hot or cold Corned Beef* and that other spicy favorite—pastrami.

PICKLED BEETS
(24 servings)

1 pint vinegar	2 teaspoons salt
1 No. 10 can (3 quarts) sliced or tiny whole beets, drained, reserving liquid	2 teaspoons celery seed
	1 teaspoon whole cloves
1 cup sugar	1 2-inch stick cinnamon

Combine vinegar, 2 cups beet liquid, sugar, salt and spices. Bring to boil. Add beets and return to boil, then cool until ready to serve. Flavor improves when marinated at least 12 hours.

Recipe may be doubled.

RED SAUCE (for shrimp or crab cocktails)
(48 servings)

1½ cups tomato catsup	1 teaspoon paprika
1½ cups chili sauce	1½ teaspoons dry mustard
3 tablespoons Worcestershire sauce	1½ teaspoons salt
2 teaspoons freshly ground black pepper	

Combine catsup, chili sauce, Worcestershire sauce, pepper, paprika, mustard and salt; let stand overnight in refrigerator to blend flavors. This will make 48 (1-tablespoon) servings.

Recipe may be doubled.

SALADS AND SALAD DRESSINGS

ACCOMPANIMENT SALADS

(*Frozen or Molded Fruit*)

CRANBERRY APPLE MOLD
(48 servings)

8 envelopes (2 ounces)
  unflavored gelatin
1 quart cold water
1 quart boiling water
2 cups sugar

1 teaspoon salt
4 cups ground raw
  cranberries
4 cups chopped raw apples
1 cup chopped orange rind

Soften gelatin in cold water. Add to boiling water with sugar and salt, stirring until dissolved. Stir in cranberries, apples and orange rind. Pour into molds or shallow pans. Chill until firm.

Recipe may be doubled if adequate refrigerator space is available. Use fine knife on grinder to chop cranberries and orange rind—putting these coarse fruits through twice gives good results. Crispy apples need only one grinding on either fine or medium knife, as preferred. For texture contrast, apples may be chopped with chef's knife into relatively larger pieces. Avoid big chunks that are difficult to cut in molds.

CRANBERRY APPLE SALAD
(48 servings)

8 (3-ounce) packages
   orange-flavored gelatin
1½ teaspoons salt
3 quarts boiling water
6 (1-pound) cans jellied
   cranberry sauce

3 (1-pound 13-ounce) cans
   crushed pineapple,
   undrained
6 large, crisp apples, diced

Dissolve gelatin and salt in boiling water. Break up cranberry sauce with fork and stir into hot mixture until smooth. Add undrained pineapple with syrup. Chill until mixture begins to thicken, then fold in diced apple. Pour into 48 individual molds or two oblong pans 13×9 inches. Chill until firm. Cut into 48 squares for serving.

Recipe may be halved or doubled safely if you check your arithmetic carefully.

CRANBERRY APRICOT MOLDED SALAD
(48 servings)

8 (1-pound) cans jellied
   cranberry sauce, chilled
4 (1-pound 13-ounce) cans
   peeled apricot halves,
   drained, reserving syrup
1 cup vinegar
1 tablespoon whole cloves

1 4-inch stick cinnamon,
   broken in pieces
6 (3-ounce) packages
   orange-flavored gelatin
Lettuce leaves
Mayonnaise, or sour cream or
   cream cheese, for garnish

Chill jellied cranberry sauce overnight. Drain syrup from apricots into measuring cup, add 1 cup vinegar, then sufficient water to make 3 quarts liquid. Add whole spices to combined syrup, vinegar and water and bring to boil. Simmer 10 minutes. Strain. Add orange-flavored gelatin to hot syrup and stir until dissolved. Place halves of apricots in 48 small molds and pour hot gelatin mixture over fruit. Chill. At serving time, unmold jellied cranberry sauce and slice each into 6 slices. Arrange slice of cranberry sauce on lettuce leaf, then top each with a turned-out mold of orange-apricot gelatin. Garnish with mayonnaise, sour cream or softened cream cheese.

Recipe may be doubled. There's a flavor surprise in the spice of this apricot salad that pleases the palate.

FROZEN FRUIT SALAD
(48 servings)

2 (1-pound 4-ounce) cans crushed pineapple, drained, reserving syrup

2 (1-pound 13-ounce) cans fruit cocktail, drained, reserving syrup

1 (8-ounce) jar maraschino cherries, sliced, drained, reserving syrup

2 pounds marshmallows, cut in small pieces

3 (8-ounce) packages cream cheese, at room temperature

1 quart chilled heavy cream, whipped stiff

2 cups slivered almonds or pistachio nuts

For garnish, if desired: maraschino cherries and pineapple chunks

Drain syrup from fruits. Add marshmallows to syrup and heat in top of double boiler until melted. Remove from heat and add slowly to cream cheese, beating smooth. Cool until mixture begins to thicken. Fold in fruits, whipped cream and nuts. Pour into two 13×9×2-inch pans or one 18×12×2-inch pan. Freeze rapidly until firm. Cut into squares to serve, garnishing with whole maraschino cherries and pineapple chunks, if desired.

Recipe may be doubled if adequate freezing facilities are available.

FRUITED FROZEN CRANBERRY ORANGE MOLD
(48 servings)

2 *pounds raw cranberries, chopped*	2 *pounds cut-up or miniature marshmallows*
8 *oranges, seeded and chopped, including rind*	6 *cups sugar*
3 *(1-pound) cans crushed pineapple with syrup*	1 *quart heavy cream or chilled evaporated milk, whipped*

Grind cranberries and seeded oranges in food chopper. Add pineapple and syrup, marshmallows and sugar. Stir until sugar is dissolved. Fold in whipped cream. Freeze in trays or in 3-ounce paper cups or individual molds.

Recipe may be doubled, if adequate freezer space is available.

GRAPEFRUIT CUCUMBER MOLD
(24 servings)

4 *(3-ounce) packages lime-flavored gelatin*	3 *cups well-drained, finely cubed cucumber*
1 *teaspoon salt*	2 *cups chopped celery*
4 *cups hot water*	*Greens*
2 *(1-pound) cans sweetened grapefruit sections with syrup*	*Unpeeled cucumber slices, for garnish*

Dissolve gelatin and salt in hot water. Add grapefruit sections with syrup. Cool until mixture begins to thicken. Stir in cucumbers and celery. Pour into individual molds or shallow pans. Chill until firm. Unmold or cut into squares and serve on crisp greens, garnished with slices of unpeeled cucumber.

Recipe may be doubled. Cool, elegant, this salad holds a delicious flavor combination in shimmering green gelatin.

GRAPEFRUIT MOLDED SALAD
(48 servings)

12 envelopes (3 ounces)
  unflavored gelatin
1½ quarts cold water
2 No. 10 cans (6 quarts)
  grapefruit sections, drained,
  reserving syrup

1½ cups sugar
1 teaspoon salt
1 (28-ounce) bottle ginger
  ale
1 quart diced, unpeeled apple
1 quart diced celery

Soften gelatin in cold water. Add hot water to grapefruit syrup to make 1½ quarts liquid. Add sugar and salt. Bring to boil. Add softened gelatin and stir until dissolved. Add ginger ale and chill until mixture begins to thicken. Add grapefruit sections, apple and celery. Turn into shallow pans or molds. Chill until firm. Unmold or cut in 48 squares.

Recipe may be doubled, if sufficient refrigerator space is available. If desired garnish with watercress or mayonnaise to which grated orange rind has been added.

HARLEQUIN SALAD
(48 servings)

10 envelopes (2½ ounces)
  unflavored gelatin
1¼ quarts cold water
2 (1-pound) cans sweetened
  grapefruit sections, drained,
  reserving syrup
1 cup white vinegar
1 cup lemon juice
2 cups sugar

2 teaspoons salt
¼ cup grated onion
1 cup chopped ripe olives
6 cups well-drained finely
  diced cucumber
Lettuce
Mayonnaise or salad dressing
  thinned with grapefruit
  juice

Soften gelatin in cold water. Drain grapefruit thoroughly. Cut grapefruit sections in quarters. Measure syrup from canned grapefruit and add enough water to measure 1¾ quarts liquid. Bring liquid to boil. Remove from heat. Stir in gelatin, vinegar, lemon juice, sugar and salt until gelatin and sugar are dissolved. Chill to consistency of unbeaten egg white. Fold in grapefruit, onion, olives and cucumber. Pour into 48 individual molds or two 18×12×2-inch pans. Chill until firm. Serve on crisp lettuce with mayonnaise or salad dressing thinned with grapefruit juice.

Recipe can be doubled satisfactorily if you have containers large enough to handle the amounts, plus needed refrigerator space.

LAYERED LIME-PEAR SALAD
(48 servings)

4 (3-ounce) packages lime-flavored gelatin	3 cups sieved cottage cheese
6 cups boiling water	1 teaspoon salt
1 quart mayonnaise or salad dressing	

Dissolve gelatin in boiling water. Cool until it begins to thicken; whip until fluffy. Fold in mayonnaise, cottage cheese and salt. Chill in shallow pans or fill 48 individual molds half full. Then prepare second layer:

4 (3-ounce) packages lime-flavored gelatin	3 (1-pound 13-ounce) cans pear halves, drained, reserving syrup
4 cups boiling water and syrup from pears	
1 (28-ounce) bottle ginger ale	

Dissolve gelatin in boiling water mixture. Cool. Add ginger ale. Slice pear halves and arrange on cheese layer, which is already set.

Pour on ginger ale flavored layer. Chill until firm. To serve, cut in squares or unmold individual molds. Serve on salad greens.

Recipe may be doubled. Salad needs no additional dressing. Green maraschino cherries or minted pears or pineapple make pretty garnish, however.

MOLDED FRUIT SALAD
(24 servings)

6 (3-ounce) packages
  fruit-flavored gelatin
5½ cups boiling water
5½ cups cold water

6½ cups canned fruit,
  drained, diced
Salad greens

Dissolve fruit-flavored gelatin in boiling water. Add cold water. Pour into shallow pans or molds, filling two-thirds full. Chill until mixture thickens slightly. Stir well-drained, canned fruit into gelatin. Chill until firm. Cut into squares and unmold on salad greens.

Reserve fruit juice from canned fruits and add part to mayonnaise for a fruit-flavored dressing to serve with this salad. For buffet service, place dressing in separate bowl for guests to serve themselves. (Fresh fruits other than fresh pineapple may be substituted for canned fruits.)

MOLDED MINTED PEARS
(24 servings)

4 (3-ounce) packages
  lime-flavored gelatin
1½ teaspoons salt
5 cups boiling water
1 No. 10 can (3 quarts) or
  4 (1-pound 13-ounce) cans
  pear halves

3 cups reserved canned pear
  juice
1 teaspoon peppermint extract
Lettuce
Cream cheese or other
  dressing

Dissolve gelatin and salt in boiling water. Cook until mixture begins to thicken. Add 3 cups pear juice and peppermint extract. Pour into shallow pans, placing pear halves in single layer, in rows, cut side up. To serve, cut in squares, each containing a pear half. Serve on crisp lettuce with cream cheese or other desired dressing.

Recipe may be doubled.

PINEAPPLE-COTTAGE CHEESE LIME MOLDED SALAD
(24 servings)

1⅓ cups water
2 (1-pound 4-ounce) cans
 crushed pineapple with syrup
2 dozen large marshmallows
2 (3-ounce) packages
 lime-flavored gelatin

1 quart small curd cottage
 cheese
1 pint heavy cream
Salad greens

Combine water, pineapple and syrup with marshmallows. Heat until marshmallows melt. Add lime-flavored gelatin and stir until dissolved. Cool until mixture begins to thicken. Fold in cottage cheese and stiffly beaten cream. Turn mixture into shallow pans or molds. Chill until set. Cut into squares or unmold on salad greens.

Recipe may be divided in half for 12 servings, double recipe for 48.

PORT WINE CRANBERRY MOLD
(48 servings)

9 (1-pound) cans whole
 cranberry sauce
1¼ quarts hot water

9 (3-ounce) packages
 cherry-flavored gelatin
1½ quarts California port

Combine cranberry sauce and water; heat to boiling. Add gelatin and stir until it is dissolved. Cool. Add wine, stirring through completely. Put sauce into 48 (½-cup) molds for individual servings or pour into 18×12×2-inch shallow pan. Chill until firm. Unmold or cut into 48 squares.

Recipe may be doubled. This brilliantly colored fruit mold will add beauty to a buffet table if chilled in one large, spectacular mold. Garnish the serving platter with small clusters of grapes, cream cheese balls and watercress or parsley.

SHERRIED APPLE MOLD WITH PINEAPPLE AND MANDARIN ORANGES
(48 servings)

8 (3-ounce) packages lemon- or apple-flavored gelatin

1½ teaspoons salt

3 quarts boiling water

1 pint sherry

3 (1-pound) cans crushed pineapple, with syrup

4 (11-ounce) cans mandarin oranges, with syrup

1 quart diced, firm, unpeeled red-skinned apples

Salad greens

Orange segments and apple slices, for garnish

Dissolve gelatin and salt in boiling water. Remove from heat. Add sherry, pineapple and oranges, with syrup. Chill until mixture begins to thicken. Stir in apples. Turn into 48 individual molds or large shallow pans. Chill until firm. Unmold or cut in squares. Serve on salad greens, garnished with additional orange segments and half slices of apple.

Recipe may be doubled. Salad needs no dressing; however, mayonnaise or salad dressing thinned with pineapple juice and flavored with grated rind is good with it. As alternate, dressing may be flavored and tinted with maraschino cherry juice.

WINE JELLY WITH FRUIT
(24 servings)

*4 (3-ounce) packages
raspberry-flavored gelatin
5 cups boiling water
3 cups California burgundy*

*4 cups diced fruit, well
drained (do not use
fresh pineapple)
Endive or other greens, for
garnish*

Dissolve gelatin in boiling water. Pour wine over fruit, let stand until gelatin comes to room temperature, then combine with gelatin mixture. Chill until mixture begins to thicken, turn into 1 large or 24 small molds. Chill until set. Unmold on platter or individual salad plates. Garnish with endive or other greens.

Recipe may be doubled. Wine jelly without the fruit may be served with a custard sauce for a light, pleasing dessert.

ACCOMPANIMENT SALADS

(*Frozen or Molded Vegetable*)

COTTAGE CHEESE MOLD
(24 servings)

4 (3-ounce) packages
  lemon-flavored gelatin
6 cups boiling water
1 pint sour cream
1 quart cottage cheese

4 tablespoons grated onion
1 cup finely chopped celery
½ cup caraway seed, if
  desired
Shredded lettuce

Dissolve gelatin in boiling water. Cool until it begins to thicken. Beat until fluffy, gradually beating in sour cream and cottage cheese. Fold in onion, celery and caraway seed. Pour into shallow pans or large or individual molds. Chill until firm. Turn out a large mold on a serving plate or cut squares for individual servings. Surround with shredded lettuce. Individual molds may be grouped as well as arranged on small salad plates.

Recipe may be increased as desired.

CUCUMBER LIME VEGETABLE SALAD
(48 servings)

8 (3-ounce) packages
  lime-flavored gelatin
3 tablespoons salt
3½ quarts hot water
2 cups vinegar
3 quarts diced cucumber

2 quarts chopped celery
2 cups chopped green pepper
Salad greens
Cucumber slices and green
  pepper rings, for garnish

Dissolve gelatin and salt in hot water. Add vinegar and chill until slightly thickened. Stir in vegetables and pour into molds or shallow pans. Chill until firm. Unmold and serve on salad greens, garnished with cucumber slices and green pepper rings.

Recipe may be doubled.

TOMATO ASPIC
(12 or 48 servings)

INGREDIENTS	12 SERVINGS	48 SERVINGS
unflavored gelatin	2 envelopes (½ ounce)	14 envelopes (3½ ounces)
cold water	½ cup	2 quarts
tomato juice	3¼ cups	4 quarts
sugar	1 tablespoon	¼ cup
salt	2 teaspoons	2 tablespoons
whole cloves	2	6
whole bay leaves	1	4
celery stalk with leaves, sliced	1 to 2	3 to 4
onion slices	1	3 to 4
lemon juice or vinegar	¼ cup	1 cup

Soften gelatin in cold water. Combine tomato juice, sugar and salt. Tie cloves and bay leaves in cheesecloth bag; add to mixture. Add large slices of celery stalk and onion. Bring to boil. Simmer 10 minutes. Strain hot liquid. Stir in gelatin until it dissolves. Add lemon juice or vinegar. Pour into pans. (Recipe for 48 fills two 18×12×2-inch pans.) Chill until firm. Cut into ½-inch cubes or larger squares to serve.

Chopped raw vegetables, including green pepper, celery and cabbage may be added to slightly thickened gelatin mixture before it sets completely. Use approximately 1½ quarts finely chopped vegetables for 48 servings recipe, about 1½ cups mixed vegetables for 12 servings recipe.

TOMATO ASPIC RINGS WITH
CUCUMBER SLICES
(24 servings)

8 envelopes (2 ounces)   ½ teaspoon onion powder
  unflavored gelatin   1 teaspoon celery salt
1 quart cold water   2 long unpeeled cucumbers,
2 quarts tomato juice   about 1½ inches in
½ cup lemon juice   diameter
1 tablespoon sugar   Salad greens
1 tablespoon salt   Salad dressing

Soften gelatin in cold water. Combine tomato juice, lemon juice,
sugar and seasonings. Bring to boil. Remove from heat. Add gelatin
and stir until dissolved. Pour into 5 No. 2 (1-pound 4½-ounce)
cans. If necessary, use greater number of smaller cans. Chill until
firm. Unmold by dipping cans briefly in hot water. Cut contents of
each can in slices, placing on beds of salad greens. "Stripe" unpeeled
cucumbers with tines of fork to flute edges. Cut into 24 slices. Arrange on slices of aspic. Top with salad dressing.

Recipe may be doubled. Good variation on usual dressing is
whipped cream cheese or sour cream, sprinkled with chopped chives,
parsley or stuffed olives.

MOLDED BEET SALAD
(48 servings)

8 (3-ounce) packages   ½ cup grated onion
  lemon-flavored gelatin   ½ cup grated horseradish
2 quarts boiling water   1 quart finely diced celery
3 teaspoons salt   Greens
1½ cups vinegar   Salad dressing or mayonnaise,
3 (1-pound) cans diced beets,   for garnish
  drained, reserving liquid

Dissolve gelatin in 2 quarts boiling water. Add salt. Measure 1½ cups vinegar into 2-quart measuring jar, then add drained beet juice and enough water to bring to 2-quart level. Add to dissolved gelatin. Chill to unbeaten egg white consistency. Stir in beets, onion, horseradish and celery. Turn into 48 individual ½-cup molds, or one 18×12×2-inch pan, or two 13×9×2-inch pans. Chill until firm. Cut into 48 servings or unmold individual molds. Serve on bed of crisp greens and garnish with salad dressing or mayonnaise.

Recipe may be doubled. Beautifully red in color and spicy in flavor is this molded salad. It is equally tasty with meat, fish or poultry entrees.

JELLIED COTTAGE CHEESE AND VEGETABLE SALAD
(48 servings)

8 envelopes (2 ounces)
unflavored gelatin
1 quart cold water
1 quart boiling vegetable
liquid or water
2 tablespoons salt
1 cup lemon juice
5 tablespoons sugar
½ cup chopped chives or
green onions

3 cups finely chopped celery
2 cups cooked or canned
green peas
6 pounds large curd,
creamed cottage cheese
Greens, paprika, radish
roses or olives, for garnish

Combine gelatin and 1 quart cold water. Dissolve in boiling vegetable liquid or water. Add salt, lemon juice and sugar. Stir until sugar dissolves. Fold in chives or green onions, celery, peas and cheese. Spoon into 48 (½-cup) molds or one pan, 18×12×2 inches or two pans measuring 13×9×2 inches. Chill until firm. Unmold individual containers or cut large salads into 48 servings. Garnish salad with greens, paprika, radish roses or olives.

Recipe may be doubled. Hearty goodness of this salad appeals to most tastes.

ACCOMPANIMENT SALADS

(Mixed Fruit)

CINNAMON APPLE SALAD WITH CREAM CHEESE BALLS
(48 servings)

48 halves Cinnamon Apples*	2 cups chopped nuts
Watercress or other salad greens	2 cups grated coconut
2 (8-ounce) packages cream cheese	

Prepare double recipe of Cinnamon Apples* or two batches, avoiding overcrowding in pans so halves remain intact. Shortly before serving time, drain and place on salad greens. Let cream cheese soften at room temperature. Combine with nuts. Shape into balls and roll in coconut. Place a cheese ball in cavity of each apple half.

Cinnamon Apples* in Relishes and Accompaniments section are sure to please, both as a salad and a spicy accompaniment.

FRUITS STAR AT BRUNCH AND LUNCHTIME

Wheeled carts can save many steps in serving a large group. Here are individual plates of salad fruits topped with sherbet, glasses of milk, Dinner Rolls, butter balls, napkins and silver grouped together. When combination of fruit for salad has been decided, consult Quantity Serving Charts, Fruit, for amounts needed. Note that fresh, canned or defrosted frozen fruits may be combined, according to individual preference or availability. See Index for Dinner Rolls recipe listing. Directions For Shaping Yeast Roll Dough include nine ways of forming rolls, including Crescents.

GRAPEFRUIT AVOCADO SALAD
(24 servings)

6 grapefruits, sectioned, or
4 (1-pound) cans
grapefruit sections
6 avocados, cut in wedges
(12 wedges per avocado)

2 heads lettuce or bunches
of romaine
1 pint French Dressing* or
Honey Celery Seed Dressing*

Arrange alternate sections of grapefruit and wedges of avocado on salad plates on greens. Drizzle with Dressing. Chill well, covered with foil or sheet plastic.

Salads may be prepared an hour or so in advance. To prevent avocado from discoloring, cover wedges well with grapefruit sections in arranging them. Cover while refrigerated. Dressing may be served separately, of course, and in any case, should not be put on salads if they must be chilled longer than an hour. This salad may also be served as a tossed salad. Separate containers of grapefruit and greens are chilled covered. Combine with avocado slices and dressing just before serving.

HONEYED GRAPE APPLE MANDARIN
NUT COMPOTE
(24 servings)

6 large apples
2 pounds red grapes
3 (11-ounce) cans mandarin
oranges with syrup

1 pound chopped pecans,
almonds or filberts
1½ teaspoons cinnamon
2 cups honey
1 cup sherry

Peel and grate apples. Halve and seed grapes. Combine with oranges with syrup, nuts, cinnamon, honey and sherry. Chill until served.

Recipe may be increased as needed.

PEAR-GRAPE SALAD
(24 servings)

*1 No. 10 can (3 quarts) or 4
(1-pound 13-ounce) cans
pear halves or 12 fresh
pears, peeled, halved,
cored, brushed with lemon
juice*

*8 ounces cream cheese
3 pounds red grapes, halved
and seeded
2 bunches watercress*

Arrange pear halves on salad plates. If using fresh pears, brush with
lemon juice or antioxidant to prevent discoloration. Whip cream
cheese until fluffy. Spread over pears and stud with halved grapes.
Surround with watercress sprigs.

Recipe may be doubled.

WALDORF SALAD I
(24 servings)

*3 quarts red-skinned apples,
diced
1¼ cups coarsely chopped
nuts
1¼ cups raisins or chopped
dates
3 cups finely chopped celery*

*2 cups mayonnaise
½ teaspoon salt
2 tablespoons lemon juice
Lettuce or other greens
Glazed cherries, nut halves or
tinted mayonnaise, for
garnish*

Combine apples, nuts, raisins or dates and celery. Mix mayonnaise
with salt and lemon juice. Gradually add the dressing to fruit mixture to desired consistency. Serve in lettuce-lined bowl or in individual mounds on greens. Garnish with glazed cherries or whole
nut halves or tinted mayonnaise put through force tube.

Recipe may be doubled. Any salad is more appealing if thought is given to an attractive garnish suitable in flavor to basic mixture. Accompanying greens must always be crisp, fresh and cool for best flavor.

WALDORF SALAD II
(48 servings)

5 pounds firm, red-skinned apples, diced

2 quarts diced celery

1 quart chopped walnuts

4 (1-pound) cans pineapple tidbits, drained

1 quart mayonnaise or salad dressing

1 quart heavy cream or 2 packages whipped topping

2 tablespoons salt

1 cup sugar

Combine apples, celery, nuts and pineapple, tossing lightly to coat apples well with residual juice clinging to pineapple. Add mayonnaise to stiffly beaten cream. (If using packaged topping, prepare according to package directions.) Add salt and sugar to dressing and fold into fruit mixture. Chill until served. Holds up well 3 to 6 hours.

Recipe may be doubled.

ACCOMPANIMENT SALADS

(*Mixed Vegetable*)

CAESAR SALAD
(48 servings)

3 cloves garlic

2 cups olive or salad oil

3 pounds (1½ gallons) mixed
salad greens (romaine,
iceberg lettuce, butter
lettuce, leaf lettuce
or endive)

2 quarts toasted bread cubes,
plain or garlic-flavored

4 (2-ounce) cans flat
anchovy fillets, diced

2 to 2½ pounds tomatoes,
peeled and diced

4 eggs, beaten

1 cup lemon juice

2 teaspoons salt

1 teaspoon freshly ground
black pepper

1 teaspoon Worcestershire
sauce

2 cups grated Parmesan
cheese

Crush garlic and let stand in oil, preferably overnight. Strain. Break salad greens into very large container. Add toasted bread cubes, diced anchovy fillets and diced tomatoes, which have been drained of excess liquid. Combine in mixing bowl, beaten eggs, lemon juice, salt, pepper and Worcestershire sauce, just before serving salad. Drizzle garlic-flavored oil over greens mixture, then add combined egg-lemon juice mixture. Toss lightly and well until greens are glistening with dressing. Sprinkle with grated Parmesan cheese and serve.

Recipe may be increased as desired. Croutons made from stale sourdough French bread are a good choice for Caesar Salad*. Toast them in a slow oven until brown or in garlic-flavored oil in heavy skillet on top of the range.

3-BEAN SALAD
(24 servings)

2 (1-pound) cans green beans
or yellow wax beans,
drained
2 (1-pound) cans red
kidney beans, drained
2 (1-pound) cans garbanzos
or baby lima beans, drained
1 cup finely chopped red
or green sweet pepper
½ cup finely chopped onion
1 quart salad oil
2 cups sugar
2 cups vinegar
1 tablespoon salt
¼ teaspoon pepper
Red and green pepper circles
or onion slices, for garnish

Combine beans in bowl and sprinkle with sweet pepper and onion.
Combine oil, sugar, vinegar and seasonings, mixing thoroughly.
Pour over beans and marinate at least 12 hours. Serve garnished
with circles of red and green peppers or thin slices of onion.

Recipe may be increased as needed.

CHERRY TOMATO-CUCUMBER SALAD
(24 servings)

3 quarts thinly sliced fresh
cucumbers
2 cups thinly sliced onions
1½ cups vinegar
1 teaspoon salt
1 cup sugar
2 cups water
24 cherry tomatoes, for
garnish
1 pint dairy sour cream,
for garnish

Arrange cucumbers and onions in alternate layers in large bowl.
Combine vinegar, salt, sugar and water, stirring until sugar and salt
are dissolved. Pour over cucumbers. Cover and chill 6 to 12 hours.
Wash and chill cherry tomatoes. At serving time, drain liquid off

cucumbers thoroughly. Arrange in serving bowls or individual salad plates, garnishing with swirls of sour cream and topping with cherry tomatoes, allowing one to each individual salad.

Recipe can be doubled if you have storage facilities. As the preparation method indicates, this salad is convenient for advance preparation. Larger individual salads may be planned by providing up to three cherry tomatoes per serving.

COLE SLAW IN LETTUCE CUPS
(12 servings)

4 pounds cabbage, shredded	½ cup minced parsley
1 green pepper, diced fine	1 cup Sour Cream Dressing*
2 carrots, shredded and cut fine	12 cup-shape lettuce leaves
	Pimento strips, for garnish

Combine prepared vegetables. Toss lightly. Cover. Chill. Add Sour Cream Dressing* just before serving. Spoon salad into cup-shape lettuce leaves. Garnish with crossed strips of pimento.

Recipe may be doubled. For best flavor, let the Sour Cream Dressing* come to room temperature before mixing with chilled vegetable mixture. Lettuce cups are picked up readily between two large serving spoons or conventional salad set of spoon and fork at serving time on buffet table.

COLE SLAW WITH CHERRY TOMATOES
(48 servings)

6 quarts shredded cabbage	3 cups salad dressing or mayonnaise
3 cups chopped celery	
3 cups chopped green onion or green pepper	1 cup sweet pickle juice
	2 pounds cherry tomatoes, for garnish

Combine cabbage, celery and onion; cover tightly and chill. Just before serving, blend salad dressing and pickle juice. Mix gently with salad. Serve garnished with cherry tomatoes.

Recipe can be doubled—but to have it crisp, do not let bowls stand any longer than necessary after adding dressing.

SOUR CREAM COLE SLAW
(24 servings)

3 quarts shredded cabbage
1 cup finely chopped green pepper
1 cup finely chopped onion
¼ cup minced parsley
1 pint dairy sour cream

1 cup salad dressing or mayonnaise
2 teaspoons salt
¼ teaspoon pepper
1 tablespoon sugar
¼ cup lemon juice
Cabbage leaves, if desired

Combine cabbage, green pepper, onion and parsley; cover tightly and chill until just before serving. Combine sour cream, salad dressing, seasonings, sugar and lemon juice. Mix gently with salad. Serve in bowls lined with cabbage leaves, if desired.

Recipe may be doubled as needed.

COOKED VEGETABLE SALAD PLATTER
(48 servings)

3 (1-pound) cans julienne-style beets
3 (1-pound) cans julienne-style carrots

3 (1-pound) cans cut green beans
3 (1-pound) cans baby limas or tender peas
Salad greens

Chill cans of vegetables thoroughly. At serving time, drain well. Arrange each kind of vegetable in separate section of platter lined with salad greens, alternating bright vegetables with green vegetables, i.e., nest of julienne-style beets, then green beans, then carrots, then peas. Serve with Russian Dressing*.

Recipe may be increased or halved as needed. It is easy to do—but pretty and delicious. Choose choice quality canned vegetables for perfect appearance.

CUCUMBER AND TOMATO SALAD
(24 servings)

24 medium-size ripe tomatoes
1 (8-ounce) package cream
  cheese
½ cup mayonnaise or salad
  dressing

6 cucumbers, peeled and
  sliced thin
Salad greens

Peel tomatoes and trim out center core as shallowly as possible. Place core side down. Make 4 cuts into each tomato crosswise only partially through, leaving uncut on bottom. Mix cream cheese with mayonnaise until smooth. Spread on both sides of cucumber slices and insert in crosswise cuts in tomatoes. Chill, covered, until ready to serve. Serve on salad greens.

Recipe may be doubled. These red-and-white striped salads have a gala look, delicious flavor.

MARINATED CUCUMBERS WITH ONIONS
(24 servings)

6 long cucumbers
1 bunch green onions or
  3 large sweet white onions
1 cup vinegar
1 cup sugar
2 teaspoons salt
1 cup water

1 pint heavy sweet or sour
  cream
¼ cup lemon juice
¼ cup sugar, additional
2 teaspoons salt, additional
¼ teaspoon pepper

Peel and slice cucumbers and onions about ¼ inch thick. Combine vinegar, 1 cup sugar and 2 teaspoons salt with water. Pour over vegetables and let stand 6 to 8 hours. Drain. Beat cream with lemon juice, ¼ cup sugar, 2 teaspoons salt and pepper. Blend with cucumbers and onions and chill until serving time. (This is better if it does not stand more than 3 to 4 hours.)

Recipe may be doubled.

POTATO OR MACARONI SALAD
(24 servings)

4 quarts diced, cooked
  potatoes or cooked
  macaroni
2 teaspoons salt
1 teaspoon freshly ground
  black pepper
1 teaspoon paprika
2 cups finely chopped celery
½ cup thinly sliced green
  onions, if desired

½ cup finely chopped
  parsley
12 hard-cooked eggs
3 cups mayonnaise or salad
  dressing
½ cup sweet pickle juice
Salad greens
For garnish, if desired:
  pimento or green pepper
  slivers

Sprinkle potatoes or macaroni with salt, pepper and paprika. Let stand while preparing vegetables. Add chopped celery, onions and parsley. Reserve 3 or 4 eggs for slices for garnish. Dice remaining eggs coarsely and add to vegetables. Toss lightly together. Thin mayonnaise or salad dressing with sweet pickle juice. Add sufficient dressing to moisten salad to desired consistency. Cover and chill for 1 hour. At serving time, mound salad in large bowl lined with greens. Garnish with hard-cooked egg slices and sprinkle lightly with paprika. Small slivers of pimento or green pepper may be used as garnish, if desired. Individual servings on plates or in small paper cups may be preferred. Garnish with one of the above or slices of pickle.

Recipe may be doubled.

POTATO SALAD STUFFED TOMATOES
(24 servings)

5 pounds potatoes
12 hard-cooked eggs, diced
1 quart chopped celery
1 cup chopped onion
2 tablespoons salt
1 teaspoon pepper
¼ cup sugar
1 tablespoon prepared
  mustard

1 cup thick sour cream
1 pint salad dressing or
  mayonnaise
8 large tomatoes
Stuffed olives or parsley, for
  garnish

Cook potatoes in skins. Peel and dice while warm. Combine with eggs, celery, and onion. Mix salt, pepper, sugar, mustard, sour cream and dressing. Stir dressing into potato mixture until thoroughly mixed. Chill salad, covered, to allow blend of flavors. Wash, peel and core tomatoes. Cut tomatoes in thirds. Lay tomato slices on individual serving plates or large platter. Arrange a mound of potato salad on each slice. Garnish with slices of stuffed olives or parsley.

POTATO SALAD ON TOMATO HALVES
(48 servings)

Double Potato Salad* recipe (above)
24 tomatoes
Salad greens

Chill potato salad 12 to 24 hours. Peel cored tomatoes and cut in half. Arrange on salad greens. Place a rounded mound of potato salad on each tomato half. This may be combined up to 1 hour before serving. Flavor is better if kept chilled in refrigerator or over broad trays of cracked ice.

Tomatoes may be peeled several hours ahead if arranged one layer deep, covered with plastic film, and returned to refrigerator. Remove core and cut in half at time of arranging salad on greens with potato mixture.

RAW VEGETABLE SALAD
(24 servings)

2 quarts (1 medium head) coarsely shredded cabbage

1 head lettuce, torn into bite-size pieces

1 head chicory or endive, torn into bite-size pieces

2 cups thinly sliced cauliflowerets

2 cups sliced celery

2 cups sliced cucumbers

1 cup diced green pepper

2 cups grated carrots

6 tomatoes, cut in small wedges

1 pint French Dressing*

Prepare vegetables, cover tightly until serving time. Just before serving, combine salad greens, cauliflowerets, celery, cucumbers, green pepper, carrots and tomatoes. Toss with dressing.

Recipe may be doubled and combination varied as desired.

TOSSED GREEN SALAD
(24 servings)

1 head lettuce

1 head romaine

1 quart thinly sliced celery

1 large green pepper, chopped

6 tomatoes, cut in wedges

3 cups croutons, if desired

1½ pints French*, Italian* or Blue Cheese Dressing*

Tear greens into bite-size pieces. Combine all vegetables except tomatoes and chill. Peel and cut tomatoes in wedges, chilling separately. Add tomatoes and croutons to other vegetables just before serving. Toss to mix. Let guests add their own choice of dressing, if possible.

Recipe may be doubled and varied as desired. Wrap prepared vegetables air-tight, chill, and they will stay crisp for hours.

MAIN COURSE SALADS

(Mixed)

CHICKEN-ALMOND SALAD
(24 servings)

2 cups mayonnaise
⅓ cup milk
1 teaspoon Worcestershire
   sauce
2 tablespoons lemon juice
12 cups diced cooked
   chicken
4 cups diced celery

4 cups grapefruit sections
Shredded lettuce or
   lettuce leaves
1 cup toasted slivered
   almonds, for garnish
4 pounds seedless grapes
   separated into small
   clusters, for garnish

Combine mayonnaise with milk, Worcestershire sauce and lemon juice, stirring well. In large bowl, mix chicken with celery and grapefruit. Add dressing, toss mixture until thoroughly mixed. Cover and chill. At serving time, mound chicken mixture on a bed of shredded lettuce or large lettuce leaf for individual servings. Garnish with toasted almonds and small clusters of fresh grapes. Salad may be arranged on platter with grape clusters in circle about it and almonds over top for buffet service.

Recipe may be doubled safely. Salad is best if freshly mixed on day of serving. For overnight storage, chill ingredients separately, then stir together 1 hour before serving.

Excellent

CHICKEN, GRAPE, ALMOND SALAD SUPREME
(48 servings)

4 quarts chopped cooked
  chicken (about 20 pounds
  dressed stewing chickens)
2 quarts sliced celery
2 quarts seeded grapes
2 quarts diced apple

2 quarts pineapple tidbits
1 quart slivered almonds
1 quart salad dressing or
  mayonnaise
Salad greens or lettuce cups

Combine chicken, celery, grapes, apple, pineapple, almonds and dressing; chill 1 to 3 hours before serving. Mound on salad greens or individual lettuce cups.

Recipe may be increased as desired. If desired to prepare farther in advance, omit apple, increasing other fruit and celery to make 2 quarts additional. This latter combination may be prepared up to 12 hours ahead of serving time.

CRAB LOUIS
(24 servings)

4 pounds fresh or frozen
  crabmeat
3 heads lettuce
1 quart chopped celery
¼ cup minced onion
¼ cup minced parsley
1 quart mayonnaise or
  salad dressing

1 pint chili sauce
1 cup pickle relish
½ cup lemon juice
2 teaspoons Tabasco
12 hard-cooked eggs, sliced,
  for garnish
Ripe olives and cherry
  tomatoes, for garnish

Remove any bits of shell or membrane from crabmeat. Chill. Arrange leaves of lettuce on serving plates. Chop remaining lettuce and prepare beds on top of leaves. Sprinkle celery over lettuce. This may be done ahead and kept chilled. Combine onion, parsley, mayonnaise, chili sauce, pickle relish, lemon juice and Tabasco. At serving time, arrange crabmeat on prepared greens. Pour sauce over crab. Garnish with hard-cooked eggs, olives and tomatoes.

Recipe may be doubled as needed, as long as refrigeration space is adequate. All but adding dressing and garnishing may be done ahead if salads are kept chilled. Lemon wedges are a colorful touch that may be added to garnishes.

SALAMI SHRIMP SUPPER SALAD
(24 servings)

1½ pounds cooked, cleaned shrimp, split in half
1½ pounds salami, cut in slivers
6 hard-cooked eggs, diced
2 cups diced celery
2 cups diced cucumbers
1 quart cooked macaroni, chilled

½ cup lemon juice
1 teaspoon Worcestershire sauce
½ teaspoon Tabasco
1 teaspoon salt
¼ teaspoon pepper
1 pint Italian Dressing*
Salad greens

Combine shrimp, salami, eggs, celery, cucumbers and macaroni. Sprinkle with lemon juice, Worcestershire sauce, Tabasco, salt and pepper. Moisten with Italian Dressing* for desired consistency. Avoid an excess of dressing. Toss lightly, cover and chill until served. Arrange in lettuce-lined bowl or mound on shredded greens or individual plates.

Recipe may be increased as desired.

MAIN COURSE SALADS

(Molded)

CHICKEN OR TURKEY SALAD MOLD
(48 servings)

10 envelopes (2½ ounces)
unflavored gelatin

2½ quarts seasoned chicken
or turkey stock

½ cup lemon juice

1 tablespoon monosodium
glutamate (optional)

1½ quarts mayonnaise

3 quarts (3¾ pounds) diced
cooked chicken or turkey

2 cups finely chopped celery

½ cup finely chopped
pimento

3 cups cooked or canned
peas

Salad greens

Soften gelatin in half the cold stock. Combine remaining stock, lemon juice and monosodium glutamate, and heat to boiling. Dissolve softened gelatin in hot stock, stirring to dissolve. Blend in mayonnaise until mixture is smooth. Chill until mixture will mound slightly when dropped from a spoon. Fold in remaining ingredients. Pour into 2 pans, 13×9×2 inches, or 48 individual ½-cup molds. Chill until firm. Cut each large mold into 24 servings, or unmold individual servings. Place each on crisp greens.

Recipe may be doubled. Assure neat squares can be cut from large pans by finely mincing celery and dicing meat and pimento into small bits.

DEVILED EGG SALAD SQUARES
(48 servings)

10 envelopes (2½ ounces)
  unflavored gelatin
1¼ quarts cold water
2 quarts mayonnaise or salad
  dressing
1 cup vinegar
1½ cups finely diced
  stuffed olives, if desired

1½ quarts finely chopped
  celery
2 tablespoons prepared
  mustard
1½ dozen hard-cooked eggs,
  diced
Salad greens
Cherry tomatoes, for garnish

Soften gelatin in cold water. Dissolve over boiling water. Remove
from heat. Stir in mayonnaise and vinegar. Chill until mixture begins to thicken. Stir in olives, if desired, and celery. Combine mustard
with eggs and add to gelatin mixture. Pour into 48 individual molds
or one 18×12×2-inch pan or two 13×9×2-inch pans. Chill
until firm. Cut into squares or unmold. Serve on crisp greens, garnished with cherry tomatoes.

Double recipe if desired.

MOLDED HAM LOAF
(48 servings)

10 envelopes (2½ ounces)
  unflavored gelatin
1¼ quarts cold water
2 quarts sweet cider or apple
  juice
½ cup vinegar

⅓ cup brown sugar
3 pounds (3 quarts) lean,
  cooked ham, coarsely
  ground
1 cup minced green pepper

Soften gelatin in cold water. Bring cider to boiling. Remove from
heat; add gelatin, vinegar and sugar. Stir to dissolve. Chill mixture

to consistency of unbeaten egg white, then add ham and green pepper. Pour into four loaf pans, approximately 9×5×3 inches. Chill until firm. Unmold and slice each loaf into 12 servings.

Recipe can be doubled.

CHILLED SALMON LOAF
(48 servings)

10 envelopes (2½ ounces) unflavored gelatin
1¼ quarts cold water
1 (1-pound) can peas, drained, reserving liquid
1 cup lemon juice or white vinegar
½ cup granulated sugar

2 tablespoons salt
48 ounces boneless cooked, flaked salmon (approximately 5 1-pound cans or 10 No. ½ flat cans)
2 cups finely chopped sweet pickles

Soak gelatin in 1¼ quarts cold water. Add sufficient water to liquid drained from peas to measure 1¾ quarts and bring to boil. Remove from heat. Add softened gelatin, lemon juice or vinegar, sugar and salt. Stir until gelatin is dissolved. Chill until slightly thickened. In using canned salmon, remove and discard skin and bones and juice. Weigh 48 ounces of flaked salmon. Fold in flaked salmon. Add peas and pickles. Divide mixture among four 9×5×3-inch loaf pans. Chill until firm. Unmold and cut each loaf into 12 slices.

Recipe may be doubled. Salmon mixture may be divided into 48 individual ½-cup molds to turn out on a bed of lettuce and garnish with salad dressing or mayonnaise.

MOLDED SEAFOOD SALAD
(24 servings)

5 envelopes (1¼ ounces)
unflavored gelatin
3 cups cold water
1 quart mayonnaise or
salad dressing
½ cup vinegar or lemon juice
1 tablespoon prepared
mustard
1 teaspoon Tabasco
¼ cup minced onion
½ cup finely diced pimento
or stuffed olives

3 cups finely chopped celery
1 cup chopped green
pepper or cucumber
3 (6-ounce) cans tuna,
drained and flaked
3 (5-ounce) cans shrimp
3 (7-ounce) cans crabmeat
Salad greens
Green pepper rings and
sliced stuffed olives,
for garnish

Soften gelatin in cold water. Dissolve over boiling water. Remove from heat. Stir in mayonnaise, vinegar or lemon juice, mustard and Tabasco. Chill until mixture begins to thicken. Fold in onion, pimento or olives, celery, green pepper or cucumber and the fish. Pour into 19×13×2-inch pan or two 3-quart molds. Chill until firm. Cut into squares or unmold. Serve on crisp greens, garnished with green pepper rings and sliced stuffed olives.

Recipe may be increased as needed. Combinations of fish may be varied to suit taste.

SALAD DRESSINGS

ANCHOVY-PARSLEY SALAD DRESSING
(About 1½ quarts)

*1 quart tart French Dressing***
4 cans flat anchovy fillets, drained and minced
1 cup minced parsley

Chill ingredients and combine dressing, anchovies and parsley just before serving. Use over mixed salad greens or shredded lettuce.

Recipe may be doubled. Garlic-flavored croutons are a welcome addition to a mixed greens salad dressed with the above mixture. Prepare croutons by browning bread cubes in garlic-flavored oil in broad, heavy-bottomed skillet while stirring; or sprinkle cubes lightly with garlic powder and toast on cooky sheet in oven.

BLUE CHEESE DRESSING
(About 2 quarts)

½ cup lemon juice
2 tablespoons dry mustard
⅓ cup powdered sugar
2 teaspoons salt
*1 teaspoon freshly ground
black pepper*

¼ teaspoon garlic powder
*½ pound blue cheese or
Roquefort*
1½ quarts sour cream

Mix lemon juice with mustard, sugar, salt, pepper and garlic. Crumble cheese and blend smooth with lemon mixture. Fold in sour cream. Chill. Serve with vegetable or fish or meat salads.

Recipe may be doubled, but do not plan to store for long periods. Blue cheese varies in saltiness. Taste dressing and add more salt, if needed, after mixture has had time to blend flavors while chilling.

CREAM CHEESE DRESSING
(about 1 quart)

1 (8-ounce) package cream cheese, at room temperature
1 pint salad dressing or mayonnaise
1 cup canned pear syrup or other canned fruit syrup
1 tablespoon finely grated orange rind

Whip cream cheese until fluffy. Gradually blend in salad dressing and fruit syrup. Sprinkle orange rind over top of serving bowl or individual servings.

Recipe may be doubled. Dressing may be made as much as 24 hours in advance. Stir well and allow to warm 30 minutes or so before serving. Particularly good on fruit salads.

FRENCH DRESSING
(1 quart)

3 cups salad oil
1 cup vinegar
1 tablespoon salt
1 tablespoon sugar
1 teaspoon pepper
½ teaspoon paprika
1¼ teaspoons dry mustard

Combine oil, vinegar, salt, sugar, pepper, paprika and mustard in quart jar with tight-fitting lid. Shake until mixture is blended. Chill. Shake well before each use.

Recipe may be increased as desired. Garlic French Dressing is made by adding a lightly bruised bud of garlic to mixture before chilling.

GREEN GODDESS DRESSING
(About 1 quart)

1 clove garlic, crushed
¼ cup tarragon-flavored
  white wine vinegar
1 cup dairy sour cream
2 cups mayonnaise
1 (2-ounce) can anchovy
  fillets, drained

1 green onion (including
  top)
¼ cup minced chives
¼ cup minced parsley

Add crushed garlic to vinegar and let stand while preparing dressing. Combine sour cream and mayonnaise. Chop anchovy fillets and green onion until very fine. Remove garlic from vinegar and add vinegar, anchovy, onion, chives, and parsley to cream-mayonnaise mixture. Serve over romaine lettuce garnished with ready-to-eat shrimp, crab, lobster or chicken.

Recipe may be doubled. Refrigerate no longer than 1 week. Justly famous, the Green Goddess Dressing was created in 1915 by a chef at the Palace Hotel in San Francisco.

HONEY CELERY SEED DRESSING
(About 1 pint)

¾ cup honey, at room
  temperature
1½ cups salad oil
½ cup lemon juice
2 teaspoons salt

1 teaspoon paprika
1 teaspoon dry mustard
½ teaspoon ginger
2 teaspoons celery seed

Combine honey, oil, lemon juice, salt, paprika, mustard, ginger and celery seed and blend well. May be made ahead and refrigerated.

Allow to stand ½ hour at room temperature before serving, then shake well before use.

Recipe may be doubled, if desired.

ITALIAN DRESSING
(1 quart)

1 cup red wine vinegar
3 cups olive oil
4 teaspoons salt
4 teaspoons sugar
1 teaspoon dry mustard
1 teaspoon black pepper
1 teaspoon paprika

½ teaspoon dry basil
½ teaspoon marjoram
½ teaspoon oregano leaves
¼ cup finely minced parsley,
   if desired
2 cloves fresh garlic minced

Combine vinegar, oil, salt, sugar, mustard, pepper, paprika, herbs, parsley, if desired, and garlic in quart jar with tight-fitting lid. Shake to blend. Chill. Shake well before each use. Omit parsley if long storage is planned. Best flavor is obtained by removing dressing to room temperature about one half hour before serving.

Recipe may be doubled. Goodness of this dressing depends on fine quality olive oil blending with remaining ingredients. Be sure to choose fresh, high quality olive oil.

ROSY ROQUEFORT DRESSING
(About 2½ cups)

1 pint mayonnaise or salad
   dressing
1 (3-ounce) package
   Roquefort cheese
⅓ cup tomato catsup

1 teaspoon Worcestershire
   sauce
Minced parsley or finely
   chopped chives, for garnish

Stir mayonnaise or salad dressing into well-blended mixture of Roquefort cheese, catsup and Worcestershire sauce. Cover. Chill. At serving time, garnish top of salad dressing with a sprinkling of minced, fresh parsley or chives.

This salad dressing is attractive served in a stark white bowl and topped with the minced green herbs for use on a buffet table as one choice among several for mixed green salads.

RUSSIAN DRESSING
(About 1½ quarts)

1 cup chili sauce or tomato
* catsup*
1 quart mayonnaise

2 cups India relish or
* finely cut sweet pickles*
2 tablespoons grated onion

Combine chili sauce, mayonnaise, relish or pickles and onion and let stand in refrigerator 24 hours before serving. This amount will make forty-eight 2-tablespoon servings.

Recipe may be doubled. Excellent dressing for hearts of lettuce salad.

SHRIMP DRESSING
(1 quart)

⅓ cup white wine vinegar
¼ cup sugar
1 tablespoon salt
½ teaspoon paprika
½ teaspoon freshly ground
* black pepper*
¼ to ½ teaspoon dry
* mustard*

1 cup mayonnaise
2 cups thick sour cream
1 (4½-ounce) can shrimp,
* drained*
½ cup finely cut parsley
Mixed greens or shredded
* cabbage*

Combine vinegar, sugar, salt, paprika, pepper and mustard, stirring to dissolve. Blend with mayonnaise, then add sour cream. Shred shrimp and add with parsley to cream mixture. Chill. Serve over mixed greens torn into bite-size pieces, or shredded cabbage slaw.

Recipe may be doubled. This creamy dressing prepared without the shrimp is a versatile salad accompaniment for vegetable, meat, fish or poultry mixtures.

SOUR CREAM DRESSING
(2 cups)

⅔ cup sugar
2 tablespoons salt
½ teaspoon paprika
½ teaspoon coarse grind
    black pepper

¼ teaspoon dry mustard
⅓ cup white wine vinegar
    (flavored with herbs, if
    desired)
1½ cups thick sour cream

Dissolve sugar and dry seasonings in vinegar. Stir in sour cream. Store covered in refrigerator. Use promptly—within a week. Use for vegetable salad mixtures as prepared or combine half-and-half with bland mayonnaise for use on fruit salad mixtures.

Recipe may be doubled. Seasonings of sour cream dressing may be varied by using tarragon-flavored vinegar or basil-flavored vinegar in place of plain white wine vinegar. Another variation is blending in crumbled blue or Roquefort cheese to taste: use approximately 1 (3-ounce) package blue cheese to 1 cup prepared dressing.

THOUSAND ISLAND SALAD DRESSING
(About 2 quarts)

1 quart mayonnaise or salad
    dressing
1 pint chili sauce
1 cup India relish

1 tablespoon powdered
    sugar
½ cup mild vinegar

Blend mayonnaise, chili sauce, India relish, sugar and vinegar together. Chill. Serve over vegetable salads.

Recipe may be increased. Long a favorite, this salad dressing is truly versatile. It is as good on hearty main dish salads made with cold, cooked meat or fish as it is over macaroni salad, cooked vegetable salads or simple greens. Combines well with hard-cooked egg slices for garnish. Keeps well in refrigerator.

SANDWICHES

COLD SANDWICHES

BASIC SANDWICH FILLING
(48 servings)

*4 cups chopped cooked
chicken, ham, roast beef,
flaked tuna or any desired
cooked or canned meat,
poultry or seafood*

*1 cup mayonnaise or salad
dressing*

½ cup finely chopped celery

*½ cup chopped nuts, if
desired*

*½ cup chopped pickle, if
desired*

Salt and pepper to taste

*Prepared mustard or lemon
juice to taste*

*Pickle or olive slices, for
garnish*

Combine ingredients and spread on buttered bread or toast or crackers. Makes 48 finger sandwiches or canapés. Garnish with slices of pickle or olives.

Recipe may be increased.

AVOCADO FILLING FOR SANDWICHES
(48 servings)

2 cups mashed avocado
  (about 3 medium)
½ cup mayonnaise or salad
  dressing

1 tablespoon lemon juice
1 teaspoon salt
Dash pepper
¼ cup minced parsley

Combine avocado, mayonnaise, lemon juice, salt, pepper and parsley and chill before spreading on bread. Sufficient spread for 2 ribbon loaves or 48 finger sandwiches or canapés.

Recipe may be increased.

BRAUNSCHWEIGER FILLING
FOR SANDWICHES
(48 servings)

1 pound braunschweiger or
  liverwurst
½ cup mayonnaise or
  salad dressing
1 tablespoon minced onion

1 teaspoon Worcestershire
  sauce
1 tablespoon prepared
  mustard

Mash braunschweiger or liverwurst and mix with mayonnaise or salad dressing, onion, Worcestershire sauce, and mustard. Sufficient for 2 ribbon sandwich loaves or 48 finger sandwiches or canapés. If using for open-face sandwiches, slices of pickle make good garnish.

Recipe may be increased.

CHEESE AND OLIVE SPREAD FOR SANDWICHES
(48 servings)

4 cups grated Cheddar cheese　　*½ cup chopped stuffed olives*
¼ cup prepared mustard　　　　*1 tablespoon minced onion,*
½ cup mayonnaise or　　　　　　　*if desired*
*　salad dressing*

Combine cheese, mustard and mayonnaise or salad dressing and mix until blended. Add olives and onion, if desired. Sufficient for 2 ribbon sandwich loaves or 48 finger sandwiches or canapés.

Recipe may be increased.

CHICKEN FILLING FOR BUNS
(About 2 quarts)

4 cups diced, cooked　　　　　*2 tablespoons grated onion*
*　chicken*　　　　　　　　　　　　*1 pint mayonnaise*
2 cups finely diced celery　　　*½ cup cream (about)*
1 cup slivered almonds,　　　　*Salt*
*　toasted*　　　　　　　　　　　　*Paprika*

Combine chicken, celery and almonds in large bowl. In separate bowl, blend together grated onion, mayonnaise and sufficient cream to give light dressing. Add to chicken mixture, blending well. Taste. Add salt and paprika if required. Use for filling 48 small buns or petits choux (paste shells), allowing 1 mounded tablespoon per serving.

Mixture may be spread on buttered bread rounds and garnished with tiny bits of pimento, parsley or lemon peel for open-face sandwiches, if preferred. Store on shallow pans covered with damp-dry cloth in refrigerator for a short while (preferably not over 2 or 3 hours).

FANCY SANDWICHES

Checkerboard Sandwiches: Use ½-inch slices of white and dark bread. Spread each slice with creamed butter and desired filling. Put together in stacks of three, alternating light and dark bread. Press together, refrigerate until filling is firm, then cut off crusts. Cut each pile into ½-inch slices, crosswise, spreading cut sides with creamed butter and sandwich filling. Lay perpendicular to original brown and white slices to form check. Again refrigerate under light weight until serving time. Cut crosswise into checkerboards.

Rolled Sandwiches: Cut crusts from fresh, thinly sliced bread. Either commercial sandwich loaf or whole loaf sliced thin may be selected. Spread a well-seasoned, smooth sandwich mixture over a slice, then roll evenly. Fasten ends with toothpicks. Cover and chill. Remove picks before serving. Tuck a sprig of watercress into ends of cream cheese-filled rolls for a garnish that is both attractive and tasty.

Fancy Shapes: Use unsliced bread, cut lengthwise into ¼-inch slices, then cut with sharp cooky cutters. Day-old bread is best. Spread with fillings. Decorate, cover, chill.

Sandwich Rings: Cut bread in rounds, then remove centers of half the rounds with small cutter or thimble. Spread complete rounds with filling and top with circle of bread or toast. Cover and chill.

Pinwheel: Cut crusts from all four sides and both ends of a loaf of fresh bread. Slice crosswise into thin slices. Roll gently over a slice with rolling pin, then fill with a sandwich mixture blended smooth for easy spreading. Roll up carefully as in preparing a jelly roll. Place on flat tray that can be covered. Chill. Before serving, cut rolls into thin slices. Ready-sliced bread if thinly cut may be used. Crusts must be removed from each slice before spreading. Garnishes may be added to pinwheels before serving: Bits of pimento, minced chives, parsley, grated egg yolk, hard-cooked egg slices, slices of pickle, stuffed olives, black olives, bits of lemon peel, colored cream cheese forced through a decorating tube and caviar—both red and black.

Ribbon: Cut crusts from all four sides and both ends of a loaf of white bread and a loaf of brown bread of approximately the same size. Cut lengthwise into four slices. Put ribbon loaf together with two kinds of prepared sandwich filling, using 2 slices of white bread and 2 slices of brown bread. Alternate the 2 breads and the 2 sandwich fillings so that a light-dark color effect is achieved. Place spread loaf on large sheet of aluminum foil or transparent freezer wrap and cover tightly. Chill thoroughly. At serving time, slice thinly across and then cut each slice in half for small sandwiches. Garnish if desired as suggested under Pinwheel Sandwiches*.

Finger: Cut crusts from thin-sliced bread. Spread well-seasoned, smooth sandwich filling over entire surface of one slice and top with matching slice. Press lightly together. Wrap in aluminum foil, thin transparent freezer wrap or freezer bags. Chill. Just before serving, cut each sandwich into thirds. Arrange on trays garnished with parsley, radish roses or other fresh, attractive vegetables for color accent, e.g., carrot curls, celery sticks, watercress and endive. Deviled eggs, black or stuffed olives and tiny crisp pickles are alternate suggestions for garnish. Avoid any additional food that will drip moisture into sandwiches. A bed of crisp, dry greens generally will prevent passage of moisture to sandwiches.

Success of these pretty sandwiches depends on careful spreading of very smooth filling over entire bread surface followed by thorough chilling. If filling has a cream cheese base, it may be frozen either before or after spreading on bread. Do NOT freeze sandwich mixtures made with mayonnaise. Cooked salad dressing may be frozen without loss of quality.

RIBBON SANDWICHES OR LOAF
(48 servings)

2 long Pullman loaves,
  unsliced
1 cup butter or margarine,
  creamed
Avocado Filling*
Braunschweiger Filling*

Cheese and Olive Spread*
2 (8-ounce) packages cream
  cheese
1 pint cottage cheese, sieved
¼ cup mayonnaise or salad
  dressing

Cut crusts from bread. For each loaf, cut into 4 lengthwise slices.
Spread middle slices on both sides with butter, top and bottom slices
on one side only. On bottom slice put Avocado Filling*. Top with
slice of buttered bread. Spread with Braunschweiger Filling*. Add
another slice of buttered bread. Spread with Cheese and Olive
Spread*. Top with remaining slice of bread. If frosted loaf is desired, mix cream cheese and sieved cottage cheese with mayonnaise
and spread on sides and top of each loaf. Chill until ready to serve.
Cut each loaf into 24 thin slices. If unfrosted loaf is desired, spread
with fillings as directed, then wrap in waxed paper and then in damp
towels, chilling until serving time, then cutting into thin slices.

Recipe may be increased as needed and other fillings of contrasting
color substituted.

HOT SANDWICHES

CHEESE-STUFFED FINGER ROLLS
(48 servings)

See recipe for Cheese and Olive Spread for Sandwiches*. Unless Finger Rolls are very tiny, double cheese mixture, allowing 2 rolls per serving. Store filled rolls in the refrigerator. To warm rolls, lay in shallow pan and cover with aluminum foil. Bake in 350° F. oven 10 to 12 minutes. Avoid overheating. Serve warm rather than hot.

CHILI BEEFBURGER
(24 servings)

2 quarts Chili Con Carne*
3 pounds ground beef
1½ cups fine dry bread crumbs
½ cup milk
1 tablespoon salt
½ teaspoon pepper
24 hamburger buns
Melted butter or margarine

Heat Chili Con Carne* until very hot, and keep warm. Combine beef, bread crumbs, milk, salt and pepper. Shape into 24 patties. Broil or pan-fry until brown on both sides. Split hamburger buns. Toast crust side under broiler, turn cut sides up and brush with melted butter or margarine. Toast lightly under broiler. Place 1 cooked beef patty on each roll and spoon approximately 3 tablespoons Chili Con Carne* over.

The young crowd will undoubtedly want seconds, so for this type of affair having a double quantity of servings may be in order.

HAM-STUFFED BUNS
(48 servings)

12 cups ground cooked ham
2 cups mayonnaise or salad
dressing
2 cups catsup
4 cups grated Cheddar
cheese

1 cup finely chopped celery
48 large French rolls, halved
and buttered

Combine ham, mayonnaise, catsup, cheese and celery. Spread thickly on halved French rolls. Bake in 375° F. oven until browned and bubbly. If serving time is uncertain, wrap tray of buns in foil before baking to avoid drying out.

Double amounts to match your crowd. Buns may be frozen ready to heat. Package in foil and they can be brought right from freezer to oven, still in foil. Allow 30 to 40 minutes at 425° F. to heat when frozen.

HOT DOG HAMBURGERS
(48 servings)

15 pounds ground beef
4 eggs
2 cups fine dry bread
crumbs
¼ cup minced onion
¼ cup finely chopped
parsley

½ cup catsup
3 tablespoons salt
¼ teaspoon pepper
1½ pounds frankfurters,
sliced crosswise
48 hot buttered buns

Combine ground beef, eggs, crumbs, onion, parsley, catsup and seasonings. Mix thoroughly and shape into 48 patties. Cut each frankfurter into about 15 to 16 slices. Broil hamburgers on one side.

Turn and press 4 to 5 frankfurter slices on top of each patty. Finish broiling. Serve on hot buttered buns.

Recipe may be doubled. For added convenience, patties may be prepared ahead and frankfurter slices pressed into patties to be frozen. If not frozen, slices are likely to drop off in turning. However, patties may be baked, rather than broiled, which eliminates turning. Bake in 375° F. oven about 20 minutes, pouring or siphoning off excess fat, during baking.

OVEN-BARBECUED HAMBURGERS
(24 servings)

8 pounds ground beef
1 tablespoon salt
¼ teaspoon pepper
1½ cups chili sauce
1 cup beer, ale or consommé

1 package (1½-ounce) dry onion soup mix
1 teaspoon Tabasco

Combine ground beef, salt and pepper. Shape into 24 patties. Place in baking pan and bake in 400° F. oven until browned. Combine chili sauce, beer, ale or consommé, onion soup mix and Tabasco. Bring to boil. Pour over hamburgers and bake 15 minutes longer.

Recipe may be increased as desired.

TURKEY SANDWICH SUPREME
(48 servings)

96 slices white sandwich bread
3 pounds sliced, cooked turkey

¾ pound butter
1 pint mayonnaise

Prepare 48 sandwiches with turkey, spreading 1 slice of each sandwich with butter and the other with mayonnaise.

20 eggs
1 quart milk
1 teaspoon salt

About 1 pound fat for
frying

Beat eggs, add milk and salt and mix well. Dip each sandwich in egg mixture. Fry until golden brown on both sides on greased griddle or in a skillet. Top hot sandwich with approximately ¼ cup hot sauce.

SUPREME SAUCE

5 quarts milk
1¾ pounds butter or
margarine

2½ cups all-purpose flour
2 tablespoons salt
1 quart California sherry

Heat milk to near boiling in top of double boiler. In separate saucepan melt 1¼ pounds butter or margarine. Blend in flour and salt with melted butter. Stir fat-flour mixture into hot milk and cook until thickened, stirring constantly with wire whisk. Add California sherry and ½ pound soft butter while stirring, beating until smooth. Avoid letting sauce boil after wine is added.

Sandwiches and basic cream sauce may be prepared ahead. Brown sandwiches and add wine and butter to gently warmed cream sauce just before serving. Do not double sauce unless professional-size equipment and experienced kitchen aides are available to assist.

SOUPS

FRENCH ONION SOUP
(48 servings)

3 pounds dry onions, sliced
  (4 quarts)
1 pound butter or margarine
3 (50-ounce) or 15
  (10½-ounce) cans
  condensed consommé or 10
  quarts beef stock

5 quarts water, if consommé
  is used
Salt and pepper to taste
1 tablespoon Worcestershire
  sauce
1 cup sherry, if desired

Sauté onions in butter until clear but do not brown. Add condensed consommé and water or beef stock. Simmer until onions are tender. Add seasonings, Worcestershire sauce and sherry, if desired. May be made ahead and reheated. Serve with Parmesan toasted bread.

Recipe may be doubled.

CLAM CHOWDER
(48 servings)

2 pounds bacon or salt pork
1 quart chopped onion
1 gallon diced raw potato
1½ gallons water
2 tablespoons salt
2 teaspoons Tabasco

1 cup chopped parsley
2 cups all-purpose flour
1½ gallons milk or
  evaporated milk
12 (7½-ounce) cans minced
  clams, with juice

Dice bacon or salt pork and sauté with onions, until onions are clear and bacon or pork is crisped. Cook potatoes in water with salt until tender. Add bacon, onions, Tabasco and parsley. Bring to boil. Blend flour with 1 quart of milk, then add remaining milk. Stir into hot mixture and cook until thickened, stirring constantly. Add clams and juice. Heat thoroughly but do not let boil. May be made ahead and refrigerated until time to heat for serving.

Recipe may be doubled.

OYSTER STEW
(48 servings)

3 quarts oysters with liquor
1 pound butter or margarine
    or half of each
2 gallons milk
2 quarts cream

2 tablespoons salt
1 teaspoon Tabasco
½ cup chopped parsley, for
    garnish
Paprika, for garnish

Heat oysters in butter until edges curl. If oysters are large, cut in halves or bite-size pieces. Do not let them boil. Add milk, cream, salt and Tabasco. Bring to simmering point (heating over hot water will eliminate danger of scorching). Sprinkle each serving or tureen with parsley and paprika.

Recipe may be increased.

RED AND GREEN MADRILENE
(48 servings)

3 (50-ounce) or 15
    (10½-ounce) cans condensed
    consommé
3 quarts water (or use beef
    stock instead of consommé
    and water)

1 (1-quart 14-ounce) can
    tomato juice
4 bay leaves
4 whole cloves
Salt and pepper to taste
2 cups diced avocado
1 cup lemon juice

Simmer condensed consommé, water, tomato juice, bay leaves, cloves and seasonings 30 minutes. Remove bay leaves and cloves. Just before serving, add avocado cubes and lemon juice. If desired, soup may be made ahead and reheated, adding avocado and lemon juice when served.

Recipe may be doubled or cut.

SPLIT PEA SOUP WITH HAM
(48 servings)

6 pounds dry split peas	3 cloves garlic
8 quarts water	4 pounds carrots, grated
1 ham bone (most of ham trimmed off)	8 medium onions
6 bay leaves	½ cup chopped parsley
2 tablespoons whole cloves	1 quart cubed, cooked ham
2 tablespoons salt	For garnish, if desired:
1 teaspoon pepper	additional chopped parsley

Soak peas in water 6 hours or more. Add ham bone, bay leaves, cloves, salt, pepper, garlic, carrots, onions and parsley. Simmer, covered, until all vegetables are tender, about 1½ hours. Sieve. Add cubed ham and return to simmering temperature, correcting seasoning as required with additional salt and pepper. Flavor actually improves if made ahead and reheated. Garnish with additional chopped parsley, if desired.

Recipe may be doubled.

TOMATO BOUILLON
(48 servings)

2½ quarts beef bouillon	3 tablespoons grated onion
4 quarts tomato juice	1 tablespoon salt
3 bay leaves	

Combine bouillon, tomato juice, bay leaves, onion and salt; simmer to blend flavors. Remove bay leaves. Serve hot. Makes 48 (½-cup) servings.

Recipe may be doubled. Protect the good flavor of this soup by dishing into warm bowls.

VEGETABLES AND PASTAS[1]

BAKED BEANS I
(24 servings)

4 pounds small dried white
or red beans
6 quarts water
1 medium onion
2 whole cloves
1 clove garlic
2 tablespoons bacon
drippings
½ pound diced bacon, ham
or salt pork

2 cups chopped onion,
additional
¼ cup prepared mustard
3 teaspoons salt
1 cup brown sugar
1 cup molasses
1½ cups catsup
1 tablespoon Worcestershire
sauce

Soak beans in water. Do not drain. Insert cloves in onion and add to beans with garlic and bacon drippings. Bring to boil and simmer, covered, 1 hour. Remove onion studded with cloves. Combine beans and cooking liquid with diced bacon, chopped onion, mustard, salt, sugar, molasses, catsup and Worcestershire sauce. Pour into two 4-quart bean pots or heavy baking dishes. Cover and bake in 250° F. oven 6 hours. Uncover, stir and bake 25 minutes longer to brown surface. Beans may be baked ahead and reheated in 350° F. oven 30 to 45 minutes, depending on size of containers.

Recipe may be increased.

[1] Macaroni, noodles, rice and spaghetti served as accompaniments to a main course.

BAKED BEANS II
(48 servings)

6 pounds dried kidney, navy,
  pea or pinto beans
2 quarts water
10 onions, chopped
3 tablespoons salt
2 cups catsup

2 cups molasses
1½ tablespoons dry mustard
1 tablespoon Worcestershire
  sauce
1 pound chopped bacon
  or ham pieces

Wash beans, cover with water and soak overnight. Add onions and, if necessary, additional water to cover. Simmer until tender, about 1½ hours. Add salt, catsup, molasses, mustard, Worcestershire sauce and bacon and pour into heavy casseroles. Bake in 325° F. oven 3 hours, adding water if beans become dry. If baking in open, shallow pans, cover loosely with aluminum foil.

Recipe can be doubled. Beans are even more flavorful made ahead and reheated.

SWEDISH BEANS
(24 servings)

2½ pounds small dried navy
  beans
½ cup molasses
¼ cup brown sugar

1 tablespoon dry mustard
¼ cup vinegar
1½ pounds bacon ends or
  salt pork, cut into cubes

Wash beans, soak overnight. Drain, cover generously with boiling water. Cook until tender. Drain liquor and save part to add to beans during baking. Combine cooked beans with molasses, brown sugar, mustard, vinegar and bacon, adding bean liquor as needed for moist consistency. Bake in 350° F. oven about 2 hours. Taste and add additional seasoning if required. It may be necessary to add a small quantity of cooking liquor during baking.

Recipe may be doubled. Ham is an alternate seasoning as well as a delicious entree for well-browned, baked beans. Prepare these ahead, if desired, for they reheat well in covered casseroles in moderate oven or at low heat on top of a range.

VINTNER'S BEANS
(48 servings)

5 pounds dried kidney beans

1 pound bacon, ham pieces or salt pork, cut fine

2 pounds onions, chopped

2½ quarts California Burgundy or claret

2 bay leaves

1 cup minced parsley

Salt and pepper

Wash beans and soak overnight in approximately 15 quarts water. Drain. Fry bacon, ham pieces or salt pork until lightly browned, then add onions and cook and stir until tender but not browned. Combine meat, onions, drained beans, wine, bay leaves, parsley and 5 quarts of hot water. Place in 350° F. oven and simmer until beans are cooked, 1½ to 2 hours. Taste, and add salt and pepper as required. Beans may be cooked in large kettles, covered, on top of the range with occasional stirring to prevent scorching.

Canned kidney beans may be substituted for dry beans. For 48 servings, drain 2 No. 10 cans kidney beans and reserve liquid. Measure beans and for each quart of beans add the following: 1 onion, chopped, and ¼ cup chopped green pepper sautéed in 3 tablespoons butter. Stir in 2 tablespoons flour, then 1¼ cups drained bean liquor and 1 cup red dinner wine. Add 1 quart beans and 2 tablespoons minced parsley. Taste and add salt and pepper, as required. Bake in 350° F. oven about 30 minutes.

BULGAR WHEAT CASSEROLE
(12 or 48 servings)

INGREDIENTS	12 SERVINGS	48 SERVINGS
butter or margarine	½ cup	1 pound
Bulgar wheat	2 cups	4 pounds
chopped onion	½ cup	2 cups
chopped celery	1 cup	4 cups
minced parsley	½ cup	2 cups
consommé or bouillon	1 quart	4 quarts
oregano	½ teaspoon	2 teaspoons
basil	¼ teaspoon	1 teaspoon
salt	1½ teaspoons	4 teaspoons
pepper	few grains	½ teaspoon
mushrooms, fresh or		
drained, canned, if desired	10 ounces	2½ pounds

In large skillet, melt butter and add Bulgar wheat. Cook and stir until kernels are golden. Add onion and celery and continue cooking until vegetables are tender but not brown. Add parsley, consommé or bouillon, herbs and salt and pepper. Bring to boil. Cover and simmer 10 minutes. Turn into casserole. Stir in small whole or large sliced mushrooms, if desired. Cover and bake in moderate 350° F. oven 1 hour or until stock is absorbed and kernels light and fluffy.

Dependable in goodness and popularity, this casserole does not mind waiting if dinner is delayed. It blends with a variety of meats as well as poultry. Additional amounts may be prepared as above.

GLAZED CARROTS
(12 or 48 servings)

INGREDIENTS	12 SERVINGS	48 SERVINGS
carrots	3 pounds	14 pounds
butter or margarine	⅓ cup	1⅓ cups
lemon juice	2 tablespoons	½ cup
white wine or		
consommé	6 tablespoons	1½ cups
powdered ginger	¼ teaspoon	1 teaspoon
salt	1 teaspoon	1 tablespoon
pepper	few grains	⅓ teaspoon
parsley, minced,		
for garnish	¼ cup	1 cup

Cut carrots into very thin slices or strips. Combine with butter, lemon juice, wine or consommé, ginger, salt and pepper. Cover tightly; bring to boiling. Reduce heat, cover and cook until tender about 12 to 15 minutes. Taste and add more salt and pepper if needed. Before serving garnish with minced parsley.

Prepare additional quantities of glazed carrots as needed, but for best results divide very large batches into at least two broad-bottom kettles.

GLAZED CARROTS AND
SMALL WHOLE ONIONS
(24 servings)

3 pounds tender carrots
1 pound tiny onions
½ cup butter or margarine

1 cup brown sugar
½ cup consommé or bouillon

Peel carrots and onions. If carrots are small, leave whole. If not, cut in halves. Parboil carrots and onions and place in shallow baking pan. Melt butter. Add brown sugar and consommé or bouillon. Bring to boil and cook until sugar is dissolved. Pour over vegetables. Bake in 375° F. oven 15 to 20 minutes, until vegetables are tender and glazed.

Increase amounts, if desired. Parboiling and preparation prior to baking may be done well in advance.

CORN FRITTERS
(24 servings)

6 cups sifted all-purpose flour	6 eggs, beaten
2 tablespoons sugar	3 cups milk
1½ tablespoons double acting baking powder	2 (1-pound) cans whole kernel corn, drained
1 tablespoon salt	Maple syrup

Sift together flour, sugar, baking powder and salt. Add beaten eggs to milk. Mix dry ingredients into milk mixture, stirring just until blended. Add drained corn. Drop by tablespoonfuls into deep hot fat (360° F.), frying until golden brown. Do not overcrowd fryer. Drain and keep hot until all are fried, placing fried fritters on paper towels in 300° F. oven. Serve hot with maple syrup.

Recipe may be doubled if adequate facilities are available for frying. Avoid overbeating.

GREEN BEANS A LA VICTOR
(24 servings)

1 No. 10 can cut green
  beans or 2 (2½-pound)
  boxes frozen green beans
2 (10½-ounce) cans
  consommé, undiluted

1 cup finely cut onion
¼ cup butter or margarine
2 fresh lemons

Heat beans in consommé. Sauté onion in butter and add to beans, simmering 10 minutes or until tender. At serving time, squeeze fresh lemon juice over beans as they are placed in serving dishes or on individual plates. Beans may be served chilled, too, in which case, omit sautéed onion. Slice lemons and layer with cooked beans and consommé in covered container. Let chill at least 6 hours.

Recipe may be doubled. Preparation may be done ahead to permit longer blending of flavors. However, if serving hot be careful not to overcook.

GREEN BEANS OR ASPARAGUS AMANDINE
(48 servings)

2 No. 10 cans green beans or
  asparagus or 12 to 16
  or 16 (10-ounce) boxes
  frozen green beans or
  asparagus or 12 to 16
  pounds fresh beans or
  asparagus

2 cups slivered, blanched
  almonds
½ pound butter or margarine
½ cup lemon juice

Cook or heat beans or asparagus as directed on can or package. Avoid overheating or overcooking. Sauté almonds in butter or margarine until golden. Add lemon juice and blend just before mixing with hot vegetables.

Recipe may be increased as required.

GREEN BEANS CAESAR
(48 servings)

2 No. 10 cans green beans, drained

6 cloves garlic, crushed

2 cups salad oil

¾ cup vinegar

1 cup onion, grated or minced fine

1 tablespoon salt

1½ to 2 quarts dry bread cubes

½ pound grated Parmesan cheese

Arrange green beans in large baking pans. Add crushed garlic to oil and let stand 1 hour or overnight. Strain. Combine 1 cup salad oil, vinegar, onion and salt and pour mixture over beans, mixing thoroughly. Pour remaining garlic-flavored oil over bread cubes while stirring to mix evenly. Spread bread cubes over beans. Bake 20 minutes in 350° F. oven. Sprinkle grated Parmesan cheese over toasted bread cubes and return beans to oven. Bake 5 to 10 minutes longer or until cheese appears slightly browned and melted.

Recipe may be doubled.

LYONNAISE GREEN BEANS
(24 servings)

1 No. 10 can green beans or 2 (2½-pound) or 8 (10-ounce) packages frozen green beans

2 cups finely chopped onion

½ cup (¼ pound) butter or margarine

2 fresh lemons

If using frozen green beans, prepare according to package directions, avoiding overcooking. Sauté onion in butter. Add to beans and heat through but cook no longer than necessary. Squeeze fresh lemon juice over beans when served, either on individual plates or in serving dishes. The fresher the juice, the more delicious.

Recipe may be increased safely with a method as simple as this. Though the lemon may seem a last-minute bother, it is worth it.

GREEN BEANS WITH MUSHROOMS
(48 servings)

1 quart sliced celery
1 quart sliced green onions
1 cup (½ pound) butter or
  margarine
4 (8-ounce) cans sliced
  mushrooms or 2 pounds
  fresh mushrooms

2 No. 10 cans green beans
For garnish, if desired:
  canned French-fried onion
  rings

Sauté celery and onions in butter. If using fresh mushrooms, sauté the slices with the other vegetables. When clear, combine celery, onions and mushrooms with beans. Bring to boil and keep warm until served. Avoid overcooking. If desired, garnish with canned French-fried onion rings, toasted a few minutes in hot oven.

Recipe may be doubled.

GREEN BEANS WITH WATER CHESTNUTS
(24 servings)

1 No. 10 can cut green beans
1 (14- to 16-ounce) can water chestnuts, sliced
For garnish, if desired: 6 hard-cooked egg yolks, sieved

Heat beans and water chestnuts to boiling point. Drain. Sprinkle with hard-cooked, sieved egg yolks as garnish, after arranging in serving dishes or on individual plates.

Recipe may be doubled.

HARVEST CASSEROLE
(24 servings)

4 medium onions, sliced
1 green pepper, chopped
4 summer squash, sliced
  or 2 cups sliced celery
¼ cup butter, margarine or
  bacon drippings
2 (1-pound) cans whole
  kernel corn

2 (1-pound) cans cut green
  beans
2 (1-pound) cans kidney
  beans or 2 (10-ounce)
  packages frozen green
  lima beans

Sauté onions, pepper, squash or celery in skillet in fat until clear. Add corn and both beans and heat through.

Recipe may be doubled. Even better made ahead and reheated so that flavors blend.

HERB-SEASONED, SKEWERED
VEGETABLES

Prepare herb-seasoned butter by mixing 1 teaspoon mixed dry herbs (one part each basil, thyme and marjoram or savory) with 1 cup melted butter or margarine. Keep warm. Thread desired vegetables on skewers to broil over charcoal or in oven broiler. Brush vegetables with prepared butter. Broil about 4 inches from heat. Turn and broil on all sides until heated through and lightly browned on edges. For best results, use cooked vegetables of uniform size when preparing potatoes, small onions and carrots (canned varieties are excellent, in many cases). These may be alternated with uncooked cherry tomatoes and large, fresh mushrooms. For amounts necessary to serve a group, consult the Purchase Guide in Chapter IV. One cup marinade is sufficient seasoning for vegetables for 24 servings.

Seasoning salts such as celery salt and onion or garlic salt and paprika are delicious additions to a vegetable marinade. Use sparingly, about ¼ teaspoon to 1 cup butter.

STUFFED MUSHROOMS
(24 servings)

24 large mushroom caps
¼ cup butter or margarine
1 (10½-ounce) can
  condensed mushroom soup
  or 1¼ cups medium
  cream sauce
½ cup finely grated
  Parmesan cheese

1 cup grated sharp Cheddar
  cheese
1 cup fine dry bread crumbs
¼ cup chopped parsley
Paprika

Sauté mushroom caps in butter 5 minutes. Combine any remaining drippings with mushroom soup, cheeses, bread crumbs and parsley. Place spoonful in each mushroom cap. Sprinkle with paprika. Bake in shallow pan in 400° F. oven until tops are browned, about 12 minutes.

Recipe may be increased as needed. Preparation may be done ahead, ready for last-minute baking. If more convenient, mushrooms may be baked in slower oven for longer time. However, too long baking dries them out.

POPPY SEED NOODLES
12 or 48 servings

INGREDIENTS	12 SERVINGS	48 SERVINGS
salt	2 teaspoons	2 tablespoons
oil	1 tablespoon	2 tablespoons
noodles	1½ pounds	6 pounds
boiling water		
poppy seeds	¼ cup	1 cup

Add salt and oil to boiling water. Drop in noodles. Boil vigorously until just barely tender. Drain well. Add poppy seeds to noodles and toss lightly but thoroughly. Keep noodles hot in covered casserole in warm oven or over hot water.

Richer flavor of this dish is achieved by using melted butter over cooked noodles. Small recipe will require approximately 4 tablespoons butter, melted. For 48 servings use approximately ¼ pound butter.

PEAS WITH ONIONS
(24 servings)

1 cup butter or margarine
6 (10-ounce) packages
frozen peas
2 cups sliced green onions
(or celery)

1 cup water
2 teaspoons salt
Dash pepper
1 tablespoon sugar

Melt butter and add peas and onions. Sauté lightly. Add water, salt, pepper and sugar; cook, tightly covered, just until peas are tender, about 10 to 15 minutes.

Recipe may be increased as desired.

BAKED STUFFED POTATOES
(48 servings)

24 large baking potatoes
2 cups milk
1 cup cream, sweet or sour
3 tablespoons salt
1 teaspoon pepper

1 cup chopped onion, green
or dry, if desired
4 cups grated Cheddar
cheese

Wash potatoes, dry, grease and prick skins. Bake in 425° F. oven until done, about 1 hour. Cut in halves lengthwise; avoid tearing skins. Scoop out centers, leaving thin shell. Mash potato "insides" until free from lumps. Gradually blend in milk, cream, salt, pepper and onion. Taste before all salt is added to correct seasoning. Watch consistency. Do not make pulp too thin. Pile into potato shells. Press spoonful of grated cheese on top of each half. At serving time, heat in moderate oven (from 350° to 400° F.) depending upon what else may need to be in oven at same time until hot through, about 15 to 20 minutes.

Recipe may be increased or decreased according to group to be served. Due to differences in starch content of potatoes, some will require additional milk, some less, so liquid to be used should be adjusted accordingly. These not only lend themselves to before-hand preparation but freeze well.

BUTTERED NEW POTATOES WITH GREEN ONIONS AND PEAS
(24 servings)

8 to 10 pounds
medium-sized new potatoes
(48 potatoes)
4 (10-ounce) packages
frozen peas

1 bunch green onions, sliced
1 cup (½ pound) butter or
margarine
Salt and pepper to taste

Scrub potatoes well and cook in skins just until tender. Cook peas according to package directions just until tender. Sauté onions in butter. Combine all and keep warm over low heat until serving time, seasoning to taste with salt and pepper.

Recipe may be doubled.

BUTTERED POTATO BALLS
(48 servings)

20 pounds small new
   potatoes or use larger ones
   and cut in balls with
   tablespoon or cube
1 pound butter or margarine

1 cup finely chopped parsley
1 tablespoon dry mustard
1 tablespoon paprika
1 tablespoon onion salt
1 tablespoon thyme

Cook potatoes just until tender in jackets. Cool enough to peel. If large, cut into balls or cubes. Melt butter and blend in parsley and seasonings. Toss with potatoes until evenly coated. At serving time, brown lightly in 400° to 450° F. oven about 10 minutes.

Recipe may be doubled.

DELMONICO POTATOES
(48 servings)

14 pounds potatoes
2 cups butter or
   margarine
½ cup onion, minced
1½ cups all-purpose flour
3 quarts milk
4 teaspoons salt

½ teaspoon paprika
¼ teaspoon black pepper
1 pound grated Cheddar
   cheese
2 cups fine dry bread
   crumbs

Pare potatoes and cook in boiling, salted water until tender. Drain and cool. Dice. Melt butter or margarine in large pan and sauté onion until limp. Stir in flour. Add milk, while stirring. Cook and stir constantly until thickened. Season with salt, paprika and pepper. Place diced potatoes in two large greased baking pans. Top with cream sauce. Sprinkle with grated cheese and bread crumbs lightly. Bake in 375° F. oven until sauce is bubbly and potatoes heated through, 30 minutes if sauce is warm or about 45 minutes if entire mixture is chilled.

Potatoes can be boiled in jackets, then cooled and peeled, if preferred. Double recipe only if very large pans are available.

RATATOUILLE
(Mixed Vegetable Casserole)
(48 servings)

4 cloves garlic, minced	1 tablespoon salt
1 quart chopped onion	1 teaspoon freshly ground
1½ cups olive oil or	pepper
salad oil	½ cup lemon juice
4 green peppers, diced	2 teaspoons rosemary
4 pounds zucchini or yellow	1 quart bread crumbs
summer squash[1], sliced	1 tablespoon garlic purée
4 pounds eggplant, peeled	1 cup butter or margarine,
and diced	melted
2 (1-pound 13-ounce) cans	1 cup grated Parmesan
tomatoes	cheese

Sauté garlic and onion in olive or salad oil. Combine with remaining vegetables, salt, pepper, lemon juice and rosemary. Cover and cook until tender, about 45 minutes. Pour into shallow baking pans. Combine bread crumbs, garlic purée, melted butter and Parmesan cheese. Spread over vegetables. Bake in 350° F. oven 20 minutes or until browned and bubbling.

Recipe may be increased as needed. Vegetables may be cooked ahead and reheated with topping at serving time.

[1] If squash is not in season, use additional eggplant or frozen or canned baby green limas.

POTATO PANCAKES
(24 servings)

12 pounds grated raw
  potatoes (6 quarts)
1 cup grated onion
½ cup finely chopped parsley
5 cups sifted all-purpose
  flour
1½ tablespoons salt

¼ teaspoon pepper
8 eggs, beaten
3 cups nonfat dry milk
  powder
2 cups water
Fat for frying

Drain potatoes well. Add onion, parsley, flour, salt, pepper, eggs, dry milk and water; mix well. Fry in shallow, hot fat, spreading to form thin pancakes. Brown on both sides. Drain on paper towels and keep warm in oven until all are fried.

Recipe may be doubled.

BOILED RICE
(24 servings)

2½ pounds raw rice
⅓ cup salt
2½ gallons boiling water

Slowly add rice to boiling, salted water so that boiling does not stop. Cover. Adjust heat so that water continues to boil briskly until rice kernels are cooked through, about 20 minutes. Drain and hold rice in colander over steam to keep warm and fluffy.

Recipe may be doubled if proper equipment is available.

STEAMED RICE
(24 servings)

5 quarts water
2 tablespoons salt
2½ pounds raw rice

Bring salted water to boiling. Slowly add rice so that boiling continues. Reduce heat to lowest level, cover and steam until rice is tender, about 25 minutes. Remove from heat and drain any excess liquid. Stir, cover and keep in warm place until rice grains are fluffy and separated. Completely cooked rice can be kept warm in lightly buttered casserole or baking pan covered with household foil and set in warm oven (150° to 200° F.).

Recipe may be doubled. Yield from 2½ pounds dry rice is 3¾ quarts or approximately 24 ½-cup servings. Boiling rice requires kettles ample in size. Rapid boil-over may be expected from too-full containers.

MOCK WILD RICE
(12 servings)

3 cups raw rice, long grain white
⅔ cup butter or margarine
2 (4-ounce) cans chopped ripe olives

1 (8-ounce) can sliced mushrooms, drained
6 cups hot water
6 teaspoons bouillon crystals or 6 bouillon cubes

Sauté rice in hot butter or margarine in broad skillet until golden. Stir in olives and mushrooms. Cover with hot water and add bouillon crystals or cubes. Bring to boil and stir until bouillon dissolves. Pour into casserole. Cover. Bake in 400° F. oven 25 minutes. Remove from oven, stir lightly from the bottom. Cover casserole and return to oven to cook 10 minutes or until liquid is absorbed and rice is tender and fluffy.

Doubling or tripling this recipe would be limited solely by the size of available containers. Heavy duty aluminum foil may be substituted for cover for casserole, if necessary.

RICE NESTS
(48 servings)

2 quarts raw rice	2 gallons boiling water
¼ cup salt	2 cups butter or margarine

Add rice gradually to boiling salted water. Cover and simmer until tender, about 30 minutes. Drain well, shaking to separate grains. Toss with butter to blend well. Pack rice firmly into oiled ½-cup individual ring molds or into four 2-quart ring molds. Set in pans of hot water and bake in 350° F. oven 30 minutes for small molds, 40 minutes for larger molds. Loosen with knife and invert on plates. If desired, 1 quart finely chopped parsley, sautéed onions or mushrooms or chopped nuts may be combined with rice before packing in mold to bake.

Recipe may be doubled if suitable equipment is available for preparation. Rice may be cooked ahead and placed in molds ready for baking, a day in advance, and stored in the refrigerator. Additional baking time is necessary, 5 minutes for individual molds, 15 minutes for larger molds.

PARSLEYED RICE
(24 servings)

3 pounds long grain raw
rice
3 gallons boiling water
4 tablespoons salt

1 cup butter, melted
2 cups finely chopped
parsley
Salt and pepper to taste

Cook rice in boiling salted water until tender, about 30 minutes. Drain. Toss with butter and parsley, seasoning to taste with salt and pepper. If desired, rice may be packed into oiled ring molds and baked in pans of hot water in 350° F. oven for 20 minutes for individual molds, 30 to 40 minutes for larger molds. Loosen edges of molded rice with knife and invert on platters.

Recipe may be increased proportionately if suitable equipment is available. Rice may also be prepared ahead and reheated, uncovered, in 350° F. oven, 30 to 45 minutes, depending on amounts in containers.

RICE PILAFF
(48 servings)

4 pounds long grain raw
rice
3 quarts boiling water
2 quarts chicken stock or
consommé

3 large onions, chopped fine
1 cup parsley, chopped fine
½ cup (¼ pound) butter or
margarine
Salt and pepper to taste

Add rice gradually to boiling water and chicken stock. Sauté onions and parsley in butter and add to rice. Bring to boil, cover and cook over low heat until rice is tender, about 40 minutes. Season with salt and pepper. If desired, rice may be prepared ahead and kept warm or reheated in covered baking dishes. Avoid stirring rice frequently but fluff gently with fork.

Recipe may be doubled if adequate containers are available.

PIMENTO RICE
(24 servings)

6 cups raw rice
1 cup butter or margarine
1 quart chopped onion, if desired
1 gallon water

2 teaspoons salt
½ teaspoon pepper
1 cup chopped pimento
2 cups slivered toasted almonds, if desired

Sauté rice in butter until golden, with onion if included. Add water and seasonings. Cover and cook over low heat until water is absorbed, about 15 minutes, stirring once or twice with fork. Add additional water if mixture is very dry. Add pimento and almonds and let stand in warm place 10 minutes. May be prepared ahead and reheated over low heat on top of range or in 350° F. oven 15 minutes.

Recipe may be doubled.

SAVORY RICE
(24 servings)

2 cups chopped onion
2 cups chopped fresh mushrooms
¼ cup chopped parsley
¾ cup butter or margarine
4 cups uncooked rice
2 quarts water

1½ teaspoons salt
½ teaspoon pepper
2 cups chicken broth or consommé
1 teaspoon marjoram
1 teaspoon thyme

Sauté onion, mushrooms and parsley in butter. Add rice and cook until golden. Stir in water, salt, pepper, broth and herbs; cover and simmer 20 minutes or until rice is tender and liquid is absorbed. Remove from heat and let stand 10 minutes. If desired, rice may be cooked ahead and reheated, covered, in 350° F. oven, about 20 minutes.

Recipe may be doubled.

SPAGHETTI
(24 servings)

5 pounds uncooked spaghetti
2 tablespoons salt
4 gallons boiling water

Cook spaghetti in boiling, salted water until tender (about 20 minutes), then drain in colander. Adding 2 tablespoons oil to boiling water before dropping in spaghetti will aid in keeping pasta separate. Cooked pasta may be rinsed with hot water and then drained, if preferred.

Ease of handling suggests cooking extra batches of spaghetti in separate containers when larger amounts than the above are required.

SPINACH A LA SUISSE
(12 servings)

1 onion, chopped
2 cloves garlic, minced
¾ cup butter or margarine
4 (10-ounce) packages
of frozen, chopped
spinach cooked and
drained very dry

1 tablespoon flour
1 teaspoon salt
¼ teaspoon pepper
¼ teaspoon nutmeg
1 cup cream

Sauté onion and garlic in butter. Add cooked, drained spinach. Sprinkle with flour, salt, pepper and nutmeg. Stir lightly. Add cream and cook until smoothly blended and heated through.

Recipe may be increased as desired for additional servings. Hard-cooked egg slices are an attractive garnish as are bits of pimento.

BAKED STUFFED TOMATOES
(12 or 48 servings)

INGREDIENTS	12 SERVINGS	48 SERVINGS
firm ripe tomatoes	12	48
salt and pepper		
bacon	¼ pound	1 pound
herb-seasoned bread cubes	2 cups	2 quarts
melted butter or margarine	¼ cup	1 cup
water	3 to 6 tablespoons	1 cup (about)
Parmesan cheese		

Wash and dry tomatoes. Carefully trim top and scoop out center pulp and juice. Reserve. Lightly season inside of tomatoes with salt and pepper and invert while preparing stuffing. Brown bacon, draining well. When crisp, crumble into slivers. Combine bread cubes with reserved tomato pulp and juice, melted butter and bacon. Only if very dry, add a bit of water to stuffing mixture. Lightly fill tomatoes. Top with grated Parmesan cheese. Place in shallow, greased baking dish. Bake in 400° F. oven until heated through and lightly brown on top, about 20 to 25 minutes.

Welcomed for their bright color as well as flavor are these. Try to avoid overcooking for best appearance. Prepare additional amounts as above.

SPINACH CASSEROLE
(12 servings)

¼ cup onion, minced
2 tablespoons butter
4 (10-ounce) packages
frozen, chopped spinach,
cooked and drained
very dry

1 teaspoon salt
⅛ teaspoon pepper
2 eggs, slightly beaten
1 cup milk
1 cup buttered bread
crumbs

Sauté onion in butter. Combine with spinach, salt, pepper, eggs and milk, and pour into lightly buttered baking dish. Top with buttered crumbs. Bake in 300° F. oven about 25 to 30 minutes or until knife comes out clean.

Recipe may be increased. Light sprinkling of grated Parmesan cheese over top of bread crumbs adds zest to topping.

BROILED TOMATOES PARMESAN
(48 servings)

24 medium-small, firm
tomatoes
Flour
Salt and pepper

2 cups grated Parmesan
cheese
1 cup fine buttered bread
crumbs

Halve tomatoes and remove core but do not peel. Dredge cut side with flour, seasoning with salt and pepper. Combine Parmesan cheese and bread crumbs. Press on cut side of tomatoes. Arrange tomatoes in shallow buttered baking pan or on greased sheet. Broil with tops of tomatoes 4 inches from heat, until cheese is browned, about 15 minutes, or bake in 425° F. oven till browned and hot through, about 15 minutes.

Prepare as many servings as needed. Preparation for broiling may be done ahead.

CHERRY TOMATOES ITALIENNE
(24 servings)

72 cherry tomatoes
(about 3 baskets)
1 (8-ounce) bottle
Italian-style dressing or
1 cup Italian Dressing*

1 cup finely grated
Parmesan cheese
2 heads romaine or leaf
lettuce

Wash and dry cherry tomatoes. Chill thoroughly. An hour or so before serving time, coat thoroughly in salad dressing. (This may be done easily by rolling them in dressing which has been poured into broad, shallow pan.) Then dust evenly with Parmesan cheese. (This is best done one at a time—be sure to drain off excess dressing first.) Arrange 3 tomatoes per serving on individual salad plates. For buffet, arrange tomatoes on greens on serving platter with dressing and cheese in bowls in center and let each guest "do it himself" style, using toothpick for individual dipping.

Recipe may be increased as needed; however, time becomes a factor if individual servings are being prepared.

GRILLED ZUCCHINI
(48 servings)

48 medium-size zucchini or summer squash
1 pound butter or margarine
Salt and pepper to taste

Wash squash and cut in halves lengthwise. Arrange in single layer on squares of aluminum foil. Dot with butter, seasoning to taste with salt and pepper. Close foil to form airtight packet. Cook over coals or in 400° F. oven, turning to cook evenly, until squash is tender, about 40 minutes. Packets of squash are easier to handle over grill if foil is cut into four 10-inch squares and squash is divided among four such packets.

Recipe may be increased as needed as long as grill space is adequate.

Appendix

POINTERS FOR BAKING

Use only shiny pans except for pies. Dark pans cause scorching. For
    pies, use oven-proof glass or dark metal pans to prevent
    soggy lower crust.

For rolls, biscuits and coffee cakes, use pans with low sides.

Do not overcrowd ovens. Air must circulate for proper baking.

Do not let pans touch one another or the sides, back or door of
    oven.

For best results, bake all doughs and batter with pans placed on
    rack about ⅓ from bottom of oven.

Better bake in two or three batches than overcrowd and spoil all
    efforts.

REFERENCE CHART FOR BAKING

Food	Oven Temp Degrees F.	Time
Cakes		
Angel	325	45–50 minutes
Chocolate	350	30–35 minutes for layers, 40–45 minutes for sheet
Cupcakes	375	20–25 minutes
Fruit cake (large)	275	3–4 hours
Fruit cake (small)	300	2–3 hours
Layers (except chocolate)	375	25–30 minutes
Loaf	350	45–60 minutes
Sheet	350	35–45 minutes
Quick breads		
Biscuits	425	12–15 minutes
Coffee cake	400	20–30 minutes
Corn bread	425	20–30 minutes
Gingerbread	350	30–40 minutes
Muffins	425	20–25 minutes
Popovers	425	45–50 minutes
Quick loaf breads	350	60–70 minutes
Yeast breads		
Brown 'n' serve rolls	425	12–15 minutes
Plain unbaked rolls	425	20–25 minutes
Plain unbaked sweet rolls	400	20–30 minutes
Pies		
Custard	400	20–30 minutes
Fruit	425	45–55 minutes
Pastry shells	425	12–15 minutes
Pumpkin	400	40–50 minutes
Ready-prepared frozen pies	425	45–50 minutes

POINTERS FOR DEEP FAT FRYING

Oil or vegetable shortening are most satisfactory fats to use for deep
   frying.
Allow enough deep hot fat to float food.
Never fill kettle more than two-thirds full.
Have foods at room temperature. Chilled food cools fat unnecessarily.
Adding food a few pieces at a time prevents excessive cooling of fat.
Drain fried foods on paper toweling after frying.
Foods may be pre-fried and reheated or kept warm in oven on
   broiling pans, uncovered, at 300° to 350°.
When frying potatoes, first drain well to remove excess moisture.
When breading foods to be fried, dip in beaten egg, then seasoned
   flour, again in egg and then crumbs. Let stand 30 minutes or
   more for breading to set before frying. Shake to remove loose
   crumbs, which cause fat to breakdown.

REFERENCE CHART FOR DEEP FAT FRYING

Food	Temperature Degrees F.	By Browning Bread Cube	Total Time In Minutes
Croquettes	390	40 seconds	1–3
Doughnuts	370	60 seconds	3–5
Fish			
Clams	390	40 seconds	1–2
Crab legs	370	60 seconds	3–5
Fillets	370	60 seconds	4–6
Fish balls	375	55 seconds	2–5
Frog's legs	390	40 seconds	2–3
Oysters	390	40 seconds	2–3
Scallops	380	50 seconds	2–3
Shrimp	375	55 seconds	4–5
Smelt	390	40 seconds	3–5
Trout	375	55 seconds	4–6
Fritters	370	60 seconds	3–5
Meats			
Breaded Cutlets	370	60 seconds	8–10
Onion rings	390	40 seconds	3–5
Potatoes	375	55 seconds	5–8

POINTERS FOR BROILING

Arrange food on broiling rack with space between pieces.

Broil with oven door ajar to permit air circulation. Otherwise, meats are roasted at high temperature, not broiled.

To obtain deep charcoal brown, broil with meats closer to broiler heat. (Smoke and odor are greater, however, from hot spattering fat.)

To broil steaks at varying degrees of doneness, start at proper times for each, marking steaks or arranging so that you know which are rare, medium and well done, respectively.

Only tender cuts of meat are suitable for broiling.

If meat is lean, brush with butter or oil before broiling and when turning.

Use tongs or pancake turner to turn meat. Piercing with fork permits juices to escape.

REFERENCE CHART FOR BROILING

Food	Thickness	Distance from Top of Food to Broiler	Total Time in Minutes (Cook Till Brown about Half the Total Time, Turn and Finish)
Bacon	Thin slices	5 inches	8
Canadian bacon	½ inch	3 inches	10
Chicken halves	1½ lb., split	8 inches	30
Chicken pieces	2-2½ lb. birds	8 inches	30
Fish steaks	¾ inch	3 inches	12–15
Ham, tenderized	½ inch slices	3 inches	12–15
	1 inch slices	3 inches	15–20
Hamburgers	1 inch	3 inches	15–20 (well done)
Kebabs	1½ inch cubes	3 inches	25–30
Lamb chops	1½ inch	3 inches	20–30
Steaks	1 inch	2 inches	12–15 (rare)
	1 inch	3 inches	15–18 (medium)
	1 inch	4 inches	20–25 (well done)
	1½ inch	3 inches	12–15 (rare)
	1½ inch	4 inches	18–20 (medium)
	1½ inch	5 inches	25–30 (well done)

POINTERS FOR ROASTING
Roasting time is for chilled meat from refrigerator.

All cuts listed are to be cooked on rack (except for standing rib roast, which has its ribs as a natural rack) in a shallow pan, with the fatter side up, uncovered and unbasted.

Beef tenderloin and all cuts of veal are somewhat lean and should be rubbed with fat or stripped with suet or bacon before roasting.

Allow 10 to 15 minutes for meat to "set" after roasting for easier carving, removing meat from oven to top of stove or other warm-not-hot area.

To obtain accurate results with meat thermometer, insert so that point reaches center of the largest muscle and is not in contact with bone, gristle or fat.

If meat is done prior to serving time and needs to be kept warm, cover loosely with aluminum foil. Do not seal meat with foil as this steams it, tending to make it stringy.

Total cooking times vary somewhat with general density of roasts. Chunky cuts will require a longer cooking time than the same style roast cut in longer, thinner manner.

Test for doneness by piercing meat with 2-tine fork. Meat should be tender, brown and juicy. Lack of juices indicates overcooking.

NOTE: Times given apply to each roast. Two roasts of 5 pounds each are to be cooked the same total time as one roast of 5 pounds, for example, even though they are cooked together in one oven.

REFERENCE CHART FOR ROASTING MEAT

Meat	Cut	Weight Lbs. of Ea. Cut	Oven Temp. Degrees F.	Meat Thermometer Degrees F. (Interior of Meat)	Doneness	Total Time in Hours
Beef	Standing 3-rib	6–8	300	140	Rare	2–3
		6–8	300	160	Medium	2½–3
		6–8	300	170	Well	3–4
	7-rib	20–25	250	125	Rare	4½
		20–25	250	140	Medium	5
		20–25	250	150	Well	6
	Rolled rib	6–7	300	140	Rare	3
		6–7	300	160	Medium	3¼
		6–7	300	170	Well	4
		16–18	250	150	Well	7–8
	Rump (high quality)	5–7	300	140	Rare	2½
		5–7	300	160	Medium	3
		5–7	300	170	Well	3½
	Sirloin tip (high quality)	4–6	300	140	Rare	2½
		4–6	300	160	Medium	3
		4–6	300	170	Well	3½
	Whole round (rump and shank off)	50	250	140	Medium	10
		50	250	155	Well	11–12
	Whole tenderloin	3–4	325	140	Rare	1½
		3–4	325	160	Medium	2
		3–4	325	170	Well	2¼
Ham	Whole	10–12	325	160	Well	3–3½
	Whole	14–16	325	160	Well	4¼
	Half	6–8	325	160	Well	2½
	Picnic	6–8	325	160	Well	3½–4

REFERENCE CHART FOR ROASTING MEAT CONT'D

Meat	Cut	Weight Lbs. of Ea. Cut	Oven Temp. Degrees F.	Meat Thermometer Degrees F. (Interior of Meat)	Doneness	Total Time in Hours
Lamb	Leg	6–7	300	170	Well	3–3½
	Rolled	4–5	300	170	Well	2½–3
	Shoulder	4–5	300	170	Well	2½–3
Pork	Leg	6–8	350	185	Well	4–4½
	Leg	10–12	350	185	Well	6–7
	Leg	12–14	350	185	Well	7–7½
	Loin	4–5	350	185	Well	3
	Loin	8–10	350	185	Well	4
Leg, loin or shoulder	Boned and rolled	10–12	350	185	Well	6–7
	Shoulder	4–6	350	185	Well	3½–4
	Shoulder	12–14	350	185	Well	6½–7
Veal	Leg	7–8	325	180	Well	3–3½
	Leg	14–16	325	180	Well	5–6
	Loin	4–5	325	180	Well	2½–3
	Rack (4-6 ribs)	2½–3	325	180	Well	1½–1¾
	Rolled shoulder	5	325	180	Well	3½–4
	Shoulder	9–10	325	180	Well	6–7
	Shoulder	7	325	180	Well	3–4
	Shoulder	12–13	325	180	Well	5–5½
	Whole Round (rump and shank off)	20	325	180	Well	6½

Roasting time is for chilled meat from refrigerator.

POINTERS FOR ROASTING POULTRY

Frozen poultry should be thawed slowly in refrigerator, allowing 24 to 36 hours.

Rapid thawing at room temperature draws out more juices.

Roast poultry on rack in open pan. Spread surface with fat, then cover loosely with foil or cheesecloth. Turkey is more juicy if roasted with breast side down.

Use meat thermometer or test by pressing thickest part of drumstick, which should feel tender. Remove from oven at least 30 minutes before serving to allow to "set" so that poultry will carve more easily.

UNSTUFFED POULTRY: Allow approximately 5 minutes per pound less time for roasting.

Variations in individual birds may necessitate shortening or lengthening suggested roasting times slightly. Time is based on refrigerator-chilled poultry.

Duck and goose normally are stuffed after half the cooking time is complete, to prevent the dressing from becoming too saturated with fat.

All poultry has a more tender skin if salt and other seasonings are added to the outside after half the cooking time has elapsed.

CAUTION: No poultry should be stuffed until just before roasting. It can cause food poisoning to do so. Once inside the bird, the moist mixture is an excellent breeding ground for bacteria. This applies to birds that are to be frozen also . . . do not stuff them until ready to roast.

In using meat thermometer with poultry, insert into center of thickest part of thigh muscle if unstuffed or into center of dressing, if stuffed. Be sure end of thermometer is not touching bone or cartilage.

To test for doneness, press thigh with fingers protected with cloth—meat should yield to touch; or move drumstick up and down—it should yield readily.

Whole birds are normally trussed by tying legs together and around tail and folding wings under so that tips rest on back of bird.

REFERENCE CHART FOR ROASTING POULTRY

Type	Weight	Oven Temp. Degrees F.	Meat Thermometer Degrees F.	Total Time in Hours
Chicken	4–5 lbs.	325	190	3–3½
Duck (domestic)	4–5 lbs.	325	190	3
Goose (domestic)	8–10 lbs.	325	190	4–4½
Turkey	6–8 lbs.	325	190	3½–4½
	8–10 lbs.	325	190	4–4½
	10–12 lbs.	325	190	4½–5
	12–14 lbs.	325	190	5–5¼
	14–16 lbs.	325	190	5¼–6
	16–18 lbs.	325	190	6–6½
	18–20 lbs.	325	190	6½–7½
	20–24 lbs.	325	190	7½–9
(Halves or quarters)	5–8 lbs.	325	190	3½–4
	8–12 lbs.	325	190	4–5
(Boned and rolled)	5–7 lbs.	350	190	3–3½
	7–9 lbs.	350	190	3½–4

POINTERS FOR COOKING VEGETABLES

Cook vegetables in small amounts of boiling, salted water. If so-
called "strong" flavored vegetables such as cabbage, cauliflower, onions and turnips are quite mature, cooking in larger
amounts of water, uncovered, makes flavor milder.

Times stated are from time vegetables begin to boil. Once boiling
point is reached, heat should be reduced so vegetables simmer.

In cooking very large amounts of vegetables, stop cooking before
completely done. Stored heat will complete cooking. Otherwise,
they will be overdone.

Seasoning vegetables with BOTH salt and sugar improves flavor and
tenderness. Use 1 teaspoon salt and 1 tablespoon sugar to 1
quart water.

FROZEN VEGETABLES: Follow package directions or use timetable above, allowing shortest cooking time. Vegetables should
be cooked in frozen state, not defrosted before cooking.

Basic facts about wine service are condensed in the following charts
for ready reference. They were developed by Wine Institute
of California and are reproduced with their permission, which is
gratefully acknowledged.

REFERENCE CHART FOR COOKING VEGETABLES

Food	Style	Total Time
Artichokes	Whole, fresh	30–45 minutes
Asparagus	Spears, fresh	10–15 minutes
Green beans	Cut or snapped, fresh	10–15 minutes
	Frenched, fresh	5–10 minutes
	Whole, fresh	15–20 minutes
Beets	Whole, fresh (diced or sliced after cooking)	45–60 minutes
Broccoli	Spears, fresh	15–20 minutes
Brussels sprouts		15–20 minutes
Cabbage	Wedges, fresh	8–10 minutes
Carrots	Diced, fresh	5–10 minutes
	Sliced, fresh	10–15 minutes
	Whole, fresh	20–30 minutes
Cauliflower	Flowerettes, fresh	8–10 minutes
	Whole, fresh	20–30 minutes
Corn	On cob, fresh	8–10 minutes
	Kernel, fresh	5–10 minutes
Eggplant	Diced, fresh	10–15 minutes
	Sliced, fresh	8–10 minutes
	Whole, stuffed	45–60 minutes
Lima beans	Fresh	30–40 minutes
Onions	Whole, fresh	15–20 minutes
Parsnips	Sliced, fresh	15–20 minutes
	Halved, fresh	30–40 minutes
Peas	Fresh	8–10 minutes
Potatoes	Whole	30–45 minutes
Spinach	Fresh	5 minutes
Squash	Sliced summer, fresh	10–15 minutes
	Winter, halved, fresh	30–45 minutes
Turnips	Diced or sliced, fresh	5–10 minutes
	Whole, fresh	20–35 minutes

WINES AND WINE SERVING

ALL PURPOSE GLASS (9 oz.)	WINE TYPES	TRADITIONAL GLASSES
APPET-IZER WINES	SHERRY VERMOUTH FLAVORED WINES	2½ to 4-ounce capacity
RED DINNER WINES (INCLUDING ROSE WINE)	BURGUNDY Pinot Noir (pea-no no-ahr') CLARET Cabernet (kab-er-nay') Zinfandel (zin'-fan-dell) "VINO" TYPES (vee-no) ROSE (Pink) (roh-zay') Red Chianti (kee-ahn'-tee)	6 to 9-ounce capacity
WHITE DINNER WINES	SAUTERNE (so-tairn') Semillon (say'-mee-yonh) Sauvignon Blanc (so-vee-nyonh blanh) RHINE WINE Riesling (reez'-ling) Sylvaner (sil-vah'-ner) CHABLIS (shah-blee') Pinot Blanc (pea-no blanh) Chardonnay (shar-doh-nay')	5 to 8-oz. capacity Rhine Wines Other White Wines
DESSERT WINES	PORT MUSCATEL (muss-kah-tell') TOKAY (toh-kay') CREAM (SWEET) SHERRY	2½ to 4-ounce capacity
SPARK-LING WINES	CHAMPAGNE (sham-pain') Brut (very dry) (brewt) Sec (semi-dry) (sehk) Doux (sweet) (doo) SPARKLING BURGUNDY	5 to 8-oz. Saucer Tulip

Wine experts agree that no wine glass should ever be filled completely. Air space left above the wine helps to concentrate the wine's bouquet, to add to your enjoyment. It is recommended that you fill the glasses to the levels shown above. Levels in the all-purpose glass in the left-hand column show the usual amount served of each wine type, when this glass is used.

WINE AND FOOD COMBINATIONS

APPETIZER WINES SUCH AS: Sherry Vermouth Flavored Wines	Serve chilled, without food or with HORS d'OEUVRE NUTS, CHEESES
RED DINNER WINES SUCH AS: Burgundy Claret Rosé (Pink)	Serve at cool room temperature, with HEARTY DISHES: STEAKS, CHOPS, ROASTS, GAME, CHEESE DISHES, SPAGHETTI (Serve Rosé chilled, with any food)
WHITE DINNER WINES SUCH AS: Chablis Rhine Wine Sauterne	Serve well chilled, with LIGHTER DISHES: CHICKEN, FISH, SHELLFISH, OMELETS, ANY WHITE MEATS
DESSERT WINES SUCH AS: Port Muscatel Tokay Cream (Sweet) Sherry	Serve chilled or at cool room temperature, with FRUITS, COOKIES, NUTS, CHEESES, FRUIT CAKES, POUND CAKE
SPARKLING WINES SUCH AS: Champagne Sparkling Burgundy	Serve well chilled, with any food: APPETIZERS, THE MAIN COURSE, OR DESSERTS (And especially good in festive party punches)

THE WINE GROWERS OF CALIFORNIA

INDEX

A

Almond-Chicken Salad, 286
  Grape-, Supreme, 287
Ambrosia, Heavenly, 149
Anchovy-Parsley Salad Dressing, 293
Angel Cake, Baking Chart, 341
Angel Loaf Cake, Chocolate Whipped
  Cream-Filled, 126
Appetizers and First Courses, 71–80
  Avocado Dip, 72
  Avocado-Stuffed Celery Sticks, 72–73
  Bacon-Broiled Prune Garnish, 73
  Bacon-Cheese Canapés, 78–79
  Caraway-Cottage Cheese Sticks, 74–75
  Celery Stuffed with Avocado, 72–73
  Celery Stuffed with Blue Cheese, 75
  Cheese, Celery Stuffed with Blue, 75
  Cheese-Bacon Canapés, 78–79
  Cheese Balls, 73–74
    Gourmet, 77
    Pimento, 90
  Cheese-Ham Deviled Deckers, 76–77
  Cheese Puffs, Broiled, 74
  Cheese Sticks, 75–76
    Caraway, 74–75
  Crab Roll-Ups, 76
  Ham-Cheese Deviled Deckers, 76–77
  Ham-Filled Cream Puffs, 77–78
  Ham and Liver Pâté, 79–80
  Meat Balls, 71
  Melon Cup, 79
  Pineapple Strawberry Kebabs, 80
  Prune Garnish, Bacon-Broiled, 73
  Wines, 81, 354
Apple Crisp, 163
Apple Crunch à la Mode, 163–64
Apple Pie, Deep-Dish, 178
Apple Salads: Cinnamon, with Cheese
  Balls, 274
  Cranberry, 261
    Molded, 261
  Grape Mandarin Nut Compote, 275
  Pineapple and Mandarin Orange, 268
  Waldorf, 276–77
Apples: Cinnamon, 256
  in Port, Baked, 164
Applesauce: Bars, 137
  Quantity of Apples for 24 Servings,
    65
Apricot Cranberry Molded Salad, 261–
  62

Apricot Loaf, 102
Apricots, for 24 Servings, 65
Asparagus: Amandine, 320–21
  for 24 Servings, 66
At Home Parties, 5–8
  Menu for 24 Servings, 47
Avocado Dip, 72
Avocado Filling for Sandwiches, 301
Avocado Grapefruit Salad, 275
Avocado-Stuffed Celery Sticks, 72–73

B

Bacon: Broiling, 345
  -Cheese Canapés, 78–79
  Crab Roll-ups with, 76
  Prune Garnish with, 73
Baking, 340. *See also* Cakes
  Reference Chart for, 341
Banana Bread, 101
Bananas: à l'Orange, 165–66
  for 24 Servings, 65
Barbecue Menus, 31, 33, 45, 51
Barbecued Chicken: Aloha, 245–46
  Charcoal or Oven, 247–48
Barbecued Hamburgers, Oven-, 308
Barbecued Spareribs, 240–41
Bavarian Cream, Orange Rum, 153
Beans: Amandine, Green, 320–21
  Baked, 314–15
    Swedish, 315–16
    Vintner's, 316
  Caesar, Green, 321
  Chili con Carne, 217–18
  Harvest Casserole with, 323
  Lyonnaise, Green, 321–22
  with Mushrooms, Green, 322
  Preparing Dry for Use, 218
  Quantity of Dried, 24 Servings, 67
  Quantity of Green, 24 Servings, 66
  Ratatouille with Lima, 328n
  Salad, 3-, 279
  Vegetable Salad Platter with, 281–82
  à la Victor, Green, 320
  with Water Chestnuts, Green, 322–23
Beef, 212–14
  Broiling Chart, 345
  Carving, 206ff.
  Chili con Carne, 217–18
  Corned, 218

Creamed Chipped, with Mushrooms, 219
Goulash, Hungarian, 219–20
Hamburgers: Chili, 306
  Hot Dog, 307–8
  Oven-Barbecued, 308
Lasagne, 222
Meat Balls: Appetizer, 71
  Burgundy, 215–16
  Epicurean, 212
  Oriental, 213
  Swedish, 225–26
Meat Loaf, 223
Meat Sauce, Italian, 220
Pie with Cornmeal Biscuits, 233–34
Pot Roast, Carving, 208
Pot Roast with Brown Gravy, 223–24
Pot Roast with Wine, 224
Quantity for 24 Servings, 64
Roasting Chart, 347
Rolled Roast, Carving, 206
Sandwiches, 300. See also Hamburgers
Sirloin Tips, Burgundy, 216–17
Skewered Cubes with Mushrooms, 234
Standing Rib Roast, Carving, 207
Stew, Burgundy, 237
Stew, Oxtail, 217
Stroganoff, 214
Tamale Pie, 227
Teriyaki, 228
Tongue, Boiled, 215
Beer, Frankfurters in, 229
Beet Salad, Molded, 272–73
Beets: Pickled, 258
  Quantity for 24 Servings, 66
  Vegetable Salad Platter with, 281–82
Beverages, 81–88
  Champagne Punch, 84
  Coffee, 83
  Fruit Punch, 85
  Mulled Punch, Hot, 86
  Quantity Chart, 63
  Rum Punch, 87
  Tea, 83–84
  Tomato Juice: Hot, 87
    Spiced, 86
  Wassail Bowl, 88
  Wine Punch, 88
  Wine Reference Chart, 81–82
  Wines and Wine Serving, 352–54
Biscuit Tortoni, 156–57
Biscuits, 95–97
  Basic, 95–96
  Cornmeal, 96–97
  Orange Tea, 96
  Quantity of Mix, 24 Servings, 67
  Reference Chart for Baking, 341
Black Bottom Pie, 176–77

Blintzes, Cheese, 188
Blueberry Crisp, 166
Blueberry Muffins, 106
Blueberry-Peach Parfait, 158–59
Boston Brown Bread, 97
Bouillon, Tomato, 312–13
Bran Muffins, 104–5
Braunschweiger Sandwiches, 301
Breads, 89–115
  Apricot, 102
  Baked Bread Specialties, 89–91
  Banana, 101
  Biscuits, 95–97
    Reference Chart for Baking, 341
  Blueberry Muffins, 106
  Boston Brown, 97
  Bran Muffins, 104–5
  Breakfast, 91–95
  Buttermilk Pancakes, 92
  Candied Fruit, 102
  Cheese, Parmesan French Bread, 89–90
  Cheese-Mustard French, 89
  Cheese Sticks, 98
  Cheese Topping for, Pimento, 90
  Cherry Muffins, 106
  Cinnamon Coffee Cake, 110
  Coffee Cake: Cinnamon, 110
    Orange, 107–8
    Reference Chart for Baking, 341
    Spicy, 108–9
  Corn, 98–99
    Reference Chart for Baking, 341
    Sesame, 99
  Cornmeal Biscuits, 96–97
  Corn Muffins, 105–6
  Currant Muffins, 106
  Date, 102–3
  Date Muffins, 106
  Dinner Rolls, 110–11
  French Toast, 94
  Frozen, 15–16
  Muffins, 104–7
    Reference Chart for Baking, 341
  Nut Muffins, 106
  Orange, 103
  Orange Coffee Cake, 107–8
  Orange Tea Biscuits, 96
  Pancakes, 93. See also Crepes
    Buttermilk, 92
    from Commercial Mix, 93
  Popovers, Baking Chart, 341
  Quantity for 24 Servings, 67
  Quick Breads and Biscuits, 95–100
    Reference Chart for Baking, 341
  Quick Coffee Cakes, 107–9
  Quick Fruit Breads, 101–3
  Raisin Muffins, 106
  Refrigerator Rolls, 112
  Refrigerator Sweet Dough, 109

Rolls, 110–14
  Reference Chart for Baking, 341
Scones, 100
Sesame Corn, 99
Spicy Coffee Cake, 108–9
Stollen, 114–15
Toast Baskets, 91
Toast, French, 94
Waffles Supreme, 95
Wheat Muffins, 106–7
Yeast, 109–15
  Reference Chart for Baking, 341
Breakfast Breads, 91–95
Breakfast Menus, 35, 46, 48–49, 59
Broccoli and Ham or Turkey en Cas-
  serole, 230
Broiling, 344
  Reference Chart for, 345
Brown Gravy, 224
Brownies, 138
  Blond, 139
Brunch Menus: for 12 Servings, 29
  for 12 or 48 Servings, 36–37
  for 24 Servings, 39, 40, 46
  for 48 Servings, 48–49, 59
Buffet Menus: for 12 Servings, 30
  for 12 or 48 Servings, 32ff.
  for 24 Servings, 36, 38ff.
  for 48 Servings, 49ff.
Butter, for 24 Servings, 67
Butter Frosting, Orange, 119
Buttermilk Pancakes, 92
Buttermilk Rolls, Quick, 111
Butterscotch Bars, 139

C

Caesar Salad, 278
Cakes, 117–34. See also Coffee Cakes
  Cheesecake, 134
  Chocolate, 122
    Reference Chart for Baking, 341
  Chocolate Whipped Cream-Filled An-
    gel Loaf, 126
  Cupcakes, 126–27
    Reference Chart for Baking, 341
  Cutting Guide, 116
    for Tiered Cake, 131–32
  Dessert Specialties Made with, 126–34
  Frostings, 135–37. See also Frostings
  Frozen, 15–16
  Gingerbread, Baking Chart for, 341
  Gingerbread, Tropical, 117–18
  Lazy-Daisy, 123–24
  Lemon, 124
  Meringue Toppings for, 123–24, 125
  from Mixes, 123–25
  Orange, 118–19
  Orange Layer, 127–28

Pans, 20
Petits Fours, 128–30
Pineapple Icebox, 161
Pineapple Meringue Torte, 124–25
Pound, 119–20
  Quantity for 24 Servings, 67
  Reference Chart for Baking, 341
  Spice, 120
Strawberry Glazed Cheesecake, 133–34
Strawberry Shortcake, 134
Tiered, 130–33
White, 121
Yellow Layer, 122
Can Sizes, 68
Canapés. See also Sandwiches
  Hot Bacon-Cheese, 78–79
Cantaloupe. See Melon
Caramel Frosting, 135
Caraway Cottage Cheese Sticks, 74–75
Carrots, Glazed 318
  with Small White Onions, 318–19
  Quantity for 24 Servings, 66
  Vegetable Salad Platter with, 281–82
Cauliflower, for 24 Servings, 66
Celery: for 24 Servings, 66
  Stuffed with Avocado 72–73
  Stuffed with Blue Cheese, 75
Celery Seed Honey Dressing, 295–96
Cereals, Quantity for 24 Servings, 67
Champagne Punch, 84
Charlotte Russe, 145
Checkerboard Sandwiches, 303
Cheese: Bacon Canapés, 78–79
  Balls, 73–74
    Cinnamon Apple salad with, 274
    Gourmet, 77
    Pimento, 90
  Blintzes with Sour Cream, 188
  Cake, Strawberry Glazed, 133–34
  Celery Stuffed with Blue, 75
  Deviled Deckers, 76–77
  Dressing: Blue, 293–94
    Blue-Sour Cream, 298
    Cream, 294
    Roquefort, Rosy, 296–97
    Roquefort-Sour Cream, 298
  Finger Rolls Stuffed with, 306
  Flounder Rolls Rarebit, 195
  French Bread with Mustard and, 89
  French Bread with Parmesan, 89–90
  Italian Pizza, 221–22
  Lasagne, 222
  Lenten Dinner Casserole, 192
  and Macaroni, High-Hat, 191
  Menus Featuring, 29, 36–37
  Mushrooms Stuffed with, 324
  and Olive Spread for Sandwiches, 302
  Puffs, Broiled, 74
  Quantity for 24 Servings, 67

Salad: Mold, Cottage, 270
  Mold, Pineapple-Lime-Cottage, 267
  Vegetable, Jellied Cottage, 273–74
Soufflé, 189
Sticks, 75–76, 98
  Caraway Cottage, 74–75
Topping for Bread, Pimento, 90
Cherries Jubilee, 157
Cherry Muffins, 106
Cherry Upside-down Pudding, 167
Chicken, 245–54. *See also* Poultry
  Alexandria, 248–49
  Barbecued, Aloha, 245–46
  Barbecued, Charcoal or Oven, 247–48
  Broiling Chart, 345
  en Casserole, 249
  Coq au Vin Rouge, 253–54
  Curried, Bombay, 241
  Fried, Oven-, 253–54
  -Ham Supreme, 250
  à la King, 254
  Livers Sauté, 250–51
  Menus Featuring, 31, 37–39, 50–52
  Polynesian, 251–52
  Quantity for 24 Servings, 64
  Salad: Almond-, 286
    Almond-Grape, Supreme, 287
    Mold, 289
  Sandwiches, 300, 302–3
  Sauté, 252
Chili Beefburger, 306
Chili con Carne, 217–18
Chocolate, for 24 Servings, 63
Chocolate Brownies, 138
Chocolate Cake, 122
  Peppermint Icebox Log, 160
  Reference Chart for Baking, 341
  Whipped Cream-Filled Angel Loaf, 126
Chocolate Chip Cookies, 140
Chocolate Glaze, 135
Chocolate Mousse, 145–46
  Mint, 146
Chocolate Pie: Black Bottom, 176–77
  Chiffon, 177–78
    Mocha, 181–82
    Rum, 184
Chocolate Pudding, Upside-down, 168
Chocolate Sauce, 162
Chocolate Spanish Cream, 147
Chop Suey Amandine, Pork, 238
Chowder, Clam, 310–11
Cinnamon Apple Salad, 274
Cinnamon Apples, 256
Cinnamon Coffee Cake, 110
Cinnamon Crescent Cookies, Mexican, 143
Clam Chowder, 310–11
Clams, Deep Fat Frying, 343
Cloverleaf Rolls, 113

Cocktail Party Menus, 47, 59
Cocktail Supper Menus, 33, 38, **57,** 60
Coffee, 83
  Quantity for 24 Servings, 63
Coffee Cake, 107–9
  Cinnamon, 110
  Orange, 107–8
  Reference Chart for Baking, 341
  Spicy, 108–9
  Stollen, 114–15
Coffee Soufflé, 147–48
Cole Slaw: with Cherry Tomatoes, 280–81
  in Lettuce Cups, 280
  Quantity of Cabbage, 24 Servings, 66
  Sour Cream, 281
Commercial Food Enterprises, **14**
Cookies, 137–44
  Applesauce Bars, 137
  Brownies, 138
  Butterscotch Bars, 139
  Chocolate Chip, 140
  Cinnamon Crescent, Mexican, 143
  Crumb Crust Made of, 174
  Date Squares, 140–41
  Matrimonial Bars, 142
  Punch Bowl, 143–44
  Quantity for 24 Servings, 67
  Spanish Sticks, 144
  Spice Bar, Glazed, 141–42
Corn. *See also* Corn Bread; Cornmeal
  Chips, Quantity for 24 Servings, 68
  Fritters, 319
  Muffins, 105–6
  Quantity for 24 Servings, 66
Corn Bread, 98–99
  Reference Chart for Baking, 341
  Sesame, 99
Cornmeal. *See also* Corn; Corn Bread
  Biscuits, 96–97
  Tamale Pie, 227
Crab: Cocktail, Servings of, 27
  Cocktail, Red Sauce for, 258–59
  Deep Fat Frying of Legs, 343
  Louis, 287–88
  Molded Seafood Salad with, 292
  Roll-ups, 76
  Suzettes, 194–95
Cranberries, Quantity for 24 Servings of Sauce, 65
Cranberry Relish, Horseradish, 256–57
Cranberry Salad: Apple, 261
    Mold, 260
  Apricot, Molded, 261–62
  Orange Mold, Fruited Frozen, 263
  Port Wine Mold, 267–68
Cream, Quantity for 24 Servings, 67
Cream Dressing, Sour, 298
Cream Puffs, Ham-Filled, 77–78
Crepes: Breakfast, 91–92
  Crab Suzettes, 194–95

Crescent Cookies, Mexican Cinnamon, 143
Crescent Rolls, 113
Croquettes, Frying, 343
Croutons, 278
Crumb Crust, 174
Crumb Topping for Coffee Cake, 108
Cucumber Grapefruit Mold, 263
Cucumber Lime Vegetable Salad, 270–71
Cucumbers with Onions, Marinated, 282–83
Cucumber with Tomato Aspic Rings, 272
Cucumber and Tomato Salads, 279–80, 282
Cupcakes: Miniature, 126–27
    Reference Chart for Baking, 341
Curlicue Rolls, 113
Currant Muffins, 106
Curried Eggs, 190–91
Curry, Bombay Chicken, 246
Custard Pies, Baking Chart, 341
Custard Sauce, 155, 171–72

D

Date Bread, 102–3
Date Muffins, 106
Date Squares, 140–41
Decorating Icing, 130, 136
Deep Fat Frying, 342
    Reference Chart for, 343
Delmonico Potatoes, 327–28
Dessert Wines, 82, 354
Desserts, 117–87
    Apple Crisp, 163
    Apple Crunch à la Mode, 163–64
    Apples in Port, Baked, 164
    Bananas à l'Orange, 165–66
    Biscuit Tortoni, 156–57
    Blueberry Crisp, 166
    Blueberry-Peach Parfait, 158–59
    Cake, Specialties Made with, 126–34
    Cakes, 117–87. See also Cakes
    Charlotte Russe, 145
    Cherries Jubilee, 157
    Cherry Upside-Down Pudding, 167
    Chilled, 145–56
    Chocolate Icebox Log, Peppermint, 160
    Chocolate Mousse, 145–46
        Mint, 146
    Chocolate Spanish Cream, 147
    Chocolate Upside-Down Pudding, 168
    Coffee Soufflé, 147–48
    Cookies, 137–44. See also Cookies

    Frozen, 156–62
    Fruited Caliloupe Mold, 148–49
    Fruits, Baked, 165
    Heavenly Ambrosia, 149
    Ice Cream Balls, 158
    Lemon Cream, Frozen, 157–58
    Lemon Crunch Pudding, 150
    Lemon Snow, 150–51
    Melon: Balls with Sherbet, 160–61
        Balls in Watermelon Shell, 170
        Mold, Fruited Cantaloupe, 148–49
        Mold, Strawberry, 155
    Mocha Soufflé, 152
    Orange Peaches, Glazed, 168–69
    Orange Puff, Tropical, 156
    Orange Rum Bavarian, 153
    Pastry and Pie Crusts, 174–75
    Peach-Blueberry Parfait, 158–59
    Peach Crisp, 169
    Peaches, Glazed Orange, 168–69
    Peaches Melba, 159
    Pears à la Cumberland, 153–54
    Pears with Custard Sauce, 154–55
    Pears Rosé, 170–71
    Peppermint Chocolate Icebox Log, 160
    Peppermint Parfait, 162
    Pies, 176–87. See also Pies
    Pineapple Icebox Cake, 161
    Rum Bavarian, Orange, 153
    Sauces, 171–73
    Strawberry Melon Mold, 155
Deviled Deckers, Ham-Cheese, 76–77
Dinner Rolls, 110–11
Dip, Avocado, 72
    Quantity for 24 servings, 67
Doughnuts, Frying, 343
Duck: Menu Featuring, 32
    Quantity for 24 Servings, 64
    Roasting, 349
    Wild Roast, 253

E

Egg Nog Chiffon Pie, 179
Egg Salad Squares, Deviled, 290
Eggs: Cheese Soufflé, 189
    Curried, 190–91
    Florentine, 189–90
    Scrambled, 192–93
Equipment, 17–22

F

Fan Tan Rolls, 113
Father-Son Banquet, Menu for, 45
Figure 8 Rolls, 113
Finger Sandwiches, 304

Fish, 194–204. *See also* specific fish
  Cocktails, Servings of, 27
  Deep Fat Frying, 343
  Fillet with White Wine, 202
  Menus Featuring, 32, 40–41, 49–50
  Quantity Chart, 64
  Steaks, Broiling Chart, 345
  Stroganoff, Baked, 196
Flounder Rolls Rarebit, 195
Fondant Frosting, 136–37
Food Preparation,
  for At Home Parties, 7–8
  and Equipment, 20
  for Organizational Events, 11–12
Food Purchasing. *See also* Quantity
    Charts
  for At Home Parties, 7
  for Organizational Events, 10–11
Frankfurters: in Beer, 229
  Hot Dog Hamburgers, 307–8
  for 24 Servings, 65
French Dressing, 294
  Garlic, 294
French Onion Soup, 310
French Toast, 94
  Oven, 94
Fritters, Corn, 319
  Frying, 343
Frog's Legs, Deep Fat Frying, 343
Frostings, 135–37
  Caramel, 135
  Chocolate Glaze, 135
  Decorator's Icing, 130, 136
  Fondant, 136–37
  Orange, 127–28
  Orange Butter, 119
  Tiered Cake, 131
  White, 129
Frozen Foods. *See also* specific foods
  Freezer-Filling Cooking, 15–16
Fruit. *See also* Apples
  Baked, 165
  Breads, 101–3
  Cake, Reference Chart for Baking,
    341
  Caliloupe Mold, Fruited, 148–49
  Frozen, Quantity, 24 Servings, 66
  Juices, Quantity, 24 Servings, 63
  Pies, Deep-Dish, 178
  Pies, Baking Chart, 341
  Punch, 85
  Preserving Values of, 25–26
  Quantity Charts, 65–66
  Salad: Frozen or Molded, 260–69
    Mixed, 274–77

G

Garlic French Dressing, 294
Gingerbread, Baking Chart for, 341
  Tropical, 117–18

Glaze: Chocolate, 135
  Spicy, for Apples, 164
  Strawberry, 133–34
Glazed Orange Peaches, 168–69
Glazed Spice Bar Cookies, 141–42
Goose: Menu Featuring, 32
  Quantity for 24 Servings, 64
  Roasting, 349
  Wild Roast, 255
Grapefruit: Avocado Salad, 275
  Cucumber Mold, 263
  Harlequin Salad with, 264–65
  Molded Salad, 264
  Quantity for 24 Servings, 65
Grapes: Melon Cup with, 79
  Quantity for 24 Servings, 65
  Salad: Almond-Chicken, Supreme,
    287
  Apple   Mandarin   Nut   Compote,
    Honeyed, 275
  Pear, 276
Gravy: Brown, 224
  Thickening with Cornstarch, 236
Green Goddess Dressing, 295
Green Salad, Tossed, 285–86

H

Halibut Stroganoff, Baked, 196
Ham, 229–32
  and Broccoli en Casserole, 230
  Broiling Chart, 345
  Carving, 209
  -Chicken Supreme, 250
  Cream Puffs Filled with, 77–78
  Deviled Deckers, Cheese, 76–77
  and Liver Pâté, 79–80
  Loaf, Molded, 290–91
  Loaf, Orange, 232
  Quantity for 24 Servings, 65
  Roasting Chart, 348
  Sandwiches, 300
    Buns, 307
  Slices with Peaches, Baked, 229–30
  Split Pea Soup with, 312
  -Veal Pot Pie, 231
Hamburgers: Broiling Chart, 345
  Chili Beefburger, 306
  Hot Dog, 307–8
  Oven-Barbecued, 308
Harlequin Salad, 264–65
Harvest Casserole, 323
Honey Celery Seed Dressing, 295–96
Honeyed Grape Apple Mandarin Nut
    Compote, 275
Horseradish Relish, Cranberry, 256–57
Hungarian Goulash, 219–20

I

Ice Cream: Apple Crunch à la Mode,
    163–64

Balls, 158
Biscuit Tortoni, 156–57
Cherries Jubilee, 157
Lemon Cream, 157–58
Peach-Blueberry Parfait, 158–59
Peaches Melba, 159
Peppermint Chocolate Icebox Log, 160
Peppermint Parfait, 162
Pineapple Icebox Cake, 161
Quantity for 24 Servings, 68
Icings. See Frostings
Italian Dressing, 296
Italian Meat Sauce, 220
Italian Pizza, 221–22

J

Jelly, Wine, with Fruit, 269

K

Kebabs: Broiling Chart, 345
Pineapple Strawberry, 80
Shish, 235
Skewered Vegetables, 323–24
Knots (Rolls), 113
Kugel, Mushroom Noodle, 193

L

Lamb, 233–37
Carving Leg of, 210
Chops, Broiling Chart, 345
Cubes with Mushrooms, Skewered, 234
Pie with Cornmeal Biscuits, 233–34
Quantity for 24 Servings, 65
Roasting Chart, 348
Shish Kebabs, 235
Stuffed Shoulder of, 236
Lasagne, 222
Lazy-Daisy Cake, 123–24
Lemon Cake, 124
Lemon Chiffon Pie, 179–80
Lemon Cream, Frozen, 157–58
Lemon Crunch Pudding, 150
Lemon Snow, 150–51
Lenten Dinner Casserole, 192
Lenten Supper Menu with Cheese, 29
Lettuce, for 24 Servings, 66
Lime Cucumber Vegetable Salad, 270–71
Lime Molded Salad, Pineapple-Cheese 267
Lime-Pear Salad, 265–66
Liver and Ham Pâté, 79–80

Livers Sauté, Chicken, 250–51
Liverwurst Filling for Sandwiches, 301
Lucky Clover Rolls, 113
Lyonnaise Green Beans, 321–22

M

Macaroni: and Cheese, High-Hat, 191
Equipment for, 21
Quantity for 24 Servings, 68
Salad, 283–84
Madrilene, Red and Green, 311–12
Maple Syrup, 257
Marshmallows, for 24 Servings, 68
Matrimonial Bars, 142
Mayonnaise, for 24 Servings, 68
Meat, 205–43. See also Beef
Balls: Appetizer, 71
Burgundy, 215–16
Epicurean, 213
Oriental, 213
Swedish, 225–26
Broiling, Pointers for, 344
Broiling, Reference Chart for, 345
Carving, 205–11
Cured, 229–32
Deep Fat Frying, 343
Loaf, 223
Menu for 12 Featuring, 30
Menus for 12 or 48 Featuring, 33–34
Menus for 24 Featuring, 41–47
Menus for 48 Featuring, 53–57
Pie with Cornmeal Biscuits, 233–34
Pizza with, 221–22
Quantity Chart, 64–65
Roasting, Pointers for, 346
Roasting, Reference Chart for, 347–48
Roasting Pans, 22
Sandwiches, 300
Sauce, Italian, 220
Wine Reference Chart and, 81–82
Melon: Balls with Sherbet, 160–61
Balls in Watermelon Shell, 170
Cup, 79
Fruited Caliloupe Mold, 148–49
Strawberry Mold, 155
Men, Luncheon Menus for, 34, 53, 57
Menus, 23–60
and At Home Party Planning, 6–7
for 48 Servings, 48–60
and Organizational Events, 10
for 12 Servings, 29–30
for 12 or 48 Servings, 31–35
for 24 Servings, 36–47
Use of, 3–4
Meringue: Pineapple Torte, 124–25
Schaum Torte, 185
Toppings for Cake, 123–24, 125

Mexican Cinnamon Crescent Cookies, 143
Milk: Quantity, 24 Servings, 63
  Substitution of Dry for Pancakes, 92
Mint. *See also* Peppermint
  Chocolate Mousse, 146
Minted Pears, Molded, 266–67
Mints, Quantity for 24 Servings, 68
Mocha Chiffon Pie, 180–81
  Chocolate, 181–82
Mocha Soufflé, 152
Mousse, Chocolate, 145–46
  Mint, 146
Muffins, 104–7
  Blueberry, 106
  Bran, 104–5
  Cherry, 106
  Corn, 105–6
  Currant, 106
  Date, 106
  Nut, 106
  Plain, 106
  Raisin, 106
  Reference Chart for Baking, 341
  Wheat, 106
Mulled Punch, Hot, 86
Mushroom Noodle Kugel Supreme, 193
Mushrooms: Creamed Chipped Beef with, 219
  Green Beans with, 322
  Skewered Lamb or Beef Cubes with, 234
  Stuffed, 324
Mustard-Cheese French Bread, 89
Mustard Sauce Supreme, 257–58

N

Noodles: Kugel Supreme, Mushroom, 193
  Lasagne, 222
  Lenten Dinner Casserole, 192
  Poppy Seed, 325
  Quantity for 24 Servings, 68
Nut Grape Apple Mandarin Compote, 275
Nut Muffins, 106
Nut Pastry Crust, 175
Nuts, Quantity for 24 Servings, 68

O

Olive-Cheese Spread for Sandwiches, 302
Olives, Quantity for 24 Servings, 68
Onion Rings, Deep Fat Frying, 343
Onion Soup, French, 310

Onions: and Carrots, Glazed, 318–19
  Marinated Cucumbers with, 282–83
  Peas with, 325
  and Peas, New Potatoes with, 326–27
Orange, Bananas à l', 165–66
Orange Bread, 103
Orange Cake, 118–19
Orange Coffee Cake, 107–8
Orange Cranberry Mold, Frozen, 263
Orange Frosting, 127–28
  Butter, 119
Orange Grape Apple Nut Compote, Honeyed Mandarin, 275
Orange Ham Loaf, 232
Orange Layer Cake, 127–28
Orange Peaches, Glazed, 168–69
Orange Puff, Tropical 156
Orange Rum Bavarian, 153
Orange Sauce, 172–73
Orange Tea Biscuits, 96
Oranges: Heavenly Ambrosia with, 149
  Quantity for 24 Servings, 65
  Sherried Apple Mold with Pineapple and Mandarin, 268
Organizational Events, 8–14
Oxtail Stew, Economical, 217
Oyster Stew, 311
Oysters: Deep Fat Frying, 343
  Quantity for 24 Servings, 64
  Shrimp Creamed with, 199–200

P

Pan Rolls, 113
Pancakes, 93. *See also* Blintzes; Crepes
  Buttermilk, 92
  from Commercial Mix, 93
  Potato, 329
Parfait: Peach-Blueberry, 158–59
  Peppermint, 162
Parker House Rolls, 114
Parsley-Anchovy Salad Dressing, 293
Parsleyed Rice, 332
Party Specialties, Menus Featuring, 34–35, 47, 59–60
Pastes (Pastas). *See also* Macaroni
  Equipment for, 21
  Frozen, 16
Pastry, 174–75. *See also* Pies
  Chart for Baking Shells, 341
  Nut, 175
  Puff Shells, 175
Pâté, Ham and Liver, 79–80
Peach Crisp, 169
Peaches: Baked Fruits with, 165
  Blueberry Parfait with, 158–59
  Glazed Orange, 168–69
  Ham Slices with Broiled, 229–30
  Melba, 159

Peach Pie, Deep-Dish, 178
Pears: Baked Fruits with, 165
  à la Cumberland, 153–54
  with Custard Sauce, Sherried, 154–55
  Grape Salad with, 276
  Lime Salad with, 265–66
  Molded Minted, 266–67
  Rosé, 170–71
Peas: New Potatoes with Onions and,
  326–27
  with Onions, 325
  Quantity for 24 Servings, 66
  Vegetable Salad Platter with, 281–82
Pea Soup with Ham, Split, 312
Peppermint Chocolate Icebox Log, 160
Peppermint Parfait, 162
Petits Choux, 175–76
Petits Fours, 128–30
Pickled Beets, 258
Pickles, for 24 Servings, 68
Picnic Menu, 38
Pies, 174–87
  Adequate Servings, 27
  Black Bottom, 176–77
  Chocolate, Black Bottom, 176–77
  Chocolate Chiffon, 177–78
    Mocha, 181–82
    Rum, 184
  Crumb Crust, 174
  Egg Nog Chiffon, 179
  Fruit, Baking Chart, 341
  Fruit, Deep-Dish, 178
  Graham Cracker Crust, 174
  Ham-Veal Pot, 231
  Heating Frozen, 15
  Lamb, Beef, or Veal, 233–34
  Lemon Chiffon, 179–80
  Mocha Chiffon, 180–81
    Chocolate, 181–82
  Nut Pastry Crust, 175
  Pans for, 20
  Pumpkin, 182
    Chiffon, 183
    Reference Chart for Baking, 341
  Quantity for 24 Servings, 68
  Reference Chart for Baking, 341
  Refrigerator Space for, 22
  Rum Chocolate Chiffon, 184
  Schaum Torte, 185
  Sherry Chiffon, 186
  Strawberry Chiffon, 187
  Tamale, 227
Pimento Cheese Topping for Bread, 90
Pimento Rice, 333
Pineapple: Apple Mold with Oranges
  and, 268
  Baked Fruits with, 165
  Cheese Lime Molded Salad, 267
  Frozen Fruit Salad with, 262
  Fruited Mold, 149

Ham Slices with Broiled, 230
  Icebox Cake, 161
  Melon Cup with, 79
  Meringue Torte, 124–25
  Sauce for Pork, 239
  Strawberry Kebabs, 80
Pinwheel Sandwiches, 303–4
Pizza, Italian, 221–22
Plum Pie, Deep-Dish, 178
Popovers, Baking Chart for, 341
Poppy Seed Noodles, 325
Pork, 238–41
  Barbecued Spareribs, 240–41
  Carving Loin Roast, 211
  Chili con Carne with, 217–18
  Chop Spaghetti, 240
  Chop Suey Amandine, 238
  Chops Hawaiian, 239
  Meat Loaf with, 223
  Roasting Chart, 348
  Stuffed Shoulder of Lamb with, 236
  Swedish Meat Balls with, 225–26
  Sweet-Sour, 241
  Tamale Pie, 227
Potato Chips, for 24 Servings, 68
Potato Pancakes, 239
Potato Salad, 283–84
  -Stuffed Tomatoes, 284
  on Tomato Halves, 284–85
Potatoes, 326–28
  Baked Stuffed, 326
  Buttered Balls, 327
  Deep Fat Frying, 343
  Delmonico, 327–28
  with Onions and Peas, New, 326–27
  Quantity for 24 Servings, 66
Poultry, 244–55. See also Chicken
  Carving, 244–45
  Pointers for Roasting, 349–50
  Quantity Chart for Fowl, 64
  Roasting Pans, 22
  Sandwiches, 300
Pound Cake, 199–20
Prawns, Baked, 196–97
Prune Garnish, Bacon-Broiled, 73
Puddings: Cherry Upside-down, 167
  Chocolate Upside-down, 168
  Lemon Crunch, 150
  Pans for, 21
Puff Shells, 175–76
Pumpkin Pie, 182
  Chiffon, 183
  Reference Chart for Baking, 341
Punch: Champagne, 84
  Fruit, 85
  Hot Mulled, 86
  Quantity for 24 Servings, 63
  Rum, 87
  Wine, 88
Punch Bowl Cookies, 143–44

Q

Quantity Charts, 3, 63–68

R

Radishes, Quantity for 24 Servings, 66
Raisin Muffins, 106
Ratatouille, 328
Receptions, Menus for, 47, 59–60
Recipes, 69–338
  Appetizers and First Courses, 71–80
  Beverages, 81–88
  Breads, 89–115
  Desserts, 117–87
  Doubling, 20
  Egg and Cheese Entrees, 188–93
  Fish Entrees, 194–204
  Meat Entrees, 205–43
  Poultry Entrees, 245–55
  Relishes and Accompaniments, 256–59
  Salads and Salad Dressings, 260–99
  Sandwiches, 300–9
  Soups, 310–13
  Use of, 4
  Vegetables, 314–38
Red and Green Madrilene, 311–12
Red Sauce, 258–59
Refrigerator Rolls, 112
Refrigerator Sweet Dough, 109
Relishes and Accompaniments, 256–59
  Cinnamon Apples, 256
  Cranberry Horseradish Relish, 256–57
  Maple Syrup, 257
  Mustard Sauce Supreme, 257–58
  Pickled Beets, 258
  Red Sauce, 258–59
Rhubarb, Quantity for 24 Servings, 65
Ribbon Sandwiches, 304, 305
Rice, 329–34
  Boiled, 329
  Mock Wild, 330–31
  Nests, 331
  Parsleyed, 332
  Pilaff, 332–33
  Pimento, 333
  Quantity for 24 Servings, 68
  Savory, 333–34
  Shrimp Creole with, 200–1
  Steamed, 330
Roasting Meat, 346
  Reference Chart for, 347–48
Roasting Poultry, Pointers for, 349–50
Rolls, 110–14
  Buttermilk, 111
  Cloverleaf, 113
  Crescent, 113
  Curlicue, 113

  Dinner, 110–11
  Fan Tan, 113
  Figure 8, 113
  Frozen, 15, 16
  Knots, 113
  Lucky Clover, 113
  Pan, 113
  Parker House, 114
  Quantity for 24 Servings, 68
  Reference Chart for Baking, 341
  Refrigerator, 112
  Shaping Dough, 113–14
Rum Chocolate Chiffon Pie, 184
Rum Orange Bavarian, 153
Rum Punch, 87
Russian Dressing, 297

S

Salad Dressings, 293–99
  Anchovy-Parsley, 293
  Cheese, Blue, 293–94
  Cheese, Cream, 294
  Cheese, Roquefort, Rosy, 296–97
  Cheese, Roquefort, Sour Cream, 298
  French, 294
  Garlic French, 294
  Green Goddess, 295
  Honey Celery Seed, 295–96
  Italian, 296
  Russian, 297
  Shrimp, 297–98
  Sour Cream, 298
  Thousand Island, 298–99
Salads, 260–92
  Accompaniment, 260–86
  Apple: Cinnamon, with Cheese Balls, 274
    Cranberry, 261
    Cranberry Mold, 260
    Grape Mandarin Nut Compote, 275
    Mold with Pineapple and Mandarin Oranges, Sherried, 268
  Apricot Cranberry Molded, 261–62
  Avocado Grapefruit, 275
  Bean, 3-, 279
  Beet, Molded, 272–73
  Caesar, 278
  Cheese, Cottage: Jellied, Vegetable and, 273–74
    Molded, 270
    Molded, Pineapple-Lime, 267
  Chicken-Almond, 286
    -Grape, Supreme, 287
  Chicken Mold, 289
  Cole Slaw, Sour Cream, 281
  Cole Slaw with Cherry Tomatoes, 280–81

Cole Slaw in Lettuce Cups, 280
Cooked Vegetable Platter, 281–82
Crab Louis, 287–88
Cranberry Apple, 261
  Molded, 260
Cranberry Apricot Molded, 261–62
Cranberry Port Wine Mold, 267–68
Cucumber Grapefruit Mold, 263
Cucumber Lime Vegetable, 270–71
Cucumber and Tomato, 279–80, 282
Cucumbers and Onions, Marinated, 282–83
Egg Salad Squares, Deviled, 290
Frozen Fruit, 262
Frozen or Molded Fruit, 260–69
Frozen or Molded Vegetable, 270–74
Grape-Apple-Mandarin-Nut Compote, 275
Grape, Chicken, Almond Supreme, 287
Grapefruit Avocado, 275
Grapefruit Molded, 264
  Cucumber, 263
Grape Pear, 276
Ham Loaf, Molded, 290–91
Harlequin, 264–65
Lime-Cucumber-Vegetable, 270–71
Lime-Pineapple-Cottage Cheese
  Molded, 267
Macaroni, 283–84
Minted Pears, Molded, 266–67
Mixed Fruit, 274–77
Mixed Main Course, 286–88
Mixed Vegetable, 278–86
Molded or Frozen Fruit, 260–69
Molded or Frozen Vegetable, 270–74
Molded Main Course, 289–92
Orange-Grape-Apple-Nut Compote, 275
Pear Grape, 276
Pear Lime, 265–66
Pears, Molded Minted, 266–67
Pineapple-Cheese-Lime Molded, 267
Potato, 283–84
  on Tomato Halves, 284–85
  Tomatoes Stuffed with, 284
Quantity for 24 Servings, 68
Raw Vegetable, 288
Salami Shrimp Supper, 288
Salmon Loaf, Chilled, 291
Seafood, Molded, 292
Shrimp Salami Supper, 288
Tomato Aspic, 271
  Rings with Cucumber Slices, 272
Tomato-Cucumber, 279–80, 282
Tossed Green, 285–86
Waldorf, 276–77
Salami Shrimp Supper Salad, 288
Salmon, Baked Whole, 198
  Cold Spiced, 198–99

Loaf, Chilled, 291
Steaks, Baked, 197
Sandwiches, 300–9
  Avocado, 301
  Beef, 300. See also Hamburgers
  Braunschweiger, 301
  Checkerboard, 303
  Cheese and Olive Spread, 302
  Cheese-Stuffed Finger Rolls, 306
  Chicken, 300, 302–3
  Chili Beefburgers, 306
  Cold, 300–5
  Fancy, 303–4
  Finger, 304
  Ham, 300
  Ham-Stuffed Buns, 307
  Hamburgers, Chili Beefburgers, 306
  Hamburgers, Hot Dog, 307–8
  Hamburgers, Oven-Barbecued, 308
  Hot, 306–9
  Hot Dog Hamburgers, 307–8
  Liverwurst, 301
  Meat, 300. See also specific meats
  Pinwheel, 303–4
  Poultry, 300
  Quantity for 24 Servings, 68
  Ribbon, 304, 305
  Rings, 303
  Rolled, 303
  Seafood, 300
  Tuna, 300
  Turkey Supreme, 308–9
Sauces: Chocolate, 162
  Custard, 155, 171–72
  Heating Frozen, 15
  Meat, Italian, 220
  Mustard, Supreme, 257–58
  Orange, 172–73
  Pineapple, for Pork, 239
  Red (Cocktail), 258–59
  Sherry Spice, 173
  Supreme, 309
Scallops, Deep Fat Frying, 343
Schaum Torte, 185
Scones, 100
Seafood Salad, Molded, 292
Seafood Sandwiches, 300
Sesame Corn Bread, 99
Sherbet, Melon Balls with, 160–61
Shish Kebabs, 235
Shortcake, Strawberry, 134
Shrimp: Baked, 196–97
  Cocktail, Ample Servings of, 27
  Cocktail, Red Sauce for, 258–59
  Creole with Rice, 200–1
  Creamed with Oysters, 199–200
  Deep Fried, 201
    Reference Chart for, 343
  Dressing, 297–98
  Molded Seafood Salad with, 292

Preparing Raw, 201
Quantity for 24 Servings, **64**
Salami Supper Salad, 288
Tallyho, 203
Smelt, Deep Fat Frying, 343
Sole Stroganoff, Baked, 196
Sole with White Wine, Fillet of, 202
Soufflé, Cheese, 189
　Chocolate, 147–48
　Mocha, 152
Soups, 310–13
　Clam Chowder, 310–11
　French Onion, 310
　Heating Frozen, 15
　Menus Featuring, 58
　Oyster Stew, 311
　Quantity for 24 Servings, 68
　Red and Green Madrilene, 311–12
　Split Pea with Ham, 312
　Tomato Bouillon, 312–13
Spaghetti, 334
　Pork Chop, 240
　Quantity for 24 Servings, 68
Spanish Cream, Chocolate, 147
Spanish Sticks, 144
Spice Bar Cookies, Glazed, 141–42
Spice Cake, Easy, 120
Spiced Salmon, Cold, 198–99
Spice Sauce, Sherry, 173
Spicy Coffee Cake, 108–9
Spicy Glaze for Apples, 164
Spinach: Casserole, 336
　Eggs Florentine with, 189–90
　Quantity for 24 Servings, 66
　à la Suisse, 334–35
Squash, Quantity for 24 Servings, **66**
Squash, Summer, Grilled, 337–38
Stollen, 114–15
Strawberry Chiffon Pie, 187
Strawberry Glazed Cheesecake, 133–34
Strawberry Melon Mold, 155
Strawberry Pineapple Kebabs, 80
Strawberry Shortcake, 134
　Strawberries for 24 Servings, 65
Sugar, for 24 Servings of Coffee, 68
Supreme Sauce, 309
Swedish Beans, 315–16
Swedish Meat Balls, 225–26
Sweet-Sour Pork, 241
Syrup, Maple, 257
　Quantity for 24 Servings, 68

T

Tamale Pie, 227
Tea, 83–84
　Concentrate, 83–84
　Iced, 84

Instant, 84
　Quantity for 24 Servings, 63
Tea Party Menu, 34
Teen-Agers, Menus for, 41, 43, 54, **56**
Teriyaki Beef, 228
Thousand Island Dressing, 298–99
3-Bean Salad, 279
Tiered Cake, 130–32
Tomato Aspic, 271
　Rings with Cucumber Slices, 272
Tomato Bouillon, 312–13
Tomato-Cucumber Salads, 279–80, 282
Tomato Halves, Potato Salad on, 284–85
Tomato Juice, Hot, 87
　Spiced, 86
Tomatoes: Baked Stuffed, 338
　Cole Slaw with Cherry, 280–81
　Italienne, Cherry, 337
　Parmesan, Broiled, 336
　Potato Salad-Stuffed, 284
　Quantity for 24 Servings, 66
Tongue, Boiled, 215
Torte, Pineapple Meringue, 124–25
　Schaum, 185
Tortoni, Biscuit, 156–57
Trout, Deep Fat Frying, 343
Tuna: Casserole, Baked, 203–4
　Molded Seafood Salad with, 292
　Sandwiches, 300
Turkey: and Broccoli en Casserole, 230
　à la King, 254
　Menu Featuring, 30, 52
　Pointers for Roasting, 349
　Quantity for 24 Servings, 64
　Sandwich Supreme, 308–9

V

Veal, 242–43
　Meat Balls with, 72, 225–26
　Paprika, 242
　Pie, Ham Pot, 231
　Pie with Cornmeal Biscuits, 233–34
　Quantity for 24 Servings, 65
　Scallopini, 242–43
Vegetable Salads. *See also* specific vegetables
　Cottage Cheese, Jellied, 273–74
　Frozen or Molded, 270–74
　Mixed, 278–86
　Platter, Cooked, 281–82
　Raw, 285
Vegetables, 314–38. *See also* specific vegetables
　Cooking Pointers, 352
　Frozen, 16
　　Quantity Chart, 67
　Harvest Casserole of, 323

Herb-Seasoned Skewered, 323–24
Pans for, 21
Preserving Values, 25–26
Quantity Charts, 66–67
Ratatouille, 328

Wine and Food Combinations, 354
Wine Jelly with Fruit, 269
Wine Punch, 88
Wine Reference Chart, 81–82
Wines and Wine Serving, 352–54. *See
also* specific dishes

W

Waffles Supreme, 95
Waldorf Salad, 276–77
Wassail Bowl, 88
Water Chestnuts, Beans with, 322–23
Watermelon. *See* Melon
Wedding Breakfast Menus, 35, 59
Wheat Casserole, Bulgar, 317
Wheat Muffins, 106–7
White Cake, 121
White Frosting, 129

Y

Yeast Doughs, 109–15
Yellow Layer Cake, 122

Z

Zucchini, Grilled, 337–38
Zucchini, Ratatouille with, 328